20th century gothic

20th century gothic

AMERICA'S NIXON

Sherri Cavan

WIGAN PIER PRESS
SAN FRANCISCO

to Frank Wills
The Watchman in the Night

20TH CENTURY GOTHIC

Library of Congress Catalog Card Number: 79-65722
International Standard Book Number: 0-934594-00-7

Lines from Bertolt Brecht, THE EXCEPTION AND THE RULE, Copyright ©1965 by Eric Bentley used by permission of Grove Press, Inc.

Excerpts from SIX CRISES by Richard M. Nixon, Copyright ©1962 by Richard M. Nixon, reprinted by permission of Doubleday and Company, Inc.

Excerpts from RN: MEMOIRS OF RICHARD NIXON by Richard Nixon, Copyright ©1978 by Richard Nixon, used by permission of Grosset and Dunlap, Inc.

Excerpts from THE NIXON NOBODY KNOWS, Copyright ©1972 by Henry Spalding, used by permission of Jonathan David Publishers, Inc., Middle Village, N.Y.

Printed in the United States of America.
Set in Plantin Medium, Bold and Italic Faces.

Observe the conduct of these people closely:
Find it estranging even if not very strange
Hard to explain even if it is the custom
Hard to understand even if it is the rule
Observe the smallest action, seemingly simple,
With mistrust
Inquire if a thing be necessary
Especially if it is common
We particularly ask you —
When a thing continually occurs —
Not on that account to find it natural
Let nothing be called natural
In an age of bloody confusion
Ordered disorder, planned caprice,
And dehumanized humanity, lest all things
be held unalterable!

What here's the rule, recognize as an abuse
And where you have recognized an abuse
Provide a remedy!

Bertolt Brecht
The Exception and the Rule

Preface

There can be no definitive account of the life and times of Richard Nixon, 37th President of the United States. Because it is a tale of the 20th century, it must illustrate the principle of relativity; true to its own logic, any rendition of the truth about these matters can only be a version or interpretation, constructed from the limited perspective of the narrator and construed in terms of the vested interests she has in telling the tale.

This book is thus a version of a story that is bound to be told and retold as long as there are persons with an interest in describing the known, assumed, inferred, alleged, and implied facts and as long as there is an audience mesmerized by one of the most extraordinary figures of the century.

I have taken the facts of my story from the public record, from documentary sources open to anyone with a strong interest in tracing what is known about the nation, its government, and the people who hold office. I have supplemented this public record with observations in Southern California. *20th Century Gothic* does not offer an expose of new facts, but rather an interpretation of familiar facts that suggest a particular pattern.

The pattern is gothic imagery—a vision of life in which good and evil are locked in mortal combat, winner take all. Theorists of strategic interaction might describe this as a "zero sum game." But to put it in that metaphoric framework is to divest the foregoing principle of its historic roots. It is not a new idea, born out of the realities of nuclear weaponry. It is an old idea, built right into the framework of Western thought. The larger questions this book addresses are the origins of gothic imagery, the interests such a world view serves, and the consequences for promulgating this particular version of reality. The more immediate topics are how Richard Nixon came to hold the gothic vision, the effect it had on his career and personality, and the consequences such beliefs have for the political system of modern America.

I do not consider myself a neutral witness to the drama I propose to describe, although I shall try to tell the story in a dispassionate voice. In the methodological appendix I have sketched out the interests I brought to this study and the way I dealt with problems of inference and interpretation. In this short preface I wish simply to acknowledge my objective and thank those who aided and abetted my enterprise.

Most important of these is Coni Tarquini. From the beginning, Coni's enthusiasm encouraged and sustained me. While her loyal friendship has been sorely tested on more than one occasion, this book would never be if it were not for what she has contributed along the way. In addition to providing me with a ready ear and critical insight during the research and writing, Coni encouraged me to publish the ensuing manuscript myself; and then she guided me through the intricacies of what I had to know in order to accomplish that task. In inspiration and design, this book is hers.

Various people have contributed their time, skill, intelligence, and good will. Some, like Gary Howard and Ken Touchet, have been involved in one way or another from the beginning, as I speculated, planned, brooded, and contracted. Others have been involved at various stages, from typing the first drafts to typesetting the final copy, from editing the manuscript to proofreading the galleys: Charlotte Canida, Marion Walsh, Lorraine DeLaFuente, Josephine Palmer, Margaret Oakly, Susan Weisberg, Deborah Hill. Frank Cieciorka's art work graces the cover and the chapter headings.

I have profited from discussions with many people: Carl Sundholm, Jacqueline Wiseman, Joe Gusfield, Harvey Molotch, Richard Flacks, Tom Ryther, Fred Thalheimer, Francisco Ramirez, Barbara Phillips, Pete Phillips, Don Leonnard, Patrick Beirnackie, Richard Rizzo, Ted Keller, Gene Weinstein, Laurie Soloman, Gaye Tuchman, Shirley Hartley, Barbara Rosenblum, Clarice Stasz, Lyn Lofland, Lois DeFleur, David Chandler, Troy Duster, Russ Ellis, Barbara Heyns, Larry Hirschorn, Arlie Hochschild, John Irwin, David Matza, Henry Miller, and Dave Vogel are those whose names come most readily to mind. In addition, there have been many whose experience contributed to my understanding of the texts I was reading: June Bailess, Edwin and Kathleen Bryant, Kenneth Chotiner, Eugene Coffin, Patricia Hitt, Dale Marshall, Robert O'Brian, Shirley Olsen, Mel Rich, and Blake Sandborn were most helpful. There were others as well, whose names I did not record or ought not record, but their cooperation is appreciated nonetheless.

Over the years the Department of Sociology at San Francisco State University has given me the freedom to explore problems of my own selection, and for this rare privilege I am truly grateful. As chair, Marjorie Seashore and John Kinch each tolerated my eccentricities, and until now, saw little expression of appreciation.

Ron Turner of Last Gasp Comix enlivened me to new forms of eccentricity, and along with the rest of the crowd at the Cafe Flore, put a little panache in my life.

Finally, there are the friends, lovers, children, and animals who brought me pleasure, shared my joys and frustrations, encouraged me, loaned me money, gave me time: Marne Campbell, Deborah Wolf, Adam Cavan, Amelia Frank, Cary Gilliam, Anne Huffington, John Marsh, Earl Nelson, and Louie Pacific.

San Francisco
July, 1979

·contents·

chronology

themes

reflections

Introduction
The Study of
Culture and Personality

In the modern world it is not inconceivable that nuclear holocaust could destroy all the living things of the earth and leave the planet a smoldering ruin of radioactivity. If such monumental tragedy were the fate of our beings, extraterrestrials might come to discover the life that was lost and inquire after its history. Most likely it would be safe to land on the moon, where they could find a bronze plaque inscribed:

HERE MEN FROM THE PLANET EARTH
FIRST LANDED ON THE MOON
JULY 1969, A.D.
WE COME IN PEACE FOR ALL MANKIND

Along with the names and signatures of the astronauts who landed on the moon is the name and signature of the incumbent President of the nation which sponsored them. So no matter what may happen to the planet earth and all of human society, Richard Nixon's name can still be immortalized.

The foregoing scenario is a travesty. If landing men on the moon is a credit to the Nixon administration, that administration has been no credit to the nation. Resignation aborted Nixon's second term in office amid charges and allegations of malfeasance so far-reaching they questioned the very legitimacy of his tenure. The practices employed by those working on Nixon's behalf, and presumably at his behest, were in no way guided by the images of justice and democracy so sacred to the American way of life. Instead, these men were willing to go to any length to insure victory and then to prevent the means they employed in achieving their goals from becoming public knowledge.

In *20th Century Gothic* I treat the career of Richard Nixon as a chapter in the unfolding saga of modern American life. Of necessity I write with the belief that the dark vision of my opening words is only plausible, not inevitable. At the same time, if there was any single, overriding objective that governed the choices Nixon made in public office, that objective was his desire to secure a place in history. So the irony compounds: no matter what may happen in the future, in light of his personal objectives, Nixon's career must be reckoned a success.

History is made by human actions that have consequences and ramifications beyond the immediate moment of their execution. It is written by sifting through the evidence that remains after time and human enterprise have had their way, providing a plausible accounting for what is known and what is likely to be true. While history recounts the life of a group, biography recounts the life of an individual, but the same principles apply. Biography orders the consequential moments of a life and so offers a description of the personality in question. Sociobiography, being neither pure history nor simple biography, proposes that the biography of the individual is not separate and distinct from the history of the groups that influence the individual through the course of his or her life.

In looking at the interrelationship of Richard Nixon's biography and the history of modern America, I have tried both to discover and to employ the method of sociobiography, although I did not start out to do either. The work emerged out of my personal experience and my scholarly interests.

In the unfolding drama of Watergate I saw a version of America I could not reconcile with the version I had learned at school. The Norman Rockwell images that colored the 1940s mentality of my childhood were shattered by the revelations of what went on during the 1972 election and through Nixon's subsequent years in office. First as a person, then as a scholar, I was overtaken by the desire to understand what it meant for an American president to electronically wire the inner citadel of his government and then record discussions of how to prevent the American people from finding out that agents of the speakers had broken into the national headquarters of the opposition party with the objective of doing the same thing: wiring that office to record the machinations that took place within it. My background in sociology led me to look for an answer in the study of culture and personality, although nothing in that literature specifically directed me to organize and interpret the material as I have.

Developed conjointly in sociology and anthropology, culture and personality theory proposes that the distinctive features of personality are formed by the influence of social forces. The most dramatic example of this process is the role of language in structuring our perception of the outer world and making sense of our inner experience. The existential moment of our being is apprehended through linguistic symbols, and these tools of analysis are a property of the group we were born into and those groups we have joined along the way. What we know about ourselves and what we know about the world is a function of the language we use to make sense of our circumstances. That language is a property of culture, not personality.

Although I have chosen to call the form of my study sociobiography, I am indebted to the existing genre of psychohistory, particularly as it is developed by Erik Erikson in *Life History and the Historical Moment* (1975).* Sociobiography and psychohistory both address the biographical facts of historical figures with the objective of illuminating the times in which those persons lived. However, the two differ in fundamental ways. In analyzing the dialectic of history and biography, psychohistory takes the dynamics of personality as the casual factor while sociobiography begins with the dynamics of culture. Where psychohistorians look to the individual's drives to construct a motivational framework, sociobiographers look to principles of interpersonal psychology and social organization. Where psychohistory invokes the language of psychoanalysis to describe the subject, sociobiography invokes the language of social science.

---

* Full source information for literature references will be found in the Bibliography, arranged by author and date (given in parentheses in the text). References to page number alone refer back to the last cited source.

With few exceptions, culture and personality theory has been used to examine and interpret the lives of ordinary people, followers rather than leaders. Research has focused on the unique personality types found in simple societies and the typical personalities associated with industrial society. In *20th Century Gothic,* I address the unique personality of one man in the milieu of an industrial nation, and so, some discussion of assumptions is called for.

Culture is not uniform. Even the simplest human groups are differentiated by age and sex, and the more complex the society, the more differentiated the culture. Contemporary America is an example of an urban, industrial nation with a polyethnic heritage and a history of regional differentiation. The study of personality in the context of 20th century America must take account of the varied texture of American life. General trends must be inferred and then investigated in terms of their particular relevance for different social groups. In addition, the unique subcultural variations that characterize groups must be considered.

Culture is not static. Historical moments can be distinguished by constellations of unique events, and the consequences of those events can be traced out in successive historical moments. The brackets defining these moments are not inherent in the ebb and flow of everyday life; rather, they are hypothetical constructs employed by the analyst to organize and summarize the historical facts of daily life. "The 1920s," for example, is thus an ideal type, constructed to order and highlight key events of a decade and used to describe the prevailing influences of the time.

Like culture, personality is neither undifferentiated nor unchanging. The features of any given individual are multifaceted: when some are highlighted, others are obscured. Thus any attempt to assess the personality of a particular person is at best a sketch and not a blueprint.

The portrait of Richard Nixon I have sketched assumes that personality is an unfolding progression affected by the forces of history on the one hand and the forces of the life cycle on the other. The progression from infancy to childhood, youth, manhood, and maturity is treated as a sequence of growth and development. Key events in each stage of the sequence are described in terms of the historical forces that molded these experiences and are assessed in terms of the consequences of their resolution in subseqent stages of personality development.

Figure 1 suggests the interrelations of historical moments of American culture and stages of the life cycle of Richard Nixon.

Figure 1. **The Intersection of Historical Moments in America and the Life Cycle of Richard Nixon**

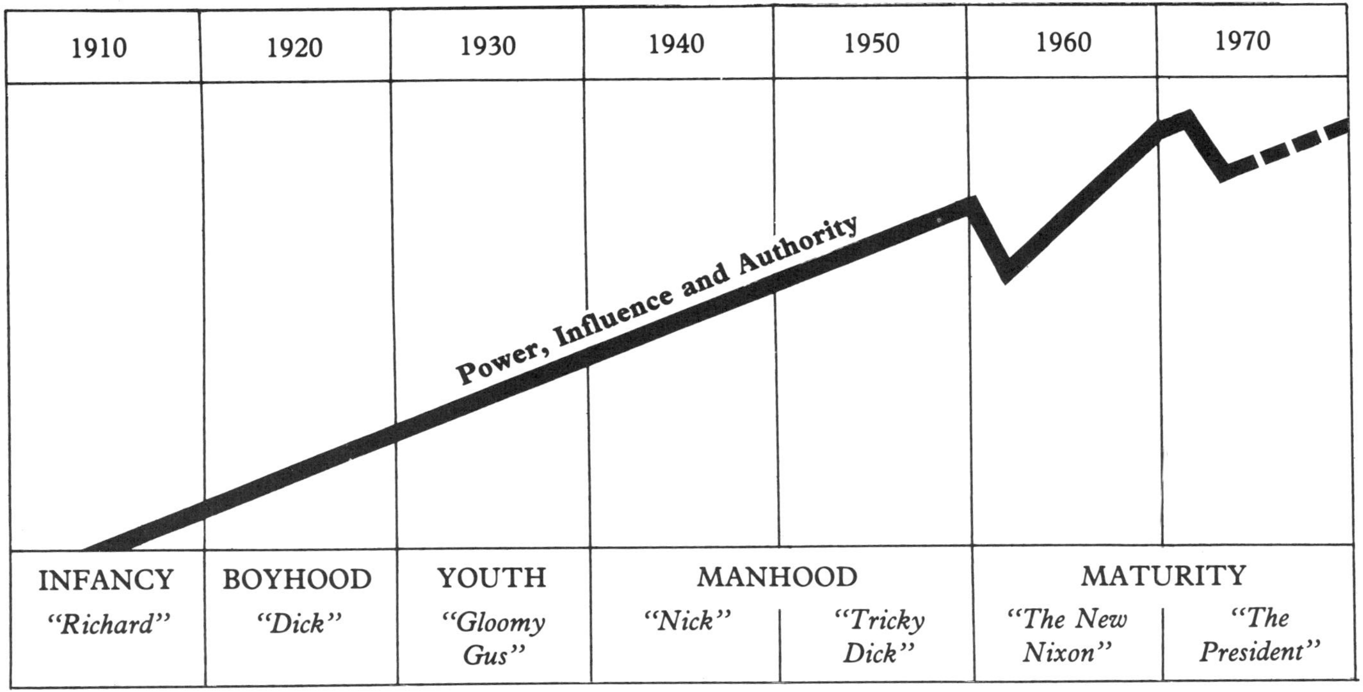

1910	1920	1930	1940	1950	1960	1970

Power, Influence and Authority

INFANCY	BOYHOOD	YOUTH	MANHOOD		MATURITY	
"Richard"	"Dick"	"Gloomy Gus"	"Nick"	"Tricky Dick"	"The New Nixon"	"The President"

The line traced across it demonstrates the shifting balance of power, influence and authority. Where once the prevailing trends of the national culture dominated the personality of Richard Nixon, eventually the personality of Richard Nixon dominates the culture. At the base of the chart I have indicated the names Nixon was called at each stage in his life cycle. They suggest an identity constantly changing to keep abreast of the times.

★   ★   ★

The first chapters address the developmental stages of Nixon's biography. I begin by looking at some of the forces influential in the lives of his parents and, by inference, in Nixon's infancy. The decade of Richard Nixon's birth was a turning point in American history. Once an isolated ex-colony on the outer fringes of the known world, the United States was becoming a global power in its own right. Like every other child born around the same time, Nixon would experience a radical shift in cultural conditioning as he made the transition from infancy to childhood. Like the offspring of immigrants, the children of the early 20th century had to adapt to a world unlike that their parents knew.

In stable, simple societies parental guidance is the dominant force in a child's life. Drawing from traditional lore and personal experience, parents tutor their offspring in the ways of the world, and the lessons learned at home are suited to the circumstances the child encounters outside the home. In a world characterized by unexpected alternatives, unprecedented opportunity, and unconventional values, parental guidance is not the dominant force in personality development. Rather, the family of orientation shares its influence with a variety of other social institutions.

Family influence is still important in molding personality in the industrial world. The vision of the world communicated in the intimacy of the domestic circle is the first vision of the world the child has. All subsequent visions are but versions or alternative interpretations of what was initally understood. Furthermore, family *imagery* remains the dominant symbol of virtue and truth.

Nixon's parents were products of an old order that was passing around the time Richard, their second son, was born in 1913. As technological innovation moved from the realm of production to the realm of consumption—autos, radios, telephones, movies—the nature of everyday life changed. The pace of action sped up; distance contracted. Images created in metropolitan centers were broadcast across the nation, and, as a result, the local community lost its distinctive focus and then its traditional force. New prospects of economic opportunity appeared, while new systems of belief evolved to justify the action taken in pursuit of economic gain. These were the conditions prevailing during Richard Nixon's boyhood, when the formative influences of his personality expanded from his immediate family to the community of Whittier, California, circa 1920.

The community may be conceptualized as a network of interrelated parts, itself subject to regional and national influences. It exerts a significant influence on all those who reside within its boundaries. The options of each family are structured by the place it holds in the community, and, in turn, these domestic options define the limit of experience for individual members. At the same time, individual family members learn most of what they know about the world from the face-to-face encounters they have with those they live around, work with, attend church with, and who otherwise cross their paths on a day-to-day basis.

The nuclear family is linked to other families through a kinship network, which may be truncated or extended. The relative influence of kin in community affairs will vary from one family to another and, accordingly, the respect paid to individual family members will vary as well. Similarly, the division of labor and the organization of economic affairs allocates people into social classes that are again distinguished by relative power and prestige. Like the kin people reckon as members of their family, the work they do influences their immediate experience and their subsequent options.

Beliefs embodied in the institutional structures of religion, politics, and education further impinge on the individual. Images and fundamental values are found in the metaphysical visions of religious traditions. Ideological metaphors associated with political parties define the virtues of the secular world. Truths associated with science are interpreted in the schools, which also serve to perpetuate an image of national purpose and international destiny.

Individually and in interaction, these various social forces impinge on the developing personality. They create structures of taken-for-granted meaning while at the same time delimiting the options available to the individual.

The world view Richard Nixon learned as a child in Southern California was a critical factor in the subsequent development of his personality. It is a key to understanding the course his career took in his mature years, although it is not the only influence in his life.

The vision of economic prosperity characteristic of America during Nixon's childhood disintegrated in his youth. For some born around the same time, the Depression was a time of critical reappraisal; but many more saw it as just an unfortunate interlude in the history of an economic system that was ultimately sound, as well as moral and just. For Richard Nixon, this was the time he became established in his own right in the community of Whittier. Though hundreds of thousands suffered setbacks and reversals during the 1930s, Richard Nixon experienced upward mobility. The son of a grocer now practiced law.

The Second World War created a structure of new opportunity. Nixon left Whittier for Washington, to work for the government; then he left his government post to enlist in the Navy. When the war was over, the fabric of American life was transformed again, just as it had been after the First World War. Richard Nixon's public career dates from this postwar era. Until this time the forces of culture that influenced his personality were relevant to a whole generation. Thereafter, more specialized forces came into play. Eventually, his personality began to influence the nation.

Selected and groomed to run for public office, Nixon made politics his lifelong vocation. First as a congressman, then as a senator, ultimately as Vice President and President, he was set apart from ordinary men. He was a leader where most were followers. He had the power and influence to set precedent, establish priorities, and in a very real sense create options that would determine the future. How he used that power and the forces that affected his decisions are the topics addressed in the thematic chapters, 7-10. The final chapters reflect on what can be learned from a close study of the 37th President.

Richard Nixon's political career thus serves as the occasion to examine the changes that have taken place in American society and to suggest the relationship of these changes to the broader historical landscape. In focusing on how cultural factors influence the development of personality, we see, in the case of powerful individuals, how personality in turn influences culture.

The future history of American society is a function in part of events that took place during Nixon's years of power. He was a key figure in the development of the Cold War mentality of the 1950s and a key figure in the development of the cynicism and apathy that has characterized the 1970s. These moments of American history are part of an unfinished story. Their ultimate significance cannot yet be assessed, but the direction they imply can be suggested.

Technological innovations of the 20th century make totalitarian rule possible in a way that could not have been envisioned in previous epochs. The enormous concentration of resources that characterizes the modern world facilitates the centralization of control, and with the centralization of control comes the possibility of usurping public power for private ends. The technology of warfare has been refined to the point where the prospect of mass annihilation by human enterprise has taken the place once held by the forces of nature such as plague and pestilence. Fear and uncertainty create conditions under which men and women are willing to trade their liberty for the promise of security. The technology of communications facilitates the dissemination of propaganda, as well as the surveillance of behavior. In subtle and direct ways, frightened people are subject to control and exploitation.

At the same time, the traditional safeguards of Constitutional rights and privileges are devalued. The existence of a document proclaiming the inalienable human rights of a free society did not protect individual privacy, assure due process of law, or permit congressional representatives to declare war during the Nixon administration. The wiretaps that were one of many "White House horrors" besetting Nixon increased under Ford. There is no reason to assume that subsequent administrations have reversed this trend.

Chapter 1
Gothic Imagery
and the Dramatization of Evil

The gothic vision is a recurrent nightmare in Western thought. It occurs in times of technological innovation, when change accelerates and unprecedented choices make life seem chaotic. Anxious people are fearful about the future, and a sinister version of reality takes root. A belief in forces of evil, dedicated to the destruction of the traditional moral order, grows; malevolent imagery begins to dominate the imagination. People come to believe that forces of evil are rampant, malicious, and ambitious and that the sole objective of these demonic forces is the destruction of those who uphold traditional virtue. Eventually, people come to believe that if the virtuous are to survive at all, they must be ruthless in their own self-defense. In this dark, metaphorical vision, all things are rationalized.

A classic example of gothic imagery and the logic it spawns are the final words Richard Nixon uttered in his role as President, as he prepared to leave the office he fought so hard to win. Explaining the circumstances that prompted his historic resignation, he cautions:

> Never get discouraged. Never be petty. Always remember: others may hate you. Those who hate you don't win unless you hate them. And then you destroy yourself. (*Washington Post* Staff, 1974, p. xxi)

Similar examples of gothic imagery dominate Nixon's *Memoirs.* Time and time again, he argues that what justified the extreme forces of destruction he let loose in Vietnam was the "vicious character of the enemy." Over and over, he repeats that what justified the secret, unlawful measures taken against demonstrators and dissenters was the catastrophic threat they presented to lawful authority. Written in exile as the public examination of his career, his autobiography routinely justifies all the questionable actions taken on his behalf (and presumably at his behest) by citing the excesses of others, whether those others are past Presidents or college students.

In his memoirs, Nixon frequently makes use of the literary device of quoting and, in particular, of quoting from his personal diary, one of the documents he fought most adamantly against having revealed to the public when the courts confiscated his papers. We may assume these diary entries record the innermost vision of the man. In the excerpts he is willing to share with the public, we read:

> From the very beginning, I wanted to fight back . . . If there was any campaign advantage to incumbency, it had to be access to government information on one's opponents . . . I dictated a diary note about this in the spring of 1972: "This has really been a shameful failure on our part, and it is hard for me to understand it, in view of the fact that I had so often pointed out that after what they did to us when we were out of office we at least owed it to ourselves in self-defense to initiate some investigations of them." (Nixon, 1978, p. 676, hereafter referred to as *Memoirs.)*

> . . . I waved out the window . . . at all the nutheads in the nasty crowd . . . I think as the war recedes as an issue, some of these people are going to be lost souls. They basically are haters, they are frustrated, they are alienated . . . (p. 685)

> We certainly have made our mistakes but perhaps the year has taught us all somewhat more compassion and understanding, although I must say that it has also brought clearly to light the unbelievable battle in which we are engaged and how high the stakes are and how bitter and fanatical the opposition is. We simply have to stick it out. (p. 1007)

> . . . as time has gone on, when we add up the Dean week which was just a year ago—and the tape issue—and then Agnew—and then following that up with the two-tapes business—the tax business—and all the other assaults—the Rebozo thing—the eighteen minutes—it's just miraculous that we are still in the game at all. (p. 1020)

He also quotes from bedside notes he made to himself in the early morning hours of his second term, when he could not sleep and fears of destruction haunted his imagination:

> Above all else: Dignity, command, faith, head high, no fear, build a new spirit, drive, act like a President, act like a winner. Opponents are savage destroyers, haters. Time to use full power of the President to fight overwhelming forces arrayed against us. (p. 971)

Reminiscing about the presentation he made before a gathering of the economic elite at Bohemian Grove, California, in 1967, Nixon writes:

> I led the audience on a tour of the world, tracing the changes and examining the conflicts, finding both danger and opportunity as the United States entered the final third of the twentieth century . . . Turning to the Soviet Union, I noted . . . "our goal is different from theirs. We seek peace as an end in itself. They seek victory, with peace being at this time a means toward that end" . . . Most important, it happens that we are on the right side—the side of freedom and peace and progress against the forces of totalitarianism, reaction, and war. (pp. 284-285)

Reviewing the televised speech he made on April 30, 1973, when he first addressed the American people about the topic of Watergate, Nixon writes:

> The instincts of twenty-five years in politics told me I was up against no ordinary opposition. In this second term I had thrown down a gauntlet in Congress, the bureaucracy, the media, and the Washington establishment and challenged them to engage in epic battle . . . Watergate had exposed a cavernous weakness in my ranks, and I felt that if in this speech I admitted any vulnerabilities, my opponents would savage me with them . . . Given this situation and given this choice—given my belief that these were the stakes—I decided to answer no to the queston whether I was also involved in Watergate. (p. 850)

In other words, he has decided to lie to the public—to dissemble the facts chronicled in his *Memoirs*—because he believes that if he tells the nation the truth, he is in trouble. In justification of his behavior, he points to the excesses of the other side:

> Most Americans are resigned to a modicum of hypocrisy in politics. I am convinced, however, the historians will eventually conclude that even the serious issues raised and abuses revealed by Watergate did not justify the abuses of power as were committed by members of the Ervin Committee. With their prejudicial leaks, their double standards, and their grandstanding behavior, they only confirmed my feelings that this was a partisan attack, a determined effort to turn something minor into something major, and we had to fight back. (p. 896)

In these and countless other ways the structure of Richard Nixon's inner vision is verbalized: a dark, foreboding place inhabited by sinister forces bent on Nixon's ultimate destruction, with Richard Nixon always aligned on the side of virtue and truth.

Gothic imagery is not just another term for paranoia. Paranoia is an attribute of the personality system, considered by psychiatrists and laymen alike to distort reality. Gothic imagery describes reality: it postulates the existence of insidious forces of evil; it attributes malicious motives to those forces; and it then rationalizes the means employed by virtue in its battle against those forces that would destroy it. Where paranoia is an individual aberration, gothic imagery is a collective illusion. When John Mitchell refers to discrediting activity as "White House horrors;" when Alexander Haig attributes the destruction of taped conversations to "sinister forces;" when Gerry Ford consoles the nation by proclaiming "our long national nightmare is over;" each testifies to his gothic imagination.

Gothic imagery dramatizes evil, not because evil is insidious, but because its dramatization is expeditious. In times of technological innovation, new opportunities for action are created, options that are either unanticipated by the traditional order or unacceptable in its customary interpretation. People of foresight, those who can see beyond the customary limits of the old order, can capitalize on the windfall opportunities of the times, if only they can convince others that their behavior is legitimate. The role gothic imagery plays in the technological transformation of the old order is the same as the role of the "convincer" in the traditional con game: it is invoked by those who stand to profit from others' fear and anxiety. It proposes that vices once considered absolute are now relative to an enemy so malicious that it will stop at nothing in pursuit of its own ambition. It proposes that in the face of overwhelming odds the forces of evil present, it is reasonable, rational and right for virtue to be ruthless in self-defense. Once such thinking takes root, anything goes.

The traditional symbols of the old order are carried along in the changing tide to justify and rationalize new behavior. But in the process they have lost their distinctive force, and eventually they lose their traditional meaning. Then peace means war, intelligence means espionage, life means death.

In order to place Richard Nixon in the context of his times, it is necessary to see how the seeds of gothic imagery were planted in the Western mind; how conditions of technological innovation gave root to that metaphorical vision; and how, most of all, a young child growing up in Southern California in the 20th century came to believe that forces of evil lurk in the world and virtue is found in sustained battle with those forces so conceived.

Let us begin by tracing—in very broad strokes—a history of Western society, and then seeing how these historic forces interact with Richard Nixon's personal experience.

Fragments of History

For thousands of years the classical form of Western society developed along the benign shores of the Mediterranean. With the ascent of Roman influence, the boundaries of that civilization were extended into the midlands of Northern Europe, a territory still characterized by Stone Age culture. Through the 1st and 2nd centuries the imperial order established under Roman dominance began to disintegrate, and by the 4th and 5th centuries the classicial vision of order was replaced by cruder forms. This was the epoch of Western civilization customarily referred to as the Dark Ages and treated as an aberration in the expanding growth of Western life.

Through military and bureaucratic efficiency, Rome had extended its influence as a source of authority into primitive barbarian culture. The Gothic conquerors of the territory once ruled by Rome adopted some aspects of the dying culture. But they disregarded others, and untimately they put the stamp of barbarian culture on the historic progression of Western life.

Organized in small, tribal bands, the Gothic conquerors' understanding of authority was personal: authority was embodied in the immediate power of whoever claimed to speak with its voice. The power of bureaucratic or appointive office had no referent in barbarian tradition. So for hundreds of years of Western history principles of bureaucratic organization governed only the affairs of the church, while personal power and inherited right governed secular life. The Dark Ages represented a period when much of what had been the classical tradition of Western civilization was forgotten, though that vision would emerge again in due time.

Roman bureaucratic administration created a network of inter-related communities, sharing in common certain taxes and obligations, subject to certain influences emanating from a central authority. Under barbarian dominance, this interrelated network broke down. What remained were isolated fiefdoms, led by powerful warriors, in constant battle with one another for land and cattle, power and prestige.

As the network tying local communities together disintegrated, so did the opportunities for trade. The merchant class vanished in the Dark Ages, as did the urban centers their enterprise sustained, the writing employed to document their affairs, and the money used to measure value and effect exchange. Gone also were the artists, philosophers, craftspeople, and intellectuals who flourished in the fertile opportunity of nascent bourgeois society. What remained of the Western tradition were warring aristocrats, laboring peasants, and a class of priestly officials and scholars whose monumental achievement was to link the civilization that began to grow in Northern Europe with the one that had once flourished along the Mediterranean.

Long after Rome declined as a center of military and administrative influence, its reputation as a center of power lingered in the popular imagination. Rome had created an empire of enormous proportions and monumental wealth, sustaining a city of over half a million citizens and almost as many slaves. It embodied a lingering ideal, even when the empire was no more and the city housed less than 200,000. In the medieval world Rome became a symbol of something that was glorious, magnificent, ennobling, and the religious practices that emanated from the Eternal City became associated with sacramental rites that promised power to the believer.

The Christianity promulgated in the last days of the Roman Empire bore little resemblance to the practices carried on in its name amid barbarian peoples who had no oppressor other than each other. Imperial Rome had been characterized by a great mass of subjugated

people and a proliferation of religious cults. Christianity was one of
the many messianic movements that promised salvation from oppression
by a reaffirmation of faith.

The faith was faith in a powerful ally, the one and only omnipotent
God who promised to bless his chosen people. It so happened that
those chosen people were the Jews, another oppressed minority in
Imperial Rome. But the Christ-figure that emerged condemned those
whose everyday practices were no longer in accord with their sacred
beliefs. He disputed the Jews' claims to the monopoly of God's
blessing and proclaimed instead that his teachings alone represented
the path to true salvation.

These claims found a receptive audience, and the Christianity that
emanated from Rome in the last days of the empire was created from
a strange amalgam. The sacred writings that played such a significant
part in the subsequent growth of the religion were in two parts. There
were the words spoken by an omnipotent God to the Jews, a loose
federation of nomadic tribes that had traversed the Sinai Desert for
thousands of years. And then there were the words spoken by Jesus
to an urban proletariat, promising a renewal of the sacred covenant that
omnipotent God made with his chosen people. The chosen people of the
new religion were self-selected. They were those who affirmed their
faith in God's power by dedication to His representative spokesmen.
Thus Christianity became a community of true believers who clustered
together in churches and practiced a variety of sacramental rites that
affirmed their beliefs and promised salvation from their miserable
circumstances.

What became the established religion among the barbarian tribes
of the north was yet another amalgam. Traditional pagan notions were
added to the beliefs promulgated in the Old Testament and the sacra-
ments sanctified by the New Testament. Those who converted to
Christianity with its promise of a powerful ally did not relinquish their
traditional understandings of the world. Rather, they merged their old
notions with the utopian vision of the new faith. The pagan beliefs
of the Goths and the Celts included demons and spirits, monsters and
improbable beasts that dwell in the dark regions of the forest, ready
to trap the unwary and devour the innocent. The sacred scriptures
of the Bible and the Apocrypha, as interpreted by a literate priesthood,
also gave testimony to evil demons, fallen angels, and incubi of
various sorts. So the sacred scriptures gave legitimacy to the pagan
beliefs they entwined with in the Dark Ages of feudal Europe.

Despite the fact that Christianity proclaims love and compassion, good faith, modesty, and devotion to altruistic causes as virtues, it also includes a substratum of belief that glorifies warfare in the eternal battle with evil. To understand the version of the gothic view Richard Nixon was heir to and in turn promulgated in the 20th century, it is necessary to see these dual aspects of the Christian world view. On the one hand, there is a principled statement about virtue and the ultimate meaning of life. On the other, there is a belief in sinister forces that oppress virtue for malevolent reasons of their own. Eventually, churchmen and philosphers would debate whether the forces of evil could exist in a world created by an omnipotent, benevolent God. But the debate would never be settled, and both notions have co-existed historically (Ahern, 1971).

Through the Middle Ages Christian expression of malevolent forces was embodied in the gargoyles and glyphs that once embellished the inside of medieval churches and later were banished to cornices and parapets. Carved from stone by skilled artisans, they symbolized pagan demonology in Christian form. They portrayed confusion, terror, fear, and horror; they generated anxiety about the night.

The gothic imagery that dominated the Western imagination from the 12th to the 16th century emerged at a unique juncture in history. The seeds of Christianity had flourished after the fall of Rome and, at the same time, complex forms of social organization were reduced to more primitive forms. Then, around the 10th century, technological developments began to transform the medieval world. The waterwheel, the windmill, and the harness generated new sources of power, and a complex social order that had previously required slave labor to permit specialization and produce a surplus reappeared. The modern plow, the European compass, the rudder, the printing press, the crank, the treadle, the lathe, and cast iron all contributed to transforming production, transportation, and communication, and thereby transforming everyday life. As the new technology created new possibilities, new opportunities were presented to the shrewd and the ambitious, who could see beyond the traditional choices.

New forms of organizations and new types of social relations emerged, while the characteristic patterns of the old order disintegrated. Eventually, a new order took form as new ideas gave direction to chaotic change. But in the centuries preceding the Renaissance, gothic imagery dominated the imagination of Western Europe. Rooted in traditional Christian imagery, it proposed a sinister version of reality.

The unprecedented changes in life's circumstances were seen as parallelling man's expulsion from Eden, and in place of the paradisical world of a fixed feudal order were the nightmare terrors of a fluid, urban society. Those who recognized that the times were changing were obsessed with the fear that such changes could only be for the worse, and belief in malevolent forces flourished. In the liturgy of the times, it was not enough for principled Christians simply to do good; they must also do battle with evil.

The Renaissance renewed interest in classical knowledge, and the scriptures lost their power as the ultimate, authoritative document. As the renewal of rationality began to supplant dedication to faith, the image of evil that dominated the imagination of the medieval world faded. But it was not exorcised.

From the Renaissance on Western life underwent a number of changes, and with each change in secular circumstance came a change in spiritual perspective. With each transformation of the social order religious groups splintered off, proclaimed a new interpretation of the old writings, and gave birth to sectarian movements. Martin Luther, John Calvin, and John Wesley were among those whose claims moved others who longed to believe in an omnipotent power allied with their own cause. Later George Fox, Mary Baker Eddy, and even Norman Vincent Peale convinced still others that the power of the omnipotent God could be found in the will of the true believer. But despite these changes in perspective, the institutionalized religion that took form in the Middle Ages remained the traditional embodiment of all ethical truth, the final authority on matters of spiritual relevance.

The discovery of the New World opened new options for those who did not fit into the old order. The early New England colonists were Puritan pilgrims of a fundamentalist sort who came to consider them-selves God's chosen people. Settlers in the Southern colonies included merchants, ex-convicts, debtors, indentured servants, and ne'er-do-wells, but all considered themselves Christians nonetheless. So despite the radical break with the aristocratic order that characterized the origins of the new nation, the Reformation faith of the Old World was imported along with the emergent philosophies of the Enlightenment. Eventually, America came to see itself as a Christian nation in a self-righteous way. The separation between church and state became a point of Constitutional principle, yet God's name was routinely invoked on solemn occasions and his blessings solicited for important national endeavors. Ultimately, the values the nation claimed as its own were those values embodied in the sacred scriptures of the past, even as more secular values were emerging from the changing circumstances of history.

By the time of Richard Nixon's birth, American society had recapitulated the growth pattern of earlier civilizations in less than two centuries. What started as an abject colony on the outer fringes of the Western world emerged as a power in its own right after World War I. For a people who began believing themselves a chosen people, global power was historical destiny. In Calvinist tradition God rewards those he chooses for salvation with success in the secular world, and success in the secular world is taken as a sign of spiritual blessing. Calvinist logic gave direction and meaning to the opportunities of the merchant class in the 17th century, who, in turn, were able to overpower the aristocracy in the 18th century. America began as an experiment in bourgeois order, and its 20th century place in international affairs gave further testimony to the principles of the Protestant ethic. Protestantism itself began as a spiritual revival in revolt against the libertine ways of the Renaissance. But it was destined to become more and more secular as the immediate gratifications of material desire became the fundamental measure of spiritual salvation. By Nixon's childhood, Christ was no longer portrayed as the savior of the oppressed, but rather as a successful salesman, as evinced by Bruce Barton's best-selling text of the era: *The Man Nobody Knows* (1924).

By the 1920s Christianity had undergone yet another transformation. Technological changes brought about by industrialization transformed the world from scarcity to abundance. The notions of Victorian piety that had characterized social life through most of the 19th century were based on a premise of denial and hence attuned to a world of privation. Sex, intoxicants, and unrestricted emotions were all taboo, as a matter of ethical principle, as were any direct references to such topics. Leisure was seen as recreation and not fun; it was a time to renew the individual for resumed battle in the marketplace, and the institutions of organized religion were the proper pastimes for those not otherwise gainfully employed. In the super-abundance of material artifacts generated by the technology of industrial production, however, such self-denial was no longer rational.

As long as material success was the measure of spiritual success, there was no reason to question the freedom of productive enterprise.

Instead, what was questioned were the Victorian notions of genteel propriety that had been proclaimed the foundation of a principled Christian life. Just in time, the writings of Sigmund Freud appeared to give authoritative documentation to the legitimacy of indulging the id. The 1920s saw the emergence of modernity, as the fundamentalist notions of the old order were challenged by scientific skepticism and the idea of relativity. The Scopes trial and Einstein's theory were contemporaries in a generation when science and education challenged the historic dominance of the church.

Modernity offered a new perspective, well-suited to ambitious entrepreneurs. Prosperity and gadgetry, mass motoring and the movies vied with church socials. The secular world was seductive, but the traditional teachings of the church were stern.

And so a critical juncture was reached. The nation could either constrain the freedom of secular enterprise in the name of sacred principles, or it could reinterpret the meaning of the scriptures to give traditional sanction to a new way of life. The citizens of the nation chose to do the latter, and thus began the epoch I have called 20th century gothic.

The Gothic Vision

Before its emergence into the 20th century, the gothic vision appears in two historical epochs. In the Middle Ages it is found embodied in beliefs about demonic forces. It is manifest in monumental architecture as well as in routine understandings of everyday life. It appears again at the beginning of the Industrial Revolution, a variant of the newly emerging literary tradition. Novels written in the gothic style recaptured the popular imagination, and through the growth of popular media such as the penny-dreadful novel, images of monstrous forces like vampires and werewolves flourished. Gothic architectural forms reappeared once again, as new forms of technology liberated new forces of energy, and the anxious became fearful of unprecedented change.

Medieval gothic, 18th century gothic, and 20th century gothic are all versions of Christian reality. Each testifies to the existence of evil forces that would destroy the pious and oppress the devout for malevolent ambitions of their own. The forces of Satan exemplify the imagery of the gothic vision, and the fundamentalist revival movements of the 1920s renewed Satan as a symbolic force in American life. Evangelical preachers evoked images of the hellfire and damnation that beset those who did not believe, while they promised salvation from their enemies to those who would commit themselves to the Christian liturgy. That liturgy proclaimed the New Testament a source of divine inspiration and the entire Bible a statement of unquestioned truth. Those who accepted Jesus, they preached, accepted the sacred writings of Christianity broadly defined. Their salvation from suffering and damnation would be assured and God's blessings forthcoming.

Devout Christians were expected to live a life enlightened by Christ's teachings. But, as every Protestant knew, when the demands of the spiritual order were in conflict with the demands of secular life, it was righteous, just, and eminently reasonable to forsake the divine inspiration of Christ's brotherhood for the practical advantage of the moment. No matter what Christ might have taught, it was God who made the final decision. Good Protestants knew that if their choices were sanctified by God, they would be rewarded with success.

At this critical juncture in history, God's blessings came down on the side of the practical opportunist. Given the choice of modifying their strategic advantage by a principled dedication to spiritual ethics, modern Americans had the option of treating the success of their enterprises as evidence of spiritual virtue. The language, imagery, and metaphors of Christian reality were carried into the new order, but religious ethics were not the guiding principles of conduct. Instead, hypocrisy became a way of life. People testified to their belief in Christian principles, but only as a rhetorical device. In the practical world—in particular, in business and politics—strategic advantage governed their interests. Just as the Victorians found sex and intoxicants unmentionable, no one spoke of self-serving interests as though they were virtues. Nonetheless, they were self-righteously pursued.

The most massive evidence of this disjunction between creed and conduct is found in the widespread violation of the 18th Amendment, itself a document of another set of scriptures. Middle class men and women who claimed to be law-abiding, righteous people, living God's will as articulated by Jesus Christ, routinely drank in one another's company while they publicly proclaimed the justice of depriving working people access to alcoholic beverages. Furthermore, they were not embarrassed by the contradiction between their private lives and their public sentiments. Rather, they considered themselves enlightened and just, knowing as they did that working class people could not hold their liquor or restrain from self-indulgence.

Throughout the 1920s and into the 1930s traditional church involvement in America declined, while the numbers who flocked to evangelical preachers to dedicate their lives to Jesus increased. Ultimately, the traditional denominations came to terms with their evangelical competitors by incorporating the imagery the revivalists promulgated. The Protestant Church in America came to sanctify war as a righteous battle against the forces of evil just in time to endorse America's involvement in World War II and all wars thereafter.

As a young and impressionable boy, Richard Nixon was exposed to the fundamentalist fervor of the 1920s. More than once his father drove to Los Angeles where he and his brothers were exposed to the fiery visions of Aimee Semple McPherson and other revivalists centered in Southern California and already giving the area a reputation for fostering eccentrics. Years later, in various testimonies to Billy Graham, Nixon describes his encounter with fundamentalism as a moving experience in his life, even though his public or official religion was "Quaker."

Having learned about the enemy in his childhood, in manhood he had the opportunity to wage war against the forces of evil that threatened the Christian democratic principles his nation stood for. In the heightened emotional context of World War II Nixon saw the "other side" as the embodiment of those forces of evil he had learned about as a child. The other side—the enemy—came to stand for all those demonic forces that beset life and made existence imperfect, uncertain, or intolerable.

The Enemy

Imagery of warfare became embedded in children's play during World War I, and it lingered for younger children as tradition. But Nixon and his brothers spent their early years on a farm, insulated from such cosmopolitan wartime images as Kaiser Bill and Big Bertha. By the time the family moved to the city, Nixon was not one to roughhouse with the gang. So the imagery of warfare and conflict that infuses the street life of city kids was not a significant part of his childhood. He suffered the loss of his younger brother Arthur in childhood, and his older brother Harold died in Richard's adolescence, but these were the only significant tragedies in his life from boyhood to manhood. Though not born into advantageous circumstances, he became a success nonetheless, first in the open competition of the school system and then in his first years of law practice. His early aspirations were never thwarted, even during the Depression. Though he had been exposed to the rhetoric of evil in his boyhood, he never had an opportunity to openly encounter the forces of evil until he enlisted in the Navy. Thus the first clear manifestation of the enemy appears in his life at the time of World War II, when the 20th century gothic vision growing in the Old World encountered itself coming around the other way.

In the 20th century, Hitler and the Axis powers came to epitomize all that was demonic, malevolent, insidious, and sinister, while the Allies, in their battle with such loathsome evil, came to symbolize all that was clean, decent, honest, just, righteous, virtuous, and true. Aligned with the most worthy of causes—the battle of democracy against fascism— the conflict with evil took on contemporary significance for both Nixon and the American nation. No longer were the demonic forces that threatened the devout spiritual forces from another world. They were now contemporaries on the same planet, engaged in mortal conflict over global dominance. Dwight Eisenhower eventually gave voice to the belief that atheism, communism, and evil were one, and the era of the Cold War mentality was sanctified. But the imagery in America had its origins long before, in the red scares at the end of World War I and the fundamental revivalism that flourished before the Depression. Though the Depression was a severe test of the traditional free enterprise system, the forces of fascism renewed Americans' faith in their society by giving expression to an enemy that threatened the sovereignty of democracy. By the end of World War II the concentration camps and the mushroom cloud took their place, along with the gargoyle and the vampire, as the symbolic manifestation of the terrible forces that threaten the world. These were the formative years of Richard Nixon's manhood.

After the war Nixon's chosen profession provided routine opportunities to encounter the enemy, and his political style developed. He began to cultivate an evangelical demeanor. Through artful speech, he conjured up images of the mortal conflict between good and evil, while he proposed his own candidacy as salvation. Through his ceaseless harangues against evil and his eagerness to do battle he brought into his reality the very demons he set out to conquer.

The sinister menace of the international communist conspiracy had been invoked to defeat his first political opponents and then used to destroy the reputation of Alger Hiss. When libertarians, intellectuals, and selected segments of the press criticized him for being in cahoots with evil by the very tactics he employed, Nixon discovered evil in his critics.

In the gothic imagination evil is insidious. Once let in, it will flourish in the most barren conditions. In their treatment of the "Checkers" speech, the press and the liberal establishment had shown Nixon their true colors. They were the enemy that would oppose him. Instead of giving him the credit that was his due when he singlehandedly staved off detractors in his own party while convincing hundreds of thousands of television viewers to come to his defense, they belittled his victory, calling it a soap opera performance by a self-serving man. They thwarted his objectives, tormented him with criticism, deprecated his accomplishments. They were not to be trusted. Time after time he confided to his intimates, "The press is the enemy," and, eventually, along with the press were all those who supported "amnesty, pot, abortion, confiscation of wealth . . . massive increases in welfare, unilateral disarmament, reduction of . . . defenses and surrender in Viet Nam" (Safire, 1975, p. 360). The disastrous presidential and gubernatorial campaigns of 1960 and 1962, respectively, reaffirmed what Nixon learned when he ran for Vice President: he had enemies who would ruthlessly destroy him for malicious objectives of their own. Thereafter, the press, the Eastern Establishment, and the intelligentsia became the enemy, the demonic forms that beset his life and made his existence imperfect. In public the enemy was courted with deference and respect; in secret efforts were made to destroy and discredit those opposing his objectives.

By the time Nixon achieved the presidency, dissent was seen as yet another threat to legitimate authority, and dissenters of various sorts crystallized into another manifestation of the enemy.

More personal, immediate enemies had emerged through his career in politics, most important among them, the Kennedys. John F. Kennedy and Richard M. Nixon entered Congress the same year. Both were young, ambitious, energetic men, but there the similarity ended. While Nixon's family was petit bourgeois, Kennedy's family was prosperous. Nixon went to Duke; Kennedy went to Harvard. Nixon's service record was undistinguished; Kennedy was a hero. Nixon was provincial, Kennedy cosmopolitan; Nixon was withdrawn, Kennedy affable; Nixon's brothers were a liability, Kennedy's an asset. It had been Kennedy's brother Robert who tarnished the reputation of Nixon's close friend and political adviser, Murray Chotiner, and, by implication, of Nixon. It was Robert Kennedy, again, who was instrumental in starting investigations of corrupt campaign practices against Nixon and his brother Donald after the 1960 election.

While John Kennedy and Richard Nixon served in Congress, they encountered one another on freqent occasions, each time on opposite sides of the issue. Nixon admired his opponent; Kennedy had nothing but disdain for his. By 1960 each had earned a reputation as a tough competitor, and the race for the White House was the big match. Nixon came off second best. From the Great Debates on, he saw himself a loser in the contest of luck and misfortune. Despite the claims of fraud and theft surrounding the final outcome, he did not contest the results. Having known he was a loser, he did not believe he could successfully challenge the Kennedy machine. He accepted the outcome with apparent good grace and prepared to renew his battle for the White House from a new political base. But he would harbor bitterness and resentment along with express sentiments of ill will.

The Kennedy ghost haunted Nixon's life. After John's assassination, Robert threatened his second race for the presidency; and after Robert's death, Teddy became a powerful foe in the Senate. Like the press, "Kennedy" became a term of heightened significance in the Nixon lexicon. It was invoked to represent the forces of evil that threatened his well-being, and, once invoked, such evil had to be managed.

More general than the Kennedys, the Eastern Establishment came to be seen among the forces that threatened Nixon's self-interests. As a young man, bright with the promise of youth, he presented himself at the citadel of the American establishment: Wall Street. But where other schoolmates from Duke were successful in securing advantageous positions, Nixon was less fortunate. His failure did not extinguish his aspirations, and Wall Street remained a symbol of real authority. After his political defeat in 1962, he turned to the East for renewal. Thirty years after his first attempt the doors of the citadel opened. But his victory was cold porridge pie. He was no longer a raw, inexperienced youth but a mature man quite fixed in his ways. Once he might have become a sophisticated cosmopolitan by just being in a cosmopolitan setting; now his provincial habits grated against his new surroundings. Despite his ambition he did not feel comfortable in New York City. His ineptness irritated him, and his discontent threatened his sense of inner satisfaction. The Eastern Establishment became another enemy.

Throughout his public career—by indirection, implication, innuendo, and inference—Nixon had accused the Democratic Party of being in cahoots with evil. Eventually, he began to act on what he had been saying for so long. By 1970 loyal opposition and illegitimate opposition merged in his vision: Democrats and demonstrators were treated the same way. Strategy and tactics appropriate to the mortal conflict between good and evil became appropriate against any and all opposition. Distinctions were no longer made between the means appropriate to one contest and the means appropriate to another, for all opposition was seen as a manifestation of sinister forces, and any power was a necessary power in support of a righteous cause. Since the forces of evil were ruthless, virtue must be ruthless in self-defense.

In assuming there was an enemy out there, committed to destroying him in pursuit of its own diabolical ambitions, Nixon routinely acted in such a way as to bring enemies into existence. He began his career as a moral crusader, a righteous warrior doing battle with all that was malevolent, depraved, and corrupt. He was instrumental in convincing large numbers of people that his cause was just. Those who did not capitulate to his vision became a source of aggravation, and a vicous cycle began. The more his objectives were opposed, the more convinced Nixon became of the power of the enemy, and the more ruthless his tactics in the cause of righteousness. As he escalated his opposition to others, others escalated their opposition to him. If they started out as critics, they eventually became the enemy. Ultimately, he fell in disgrace, a victim of the very forces he invoked.

By the very nature of the drama, some in the audience will always believe Nixon was the innocent victim and not the wily magician. At each stage in Nixon's career they will be convinced that there are forces of evil extant in the world, that known manifestations of those forces have done battle with Nixon in the past, and that those same parties are involved in the present. They have seen the drama, but they have missed the action. They have not seen how Nixon's own behavior either conjured up the enemy or exacerbated the conflict. So they will buy Nixon's line that he is the underdog, beset by vicious enemies, and their sympathy will go out to him. They share the gothic vision.

Others more critical of Nixon's role in his own demise will interpret his failing in different terms. They will see him as basically weak, ineffectual, impotent, or sick. Admitting they might have been fooled for a little while into believing he was the strong leader America deserves, they will be forced to acknowledge that, after all, he is just another version of Willie Loman, the pathetic hero of Arthur Miller's *Death of A Salesman.*

Those who are most critical might question the drama itself, its scripting, its backers, and, most of all, its assumptions. Though every human culture must deal with the exigencies of life, evil is not always embodied as misfortune. Furthermore, even where evil forces are acknowledged as one of life's hazards, they are not always portrayed as locked in mortal conflict with good. The Yin and Yang of Eastern thought posits good and evil as coexistant. Virtue is found in an expeditious path between them. This is not to say that warfare and battle have not been sanctified in the East, only that the philosophic assumptions about the universe are different.

The West was heir to a dualistic version of the world in which the fundamental precept was the rule of the excluded middle: positive and negative cancel one another; they do not form a synthesis. Aristotelian logic, based on the rule of the excluded middle, was cultivated during the Middle Ages when the gothic image first took form. The two survived through the Renaissance, the Reformation, and the Enlightenment. In the 20th century relativist thought threatened Aristotelian dominance. But even while the logic that gave the gothic image its force began to lose influence, the vision it fostered flourished. Starting in the early part of the 20th century, that vision came into its own, and by mid-century it was our dominant metaphor.

·chronology·

Chapter 2

Growing Up
in Southern California

The tide of westward exploration and expansion that began in Europe in the 15th century came to rest on the Pacific shores of the New World in the 20th century. In the flowing mass of humanity, Nixon and Milhous ancestors came from Ireland to America in the 18th century, their descendants moved from the East Coast to the broad valleys of the continental interior in the 19th century, and eventually Frank Nixon and Hannah Milhous went from the Midwest to Southern California. On January 9, 1913, in a clapboard house on the side of an irrigation ditch, Richard, their second son, was born. There was no reason to suppose that infant would eventually make his mark on Western history. Yet as insignificant and inconspicuous as his birth and boyhood were, Richard Milhous Nixon did indeed make history, just as he himself was the product of historic forces.

The most notable of those forces in the decade of his birth were the forces of change. The traditional forms of social life that emerged in America after the Civil War influenced Nixon's father and grandfather in very similar ways; but by the time of Richard's birth those forms were undergoing radical transformations. Before World War I time and space had posed considerable barriers to transportation and communication. Most people lived their lives among familiar people and familiar events, insulated by the peculiar values of the local community. Outside the local community there were few common denominators between people. Mass media and mass advertising were yet to become routine parts of life; radio, television, and other electronic phenomena were no influence. These were horse and buggy days, when the average speed of a wagon was six miles an hour and those who were disillusioned with urban life could still find alternatives in rural regions.

In the days of Richard Nixon's father and grandfather, urban life had been characterized by the influx of millions of immigrants, ignorant of the language and customs of their new country; by ever-growing masses of people with limited skills and meager resources, clamoring for a share of the good life. Tenements and sweat shops were the customary lot of these urban poor. Those in the hinterland did not fare much better. In the thousands of milltowns and minetowns, workers were impoverished by low wages and imprisoned by poor working conditions, often dependent on the inferior living conditions company towns regularly propagate. In most parts of the country people were without fresh fruit and green vegetables from late autumn to late spring. Thus added to the harsh conditions of labor were the further discomforts of inadequate nutrition: sluggish health and poor disposition for at least a part of every year.

As a carpenter, a telephone lineman, an oilfield roustabout, Frank Nixon experienced many of these hardships. Yet the era was not without hope. From the Civil War to the First World War, Horatio Alger stories presented millions of American boys with an idealized picture of American life, one where even the most impoverished could rise to economic power and corporate influence by hard work and luck. Men such as John D. Rockefeller, Andrew Carnegie, and J. Pierpoint Morgan presented living examples of the mythical heroes embodied in the pages of *Bound to Rise, Luck and Pluck, Sink or Swim.* Books like these produced successive generations of men who sincerely believed that wealth was the fruit of hard work and virtue, while poverty was the result of indolence and sloth. Like the millions of other young men of his generation who had been raised on the imagery of the dime novel, Frank Nixon could sustain a vision of the future that would more than compensate for the hardships of his present condition. When he migrated from Columbus, Ohio, to Whittier, California, he could anticipate not only a more benign climate but also renewed opportunities for economic success.

Frank Nixon came to Whittier for reasons of money and comfort; Hannah Milhous's migration was less worldly. Dating back to the 18th century, Milhous folk had been Quakers; and at the turn of the 20th century, Whittier was one of a small number of intentional Quaker colonies. Hannah's family migrated from their Indiana farm to the community of Friends in 1897 and the Milhouses were respected and influential members of the community from its inception. Eventually, Frank Nixon met Hannah Milhous at a community social, and they were married soon afterward.

The Nixon boy and the Milhous girl were an unlikely match. She was a Quaker; he was a Methodist. She came from an influential family; he was an itinerant laborer. She was a graduate of Whittier College; he had left school in the sixth grade. She was patient and gentle by temperament; he was harsh and argumentative. Nontheless, they were wed and began life together on a citrus farm in Yorba Linda, a few miles south of Whittier. They were married for almost 50 years, until Frank's death in 1956. They produced five sons, three of whom lived to maturity.

The decade of Richard Nixon's birth was characterized by massive technological and material changes, and American social life was in a ferment of adaptation. In the 1890s corporate control of government had begun in earnest. Through hints, suggestions, loans, and gifts, as well as through an occasional bribe, corporations had begun to make legislators, elected officials, and even judges do their bidding. For the most part, this alliance went unchecked. The most vocal antitrust speakers were aligned with the cause of socialism, and the foreign flavor of their proposals raised suspicion in more provincial minds. There were few people outside of business or corporate law who understood how extended business combinations were set up, how they functioned, or how they exercised their political leverage. The general isolation of communities made it difficult for people to see how the interdependence of business and political activity ultimately affected their everyday lives. Thus the changes in the social structure that began before the turn of the century continued. Industrialism expanded, and with it the growth and influence of business interests.

Then in the 1910s, a wave of idealism and reform swept the country. Radical voices were louder, more widespread. Their objectives were more focused. Ferment spread. Women and workers organized in protest of their oppressive conditions. Women were given the right to vote. The graduated income tax was introduced as a technique to redistribute the wealth that had become more and more concentrated in fewer and fewer hands. Change was everywhere.

American involvement in the First World War intensified the changes that had been taking place in the prewar years. First of all, the war produced strong pressures for a national identity as a model of patriotism. It fostered the notion of the 100% American, who had no ties to foreign loyalty in culture or custom. It was a decade when antisemitism flourished and the Ku Klux Klan grew. The existence of an alien enemy simply gave substance to the fear of un-American sentiments that had begun before the war.

Despite the economic interests that were represented by the conflict in Europe, the domestic image of American involvement was couched in the language of idealism best expressed by Woodrow Wilson. From Richard Nixon's childhood through his youth, this idealism gradually eroded. But during his early years, at least, there was a widespread belief in enlightened self-government and a strong sense of confidence and optimism. People believed American Christian Democracy could and should be universally applied for the betterment of humanity. World War I reinforced the conviction that if there was evil in the world, that evil came from sources outside America, from foreign shores. After the war the image of Kaiser Bill was replaced by that of the bomb-throwing anarchist, and thus the red scare continued to heighten ethnocentrism.

By the 1920s the active anticommunism movement had abated, but it left in its wake bitter suspicion of aliens, distrust of organized labor, hostility toward reformers, and a general insistence on political and social conformity. These were the sentiments that permeated American life when Nixon was growing up in Yorba Linda and later in Whittier.

In addition to channeling moral sentiments, the war also influenced the relationship beween business and goverment. The informal alliance between economic and political interests that characterized the earlier decades was formalized when, in the face of the war effort, government agencies began large-scale control of the economy. It was clear that government intervention need not tether the invisible hand guiding the marketplace, but instead might move it in more profitable directions.

Fortunes were made through the course of the war; and afterward business interests supported Warren Harding for President as the man most likely to be congenial to the concerns of business.

Harding presented a figure of bourgeois prosperity. He was a gregarious person with great interest in, and liking for, other people —particularly his buddies from Marion, Ohio. He appointed his old friends to high political positions regardless of expertise or even experience; and his friends played fast and loose with their new-found power. They kept a brothel in the heart of the capital; they dealt in bootleg liquor. They peddled influence in litigation and contracts. They manipulated government resources for private profit. In the first years of his administration there were rumors of graft and corruption, but Harding presented a seemly front. Thus when on a tour of the West he was taken ill and suddenly died, people throughout the country mourned the goodhearted man who had died as a martyr in the service of his country. His successor declared a day of public mourning. Businesses were closed and memorial services were held all over the country, including Whittier, California.

Over a period of years testimony of what went on behind the closed doors of the Harding administration came out. But unlike the story of Harding's funeral entourage, the stories of graft and corruption came out intermittently, not in a continuous tale. The facts were confusing; the account hard to piece together. As time went by, later investigations seemed like washing old dirty linen. Those who tried to arouse interest in the story were labeled scandalmongers and character assassins. Eventually, however, even resentment toward the scandalmongers passed, and in its wake settled public apathy and a certain apprehension about the critical objectives of a free press.

Years later, Hannah Nixon described the scandals of the Harding administration as a key point in her son's early development:

> Richard could not help but hear and to some extent share his father's indignation about the Teapot Dome scandals. One evening Richard was lying on the floor, the newspaper spread out around him, reading an account of the corrupt officials and attorneys who had been on the front pages . . . Suddenly he looked up and solemnly announced, "Mother, I just made up my mind; I'm going to be a lawyer—a lawyer who can't be bought by crooks." (Spalding, 1972, pp. 52-53.)

In his post-Watergate memoirs, the incident is never mentioned.

★   ★   ★

By the time the stories about the Teapot Dome began to make headlines across the nation, the Nixon family had moved from Yorba Linda to Whittier. This was the first significant change in young Nixon's immediate circumstances. Home in Yorba Linda had been a cottage on the side of an irrigation ditch in an isolated rural area. Home in Whittier was adjacent to the family gas station on East Whittier Boulevard. Soon afterward, Frank Nixon purchased the building of the old Friends Church, moved it to his lot, and expanded the family business to include a grocery store as well as a filling station. Thereafter, the Nixon boys were known as the grocer's sons in the thriving Southern California community.

If Frank Nixon grew up in the horse-and-buggy days, Richard Nixon's experience with the old order was brief and dramatic. Biographers note that among his childhood misfortunes was a buggy accident at the age of three, in which he was thrown from the wagon when the horses bolted. He suffered a severe laceration of his scalp and might have died if a neighbor with an automobile had not rushed him to a local hospital. The automobile thus played for the first time a critical role in his life; years later he would decribe cruising on the freeways at high speed as a favored form of relaxation.

The automoble had been one of the major technological changes introduced in the previous decade. Commonly referred to as the "Tin Lizzie," it quickly replaced the horse in both urban and rural life. Employing radically new methods of production assembly, by 1910 Henry Ford had produced millions of Model Ts. The Model T was a cheap, relatively reliable method of transportation. Anyone with a grasp of mechanics could keep it in repair and running, even over the inferior dirt roadways that characterized the times. Once it got started, the Ford automobile could do 40 mph on a flat stretch. The horse-and-buggy days were passing. The distances that had been an integral part of the old order were dramatically reduced.

As an example of technological adaptation and diffusion, mass motoring in America was phenomenal. When it was first introduced, it was assumed that the automobile would be the prerogative of the rich alone. However, cheap gasoline and the introduction of installment buying in the 1920s would change this; by 1930 mass automobile ownership began to characterize the American experience. Automobile registration went from nine million cars in 1920 to 26.5 million in 1930, and the numbers increased enormously every decade thereafter.

Mass motoring required relatively reliable, relatively inexpensive machines, and means such as installment buying by which large numbers of people could afford them. It also required a network of good roads and highways and enough garages and filling stations to service those who took to the roads. It was the latter necessity that offered a new opportunity to Frank Nixon when it was clear that his citrus farm in Yorba Linda would always be marginal.

Hannah Nixon looked back on Yorba Linda as a good place to raise children, but not to make a living. Before her husband became a farmer in Southern California he had worked at a variety of tinkering trades. So it must have seemed reasonable that a man with his talents who wanted to get ahead in the postwar world might think of opening a gas station on the highway outside his wife's home town.

Reflecting the times, the little community of Whittier was itself changing. Where agriculture had dominated the economic structure of the town before the war, oil, and then land became the major economic influences in the 1920s. One of the early Standard Oil finds was in the hills east of town. Soon ads for automobiles began to dominate *The Whittier News*. Articles in the local newspaper noted "Tourist travel to be the greatest in history," and "The price of gasoline is going up, but supplies are adequate for consumer needs." In addition to the proliferation of ads associated with expanding oil interests, *The Whittier News* included innumerable advertisements for subdivisions and land developments. One large ad for a local subdivision read, "By actual count 300 autos pass this corner in 15 minutes on regular work days."

Oil and real estate interests intertwined in Whittier, as they did in the nation at large. Before the advent of the automobile, accessible trolley lines limited the growth of suburban settlements. After the advent of the automobile, land that had previously been inaccessible suddenly became marketable. Soon after the subdivision ads appeared in *The Whittier News*, ads for savings and loan associations and for contractors began. Through this interdependence of economic interests, the community of Whittier grew from 8,000 in 1920 to 15,000 in 1930.

Prosperity was now the keynote of the times, and everywhere young Nixon looked he could see examples of how, in these changing times, some were rewarded with wealth and influence while others withered on the sidelines.

By the prosperous standards of Whittier, Californa, c. 1920, the Nixon family enterprise could not be counted a success. Like the thousands of other roadside stands that began to dot the landscape of the nation with the advent of mass-motoring, they sold milk and bread, ice cream and candy, gasoline and automotive services. As the enterprise was well situated on the main highway at the edge of a growing community, townfolk, farmers and wealthy Southern California tourists created a ready market for gas and refreshments. Nonetheless, Frank Nixon never struck it rich.

Gradually, under Hannah's adroit management, the grocery section was expanded. She baked pies, kept the books, and mediated between her argumentative husband and the customers. The Nixon boys began to take an active part in maintaining the family business; eventually they took charge of various departments. Richard's responsibility was produce. Throughout high school and college he rose in the morning, drove fourteen miles to the wholesale market in Los Angeles and fourteen miles back. He cleaned his fruits and vegetables and arranged them in attractive displays. Then he went to school and began his studies of civics, Latin, history, and debating. But despite the enterprise, energy, and initiative the Nixons displayed, the Nixon grocery was not a financial success. Throughout the 1920s a number of local grocery stores regularly advertised in *The Whittier News,* but the Nixon grocery was not among them.

In an era when many in similar circumstances were beginnning to experience prosperity and affluence, the Nixon family remained petit bourgeois. They were a part of the business class of the community, yet the social distance between themselves and the class of laborers and farmers was marginal. Success seemed to be systematically eluding Frank Nixon. Not long after he sold the citrus farm in Yorba Linda, oil was discovered on the land he once held title to. When he deliberated over two locations for his new business in Whittier, oil was later discovered on the one he rejected. Frank Nixon *almost* struck it rich; yet success was not his. His misfortunes may well have contributed to the vituperation he demonstrated in his attacks on the participants in the Teapot Dome scandals, and may have served to heighten the salience of the event for his son.

Dreams of honor and fear of failure appear quite early in Richard Nixon's life. In grade school he became interested in, and showed considerable talent for, debate. This was a time when local high school debates still made front page news in the daily paper. He was encouraged by his father, who helped his son assemble the facts he employed in his first debates and later drove him to citywide meets. Thus by the seventh grade Richard had learned that a few facts and a facile tongue could win him personal respect and esteem.

Nixon's mother remembers her young son of this period as resolute, determined, and eager to please. Others in the community recall him as solemn, shy, studious, and sensitive. His brothers remember him as studious, solemn and likely to hold a grudge. There are no stories of him as a mischievous boy. In biography and autobiography alike, he is portrayed as a boy dedicated to work and study, obedient and always respectful of lawful authority. Though he learned to play the piano and for a while took lessons on the violin, there is no sense of *joie de vivre*. Where he excelled was in the arena of formal talk, trained to take either side of an issue without principled commitment.

Childhood and youth are a time when one's impressions of the world are established. Thereafter, these early experiences become the benchmarks for assessing life and the meaning it holds. Sometimes early impressions are modified or radically altered in the light of new experience. More often these early experiences serve to interpret and make sense of the present, as well as to give direction in the future. Thus theorists of ego development such as Freud, Erikson, Perls, and Laing consider the experiences of childhood and youth critical: they set the foundation for all future development.

Sensitive and ambitious, young Nixon must have been keenly aware of his family's position in the town of Whittier. During the '20s the class lines that characterized virtually every community were easily visible. Styles of dressing and the economics of clothing had not yet been transformed by mass production and marketing, as they would be in the '30s. The local community was still small, and a family's place in the class structure was common knowledge among the people encountered through the course of the day; there was little anonymity, few secrets. People were accorded respect appropriate to their station in the community. Hannah Milhous was respected because she was the daughter of one of the influential families of the original community. Frank Nixon was paid less respect because he had no independent links of kinship to tie him to the central core. Furthermore, in a thriving community dominated by substantial oil and real estate interests, the corner grocer is due little regard in his own right. Though Richard bore his mother's name, he was nonetheless the son of his father in a culture where kinship is reckoned by patrilineal descent. Thus it is likely that the deference and respect accorded to Richard Nixon in his youth was that appropriate to the grocer's son—even if he was a respectful, obedient, hard-working child who won honors at school and was well behaved at home.

Moving from the isolated rural hamlet of Yorba Linda and finding his place in the prosperous community of Whittier was one of Nixon's critical childhood experiences. Growing up in the 1920s was also important. Throughout this period, new methods of production and distribution continued to transform the old order. President Woodrow Wilson represented an era of naive idealism that would soon pass. The noble sentiments that had been proclaimed as the objectives of the first war of the 20th century were far from realization at the war's conclusion. The mood of the country shifted from utopian dreams to practical considerations. Warren Harding's inauguration signaled a renewed interest in business affairs; and, after him, Calvin Coolidge came to utter and then symbolize the motto, "The business of America is business." Whereas Harding's alliance with business interests had been of the informal, backroom order, Coolidge treated the relationship between government and business as a matter of principle. He assumed that, given full support of a cooperative government, business interests alone would maintain economic prosperity, and from economic prosperity would flow domestic tranquility. Business was booming when Coolidge took office, and it continued at a relentless pace under his administration. It was further abetted by a variety of technological and organizational changes that were taking place.

Like the automobile, the telephone was cutting down distances between people and hence speeding up exchanges. Formerly, business transactions were limited by primitive methods of communications, which might cause a simple transaction, such as an order to sell, to extend over a protracted period as the message was sent from one place to another and back again. The expanded growth of the telephone network increased the number of transactions that could take place in a day, a year, or a lifetime, and thus increased the potential for profit. Through the decades diesel trains and airmail planes further multiplied the rate of exchange and prospects of profit.

At the same time, the introduction of installment buying encouraged the widespread possession of consumer goods. In the old days of frugal privation the consumer had to save in order to possess. "Buy now, pay later" became a sign of the new times. Ownership of radios, electric refrigerators, and new livingroom furniture became commonplace. Chain stores provided lower consumer prices by dealing in volume and thus provided greater opportunity to possess the material abundance of this most advanced, most prosperous nation.

In the midst of this heightened economic activity, advertising took hold in earnest. Through most of American history sales practices had been governed by a peddler mentality epitomized by the image of the Yankee trader. Goods were displayed decorously, and newspaper advertising focused on the properties of the object offered. In the late 1800s, P.T. Barnum first demonstrated the successful uses of ballyhoo in marketing commodities from midgets to medicine. But the temper of the prewar world was distinctly sedate, and most merchants shunned such aggrandizement of their wares. In the 1920s, however, advertising would transform American marketing practices. Rather than focusing on the virtues of their products, the new generation of marketing experts linked products to such ephemeral values as being young and desirable, being rich, keeping up with the Joneses, being envied by others. Bolstered by innovations in printing, and in particular by the introduction of the four-color press, Americans were bombarded by appeals for all sorts of consumer goods. The growth of radio supplemented the press, providing a new medium for sales pitches.

Increasingly, advertising began to employ principles of psychology and appeals to emotion to motivate consumer spending. One of the most dramatic of these advertising campaigns was for Listerine mouthwash, which promoted the theme of "social acceptability." In a long series of full-color ads in slick magazines like the *Saturday Evening Post,* the dire effects of halitosis were chronicled: how, because of bad breath, women remained spinsters, lovers were abandoned, salesmen offended prospects. The effect of these and other such advertisements was not only to speed up consumer spending, but to transform American grooming habits and add a new dimension to social respectability. Prior to World War I bathrooms were rare and bathing infrequent; after the war the ritual of cleanliness took a special place in American life. In an interview in 1960, Hannah Nixon notes of her son:

> As a boy riding to Fullerton High School in a crowded bus, he used to be very fastidious. Every morning he would take great pains in brushing his teeth, was careful to gargle, and asked me to smell his breath to make sure he would not offend anyone on the bus. (Nixon, 1960, p. 208)

Young Richard was not alone in his concern for not offending anyone, for during the 1920s the seeds of the other-directed character that would flourish in the 1950s were just beginning to germinate. By midcentury David Riesman wrote of the other-directed person:

> While all people want and need to be liked by some of the people some of the time, it is only the modern other-directed types who make this their chief source of direction and chief area of sensitivity . . . As against guilt-and-shame controls, though of course these survive, one prime psychological lever of the other-directed person is diffuse anxiety. (Riesman, 1955, pp. 38, 42)

This anxiety is for the most part directed toward acceptability in the eyes of others. The homogenizing effect on character and style that had begun with the vision of the 100% American in the 1910s was to become an intense preoccupation in the 1920s. *What others thought of you, as a person, came to replace what you, as a person, thought.*

In addition to advertising campaigns focused on social acceptability, the era saw a renewed growth in self-improvement manuals—the classic ad, "They laughed when I sat down to play the piano" was a product of the times. Manuals on how to be popular, how to be proper, how to be strong, were not a new genre, but the new marketing practices made them easily accessible and served to heighten notions of self-improvement in the public eye. Thus the image of the self-made man, emerging in his grandfather's generation in the books of Horatio Alger, was revitalized in Richard's youth. As a serious, hard-working boy, he most likely took these messages to heart, like millions of others in his generation who learned to attune their inner senses to the prevailing social current and to create of themselves an image that others in the community would accept and respect.

At this same time business was receiving a new measure of respectability and acceptability. In earlier eras business had been considered less dignified and less distinguished than the learned professions such as medicine and law. In the 1920s attitudes began to change. The salesman was treated with new respect, and techniques of salesmanship were defined as a virtue. This was, in effect, the era of the supersalesman, the time when Bruce Barton wrote a book titled *The Man Nobody Knows,* extolling the virtues of Jesus Christ by showing how he employed principles of salesmanship and promotion in his organization and distribution of Christianity. *The Man Nobody Knows* became a best seller in the mid-twenties. Fifty years later there was still a copy of it in the Whittier City Library. Henry D. Spalding, one of Nixon's favorable biographers, chose to title his 1972 book: *The Nixon Nobody Knows.* His choice of titles is inexplicable, unless

Spalding was implying Barton's book was a significant influence on Nixon's life.

It behooves us to look at the Barton text closely, for clues to Nixon's childhood are few and far between, and what a boy is likely to have read is likely to influence what a man knows and assumes.

Bruce Barton was the son of a poor Tennessee preacher. He sold newspapers to put himself through college and then in association with some wartime acquaintances, he founded the firm of Batten, Barton, Durstine and Osborn, which firm was to become one of America's most influential advertising agencies. In 1956, Batten, Barton, Durstine and Osborn managed Eisenhower's campaign for reelection. In *The Man Nobody Knows* Barton tells the traditional story of Christ's life and the influence it had upon the Western world. The story he tells is without creed or ideological dogma. It is a simple narrative of a poor boy, growing up in a peasant family, working in a carpenter shop. As a young man, Christ gradually feels his powers expand. He begins to have influence over his neighbors. He recruits a few followers, suffers disappointments, reverses, death, and then immortality.

However, what is important in Barton's account of Christ's transformation from a simple peasant boy to a powerful world leader is not a spiritual dedication to religious principles but "the awakening of the inner consciousness of power" (Barton, 1924, p. 11). Barton does not see this awakening as a rare gift, but as the potential of everyone and anyone. He gives an account of various distinguished businessmen who all rose from obscure origins to positions of influence and power. He writes:

> At what hour, in the morning, in the afternoon, in the long quiet evening did the audacious thought enter the mind of each of them that he was larger than the limits of a country town, that his life might be bigger than his fathers? When did the thought come to Jesus? (p. 12)

And so in the Barton account Jesus was convinced that he was "linked with the Eternal, and that God had sent him into the world to do a work which no one else could do" (p. 17). The rest of the book focuses on how Jesus does his work.

As a leader, he must draw followers, and this he does through the sheer strength of his personal magnetism:

> The essential element in personal magnetism is a consuming sincerity—an overwhelming faith in the importance of the work one has to do. (p. 19)

Sincerity becomes the key to Christ's success, just as a few years later Dale Carnegie would suggest (in *How to Win Friends and Influence People*) that sincerity is the key to *everybody's* success.

Barton notes Christ's second talent in addition to being sincere: the ability to pick men and to recognize hidden capacities in them. Christ took a motley collection of fishermen and small-town businessmen and turned them into effective disciples in his cause. Clearly, the capacity for organization is an important element in success.

For Barton the growth of Christianity was predicated not on the merits of its case, but on the salesmanship of its promoters. He attributes the following statement to St. Paul:

> Let me tell you an interesting coincidence, gentlemen. This God whom you worship, without knowing his name, is the very God whom I represent. (p. 103)

Christianity did not conquer the world because it offered a truer vision of life, but because it employed sophisticated techniques to convince the world of its desirability. Again, Barton writes:

> He would be a national advertiser today, I am sure, as he was the great advertiser of his own day. Take any one of the parables, no matter which—you will find that it exemplifies all the principles on which advertising text books are written . . . First of all they are marvelously condensed, as all good advertising must be . . . His language was marvelously simple, a second great essential . . . Sincerity glistened like sunshine through every sentence he uttered . . . Finally he knew the necessity for repetition and practiced it. No important truth can be impressed upon the minds of any large number of people by being said only once. (pp. 140-155)

Thus through dedicated adherence to principles of salesmanship, Jesus was able to get his message across.

Barton's work clearly aligns the principles of business acumen on the side of the spiritually devout. Being a Christian and being a businessman can be taken as synonymous. There is no need to question the ethics of market practices because those exact procedures were used by the most holy of all.

I do not know for certain that Richard Nixon read *The Man Nobody Knows* in his impressionable youth. I do know that he was an avid reader, that the book was a popular best-seller and that it was available to him at his local library. Furthermore, even if he did read the book, there is no way of knowing just what lessons he learned from it. The best we can assert is that the Barton text was available to him in his youth and if he was not impressed with it, many young people of his generation were. At the same time, from the account of his youth he presents in his *Memoirs,* as well as other biographical sources, we do know that he was influenced by the fundamentalist revival movement that was centered in Southern California in the 1920s, and, in particular, by Aimee Semple McPherson, whose style and message both parallel the Barton text and presage the later Nixon style.

There is nothing in the Barton text or in the fundamentalist revival movement that in any contradicts the teachings Nixon was regularly exposed to at the East Whittier Friends Church. Although the Quakers began as a radical Christian sect in the 17th century in England, by the end of that century a certain tolerance for their religious style set in, and the revolutionaries became bourgeois. By the 18th century, Quaker meetings included the richest trading families in London. Thus business interests and established Quaker precepts were never in conflict. Gradually, even the distinctive style of their worship changed, so that in some communities the "steeplehouse" replaced the "meetinghouse," and a conventional ministry became a routine part of the church. The community of Whittier was characterized by both a "meetinghouse" and a "steeplehouse" congregation; the Nixons belonged to the latter. Furthermore, they were faithful churchgoers. Hannah, Frank, Richard and his brothers attended services three times each Sunday and once on Wednesday night. So throughout his youth Richard was exposed to fundamental religious precepts: how, as a Christian, he should not yield to temptation and how, as a Quaker, he should yield to his own inner light. Beyond its own distinctive style of worship, beyond its denial of dogma and pageantry, there is in Quakerism an affirmation in the inner light of consciousness. God speaks to everyone, directly, in ways that he or she can understand without mediation of a priesthood, without liturgical prayers, without public affirmation. It is not far from the Quaker belief in the inner light of revelation to the Barton belief in the revelation of the inner consciousness of power. There is all the more reason to suppose that the currents of the era epitomized by the Barton text were a significant feature of Nixon's boyhood experiences.

Throughout the 1920s, the technological innovations of the era continued to transform the conventional culture. Radio had become not only an important consumer good but a major medium for home entertainment. The programming was dominated by music, and so millions of Americans were introduced to the speeded-up tempo and the syncopated beat of jazz, as it was interpreted by the white band leaders of the era. In addition to music, radio carried news and dramatic programming, although through the '20s the dramatic fare was mainly comedy; it was not until the 1930s that the crime show became an important staple of home entertainment.

The previous decade had seen the birth of the motion picture industry in the community of Hollywood, not far from Nixon's home town. By 1914 the "movie" had entered the repertoire of cultural pastimes, and families who would not have gone to the theater began attending such attractions with increasing frequency. The early motion picture featured madcap chase scenes and maudlin romances, as well as historical extravaganzas on biblical themes. Americans took to the movies in great numbers, and from the adulation of this new audience, the celebrity system emerged—the star, admired and respected by millions everywhere.

In the 1920s romance and adventure continued to be entertainment staples. By 1927 sound had been added to motion, and a more intense experience was to be found in the local theater of virtually every city and town. The movies began to dominate the popular imagery as the dime novels had for an earlier generation. In many larger cities "movie palaces" were built, auditoriums as elaborate and grandiose as the gin palaces built by distillers in Victorian England. On the screens in these elaborate art deco palaces of entertainment viewers could watch the glamorous images of Gloria Swanson and the swashbuckling images of Rudolph Valentino. By the end of the decade, they could watch images of conflict between sinister gangsters and courageous G-men.

Combined with the growth of mass advertising, the growth of Hollywood imagery had significant consequences for the nation. Urban tastes, urban dress, and urban values quickly spread throughout the country. The rube and the hayseed began to vanish from the provincial town and the rural village. Guided by the images of the mass media, the urban proletariat began to lose its distinctive style, first in dress, then in domicile, then in manners. As the outward markers of class distinction began to fade, so did class consciousness. As the buying power of wages for skilled workers swelled, the ferment and organization that characterized labor at the end of the previous decade began to recede. It seemed, indeed, that there was an intimate link between business prosperity and domestic tranquility.

Business interests dominated the mainstream of American life in the 1920s, and new forms of leisure were gaining widespread acceptance. There was also an unconventional side to the American experience of the time that was not symbolized by the pious virtues of New England Puritanism but by the jazz-age pursuit of hedonistic pleasure and the flagrant disregard of the laws of prohibition. In urban settings in particular the tempo of life that had been altered by automotive transportation and telephonic communication seemed to be orchestrated by the music of jazz. College professors denounced jazz as "the attempt of a joyless industrial civilization to arouse its fatigue-poisoned minds and its drudgery-jaded bodies," and ministers proclaimed: "Jazz may be analyzed as a combination of nervousness, lawlessness, primitive and savage animalism and lasciviousness." (*Time-Life Books,* V.3, p. 78) Nevertheless, the music of the jazz musician came to symbolize the youthful mood of the '20s, just as the music of the rock musician was to symbolize a generation 40 years later.

Vitalized by a new drummer and a new beat, the ongoing ferment of social change was dispersed and transformed. In the 1910s Emma Goldman had been proclaiming the virtue of freedom in clothing and in sex to a generation still tightly corseted in Victorian notions of dress and demeanor. By the 1920s a new term had to be coined to refer to that class of women who had discarded their corsets, smoked cigarettes openly, and danced cheek to cheek with young men. Along with the term "flapper," a new vocabulary emerged to refer to relations between the sexes: "blind date," "sex appeal," "drugstore cowboy," and "necking" all appeared. The theories of Freud and Einstein were challenging old notions of life and matter, and the ideas held only by "bohemians" a generation before were becoming commonplace.

The '20s was a time of slang, when new words were being introduced to refer to new phenomena. In addition to terms addressed to sexual relations were terms addressed to drinking and prohibition, for, along with the music, these themes constituted the dominant motif of the jazz age. The wave of idealistic reform that had swept the country the decade before had introduced prohibition as a national fact of life. Prohibition transformed drinking into a federal offense, and, as a consequence, millions of Americans began regularly and routinely to violate the law. Prohibition also provided opportunities for wide-scale bootlegging enterprises, and the gangster transformed law violation into big business. The image of Al Capone was as much a part of the decade as were the images of Coolidge and Lindbergh.

The jazz age was manifested in cosmopolitan settings. How much of its influence spread to the provinces, and to what extent it might have affected Richard Nixon, are hard to assess. Certainly the mood of the era was more likely to be felt in Southern California than, say, in Midwestern Kansas, for by the 1920s Southern California already had a reputation for eccentricity. Richard's responsibility for the family produce concession took him to the cosmopolitan center of Los Angeles daily. The radio, the movies, and the slick magazines all transmitted conventionalized versions of the new lifestyle, reinforcing whatever he might have learned from his own experience. Yet despite the opportunity for young Richard to encounter the lawless, fun morality of the decade, there is little evidence in descriptions of him, either as a child or an adult, to indicate that it had any effect.

Furthermore, *The Whittier News* of the times suggests that the fun morality was not the most salient issue in his community. The stories of national and local significance focus for the most part on business and prohibition, lauding the transactions of the former and deploring the transgressions of the latter. Drinking, and the lawbreaking it entailed, was not the sole province of the young in the '20s. Respectable business leaders were just as likely to violate the 18th Amendment as were flappers and drugstore cowboys. However, despite the play the local newspaper gave to the pervasive disregard of the law in general, there is little evidence that lawlessness was characteristic of Whittier in particular. Its origins as an intentional religious community suggest that the traditions of the influential citizens would inhibit drinking and thereby curtail systematic lawbreaking. As the Lynds write about the small midwest community of Middletown, c. 1920:

> Drinking as a convivial activity has not been common among the businessmen of Middletown since the coming of prohibition, due largely . . . to the abstinence of a group of men powerful in industrial, social and civic life both in 1890 and today. (Lynd and Lynd, 1929, p. 277)

This mode of abstinence most likely characterized the influential men of Whittier as well. It is possible that, as a grocery boy, making deliveries to back doors and having entrance to kitchens and pantries, young Richard had some opportunity to see evidence of disregard of the law on the part of some prosperous, respected members of the community, but it is unlikely that he would be introduced to *systematic* violation of the law. And it was not until college that he himself finally violated the 18th Amendment by drinking in a speakeasy in San Francisco while on a tour with his debate team.

However, Nixon did not need to wait until college for his first introduction to lawlessness. When his older brother, Harold, became ill with tuberculosis, Hannah took him to Prescott, Arizona, in the hope that the dry air would arrest the disease. There she opened a boarding house for other tubercular patients, and in the summers Richard came to stay with them. To help make ends meet, he took a job as a barker for a wheel of fortune at the Slippery Gulch Rodeo. One of his biographers notes:

> It was a strange and mystical game they played. Hannah and her son. She must have known how Richard was earning his wages, but she said nothing. When he brought her his pay, she lovingly patted his cheek—and they both thought of Harold who was visibly sinking. There are times when the tongue and heart are poorly connected, and this was such a time. But they both knew. (Spalding, 1972, p. 73)

As a Quaker, Hannah most likely disapproved of gaming in any form. And as a Quaker, Hannah would not pray out loud for the Lord to understand why, in the circumstances they were in, they had to do what they did; and why, understanding the nature of their situation, the Lord should forgive them for having done so. Such is not the tradition of Quaker prayer, which is silent and inward. Yet her silence must have left open the interpretation of the moral lesson. Richard may have learned *not how conscience is sacrificed to expedience, but how the path of expedience can be taken in good conscience.*

In addition to learning how to interpret the meaning of his work, he had the work itself. Although never one to be part of a close, intimate network of friends, he was seventeen and away from his local community. He was living with his mother, his dying brother, and the tubercular patients his mother was caring for. He was working in a carnival, symbolically suspended between life and death. But the version of life the carney presented was not the conventional version he had learned in East Whittier.

Carney life and the underworld tradition of lawlessness have a long association. On the American scene the carnival was a meld of boisterous hedonism and unseemly perversions, and the con game was added to this as a regular feature. The facile tongue and the way with words that won Nixon honors in debating in Whittier provided him with instant mobility in the world of the carnival. While other young boys were starting as sweepers and roustabouts, young Richard began his career in a most prestigious position: as a pitchman at a gambling concession. One carney pitchman recalls:

> To be able to sway a crowd of strangers and turn them into friends, make them do your bidding, all within a matter of minutes gives you a marvelous sense of dramatic power. (Lewis, 1971, pp. 221-222)

There was prestige and influence in the job he was doing. In the context of his new associations he was introduced to experiences of power that he probably had not experienced in the old home town.

It is also likely that carney life introduced him to attitudes that he had not known before. The carney is a world of manipulated illusion, where crowds are tipped to the seller's advantage. It is a place where gambling and drinking, swearing and sex are routine, and where bribery and graft are frequent. In the carney it was possible to learn attitudes about the law that were not salient features of the Whittier community. Such attitudes are embodied in the words of the proprietor of a carney kooch show:

> Flexibility . . . is the basic ingredient of the law, a fact most people in my profession recognize, or perish. The Law can be stretched so far you'd think it would break. The Law can be contracted so tightly you're sure those who are enmeshed in it will be strangled. And the Law possesses the prime element of intertia—"stay-as-it-isness." (p. 243)

Whatever Nixon might have learned about the law from living in Whittier and reading his civics text, there was something new to be learned in Prescott, Arizona, and a new dimension to be added to his psyche.

We need not suppose that young Richard was radically transformed by his experience with carnival life. After all, it was only a summer or two in a protracted adolescence, an interlude in the passage between boyhood and youth. Unlike some who yearn to be part of that nomadic underworld and run away to join the circus, Richard returned to Whittier, enrolled in the local Quaker college, and majored in history.

Chapter 3
War and Opportunity

Through the 1920s Americans believed in, expected, and desired ever-expanding economic opportunities. Children who grew up in those times were constantly assured that through hard work and determination they could be a success; that through keen investment and judicious speculation they, too, could make a profit in the game of life. Then, in 1929, the crash of the stock market arrested the sense of ebullient affluence that had permeated the nation for as long as anyone could remember. In the last few years of the decade the material desires of consumers had been inflamed by advertising and their resources extended by credit. Millions were in debt, expecting next week's paycheck to cover this week's purchases. The flurry of consumer activity led to increased market speculation. Big money interests bought on margin, and ordinary folk invested their life savings. Newspapers in communities like Whittier ran stories explaining how speculators were "different" from gamblers and thus made the prospects of windfall profits reasonable for even the most religiously devout. Ministers and school teachers, barbers and housewives all began to invest in the market with the hopes of being lucky and getting rich. Then suddenly, the prospects for profit that had looked so good for so long were dashed by the news from Wall Street. The bottom had fallen out of the economy. Banks were closing their doors, and bankers were jumping from their penthouse windows.

The meaning of these disasters in the East were slow in getting to Whittier. The day after the crash the major headline of *The Whittier News* was "Second Big Shipwreck on Lake Michigan Within Single Week." In the upper left-hand corner of the front page was a story that said, "Officials here are not much concerned about the break in the stock market." Readers were assured that those who knew about and were responsible for the economy were not alarmed. So the stock-market crash first came to Whittier not as bad news, but at most as a mild alarm.

Through the bleak months that followed the crash, millions all over the country were trying to interpret the meaning of what had happened to the system they all had faith in. In Whittier the papers gave considerable coverage to the meetings between the President and the captains of industry. A mid-November headline proclaims: "President Gets Back to His Favorite Roll (sic), Godfather to the Nation." The story goes on to reaffirm the Coolidge doctrine of the relationship between business and government. The role of government is not to regulate but to encourage business interests, and from this congenial relationship, domestic tranquility will reign through the land. The Hoover administration took no active measures to control the economy that was massively dominated by corporate interests. Instead, the President repeatedly proclaimed, "We have now passed the worst and with continued unity of effort we shall rapidly recover." (Allen, 1959, p. 244) But things continued to get worse. Despite promises made by the leaders of industry that they would not cut wages, wages were ultimately cut. In a downwardly spiraling cycle, ebbing sales were followed by declining corporate profits. In attempts to restore the rate of profit that was believed proper and fitting to the corporate interests, salaries and wages were cut and workers were laid off. This reduced sales even further, which led to increased business losses, which led to further wage cuts and further layoffs, and so on. By 1932 workers' wages had been cut 60 percent and some two million men wandered the country aimlessly, in quest of a job, or relief, or just a sense of motion. While millions of people were being displaced and millions of others were ill-housed, ill-clothed, and ill-fed, *The Whittier News* continued to proclaim that prosperity was right around the corner and to give as much, if not more, space to stories about prohibition as to stories about the economy.

Ultimately, the standard of living of a third of the nation was depressed and disrupted by the downward spiral of the economy. But the Soutern California community of Whittier, and the Nixon family within it, were among the more fortunate two-thirds of the nation. Years later, as Vice President, Nixon was asked about the circumstances of his youth. He replied:

> We were poor, but we didn't know it. We never had the feeling we were poverty stricken. As a matter of fact, Father was fairly successful. The filling station, and later the market, provided our immediate needs. If it hadn't been for the expense of my brothers' sicknesses, we wouldn't have had any problems at all. (Kornitzer, 1960, p. 114)

Thus the misfortunes of the decade that touched Nixon directly were not the misfortunes of the nation at large but those of his immediate family. While other young men were drifting without resources or opportunity, young Richard was going to college and law school. While he may have seen himself as less fortunate than some, he was clearly more fortunate than others.

In the 1920s the image of the college man had emerged as a prominent feature of the jazz age. He was portrayed as cynical and irreverent, in hedonistic pursuit of dancing and drinking to the exclusion of all else. Small religious colleges maintained stricter standards and more stringent control; nevertheless, the popular idea took hold that formal education should be a time for more than just scholarly pursuits. Through high school Richard had been a diligent scholar and an active participant in various clubs and organizations. Alongside his graduation picture, the yearbook notes that he took part in the oratorical contest, was involved in the scholarship and Latin clubs, served as student-body manager, and worked on the school newspaper. In college he continued to be an activist. He participated in debating. He became involved in acting and campus politics. He continued his interest in journalism and added football to everything else. Though his biographers describe him as a "loner" in terms of making few friends and having few intimates, his involvement in extracurricular affairs suggets an eminently sociable nature. Clearly, young Nixon had a desire to be a part of things, to be in the center and not on the periphery.

As a microcoism of the larger community, the school system provides an arena in which talents can be recognized, abilities can be developed, and success can be measured by the position one achieves. Richard Nixon graduated at the top of his college class. With the exception of his courses in journalism, he was a straight A student. He won oratorical contests and had the lead role in the school play. He was elected freshman class president, senior class president, and, on a promise of dance reform, student body president. Following this election, he argued convincingly before the board of trustees of Whittier College that students ought to be permitted to dance on campus, lest they drive to Los Angeles and frequent dens of iniquity in pursut of their pleasure. He was also active in organizing a campus group called the Orthegonians, in opposition to the elite Franklins, whose membership had been open only to the sons of the most wealthy families in town. The Orthegonians prided themselves on their democratic conviviality. They were the "good guys" as opposed to the "rich guys," and their motto was *Ecrasons l'infame:* stamp out evil.

The only endeavor young Nixon did not succeed in was sports. Through the 1920s American interest in sports had grown. In Whittier high school and college athletics had begun to replace debate as frontpage news, and by the early '30s the newspaper had added a separate sports section with a logo the same as the one displayed on the front page. Sports had come to be seen as a training ground, where young men could be prepared for future combat in the marketplace, where, ultimately, the fit would survive and the losers perish. In sports the masculine virtue of competition could be demonstrated and one's fitness tested. For four years Richard attempted to distinguish himself in football, but without success. His coach said:

> What an inspiration he was to the team! Weeks would go by and he wouldn't even play a minute, but he almost never missed a practice and he worked hard. He was really wonderful for morale. (Spalding, 1972, p. 88)

On those few occasions when he did get the opportunity to play, his light weight and poor physical coordination put him at a distinct disadvantage. One teammate reminisces:

> Dick didn't play very often, but once when he was called into play in the last few minutes of the game I said, "Let's get out the five-yard penalty marker." What I meant was that Dick was so eager to win he'd be off side about every play. (p. 87)

For a young man who regularly excelled at all he attempted, his failure in sports stands out as a notable exception. Nonetheless, he diligently attended practice and from the bench he provided an enthusiastic audience for others. He was able to maintain a sense of himself as part of the action. Even if he did not succeed at being a football hero, he was still a team member.

School and various extracurricular activities dominated his time and energy. In addition to school there was home and family, work and church, and, through his college years, a girl friend named Ola Walsh, the daughter of the local chief of police. At home his mother had returned from Arizona with his ailing brother, Harold. In a year or so Harold would die, and the Nixon family would consist of Frank and Hannah and three sons. Arthur, a younger brother, had died a few years earlier. When Harold died Richard ascended to the role of "eldest son" with all the responsibility and honor such a position implied.

Work continued pretty much as it had been in the 1920s. The Depression was experienced variously by different social classes. Laborers were more likely to be hurt than the petit bourgeoisie, and, generally speaking, the Nixon family enterprise was well situated. They dealt in food and gasoline, and by the 1930s both were considered necessities of life. Possessing a car was evidence of possessing a bit of the American dream. The mobility it provided symbolized freedom. Even the impoverished Okies who migrated from the Dust Bowl to California in broken-down jalopies required a constant supply of gasoline. The Nixons were there to serve them. Townsfolk continued to need milk and bread, produce and pastries. Thus throughout the Depression Richard was insulated from the immediate effects of cut wages and lost jobs. All around him people needed what his family had to offer, and the Nixons were relatively better off during the Depression than they had been in times of prosperity.

By the time Richard was ready to leave for Duke University Law

School, the Nixons were well enough off to dispense with his services at the store, and to provide him 35 dollars a month spending money and occasionally a little extra. Later they were able to support his younger brother, Donald, at prep school in South Carolina. If the Depression was felt by Nixon at this time, it was felt more as the mood of a distant nation than an immediate life experience and in his *Memoirs* the only mention of the Depression is his having seen the play *Tobacco Road* on a trip to New York City. While other young men of his generation began to question the relation of corporate capitalism and domestic tranquility, there was nothing in Richard's experience to lead him to such radical thinking. Even though the expanding economic horizons he had come to expect as a boy were beginning to contract just as he was becoming a man, there was no immediate reason for him to question the assumptions about the world that he took for granted. Hence throughout the Depression he continued to be committed to principles of free enterprise and individual initiative.

Finally, through his budding manhood there was his girl friend, Ola, whom he had met when she played the romantic lead opposite him in a high school Latin play. They dated steadily in college. They went to movies in the evening; on Sundays, after church, they would drive to the beach. She liked dancing, but he never learned to dance, so sometimes they would argue and break up, and then they would come back together. Ola was fun-loving and Dick was serious; when he left town for law school, they gradually drifted apart. But along with home and school, work and church, there had been romance for young Richard in the early part of the 1930s.

In 1934 Nixon left Whittier to attend Duke Law School on a scholarship he had won for outstanding work at college. It was the nadir of the Depression, and his impoverished life as a student was not much different from the style of life millions of other Americans were experiencing. But unlike those who had been displaced by the Depression, Nixon had the role of other-worldly scholar to insulate him from hard times. He lived in a ramshackle farmhouse with three other law students. He bathed at the school gymnasium and studied in the library. He lived on peanut butter sandwiches and candy bars. Money from home, plus the money he earned doing research for Dean H. Claude Horack of the law school, supplemented his scholarship.

He was determined to earn a degree and fulfill his childhood ambition to be a lawyer, a man of principle who could not be bought.

During this period he got the nickname of Gloomy Gus. To his mother he had always been Richard though his brothers and peers in Whittier called him Dick. At college he was sometimes called Nicky; and though it angered him then, that is what he would eventually be called in the Navy. But in law school he was Gloomy Gus and his roommate, explaining the moniker to a biographer, said:

> He never expected anything good to happen to him or anyone close to him, unless it were earned. Anytime someone started blowing rosy bubbles, you could count on Dick to burst them with a pin prick of reality. (Kornitzer, p. 119)

Though Nixon pursued his studies in business law and taxation with grim determination, the pattern of extracurricular involvement he had established in college continued at law school. He became a member of the *Law Review,* and he contributed essays to the *Duke Bar Association Journal.* He was elected to the exclusive honor society and joined the local law fraternity. In his senior year he ran for, and was elected, president of the Duke Bar Association. When he graduated in 1937, it was with honors and distinction.

By the time Nixon earned his law degree, the worst of the Depression was over. Roosevelt signaled a change in the relationship between business and government, suggesting that the interests of workers and the interests of the unemployed were as much a concern of the government as were the interests of the entrepreneur. Roosevelt began to actively manage the economy through a patchwork of reforms and initiatives that came to be called "the New Deal." The New Deal envisioned a redistribution of economic opportunities, restricting some of the advantages business had always maintained, eliminating some of the disadvantages that had always been on the side of the workers. The most dramatic of these measures was the introduction of unemployment and social security benefits; but support was also provided for collective bargaining. During the Roosevelt administration union membership tripled.

If the New Deal had taken some of the risk out of life for the underdog, there was far from general support for the measures it proposed. The image of the bona fide American citizen as a rugged individualist had held sway for decades, supported by the belief that the unfortunate were to blame for their own condition. Charity was considered a private affair, suitable for the church but not the state. In their description of Middletown in the 1930s the Lynds sum up this prevailing sentiment as follows:

> This is a free country of boundless opportunity which guarantees an equal chance to everybody. If people don't get ahead it isn't the fault of society.
> Unfortunately there has always been in this and every other society a fringe of "unfortunates." Things like this just happen.
> But these things "happen" usually in part at least because the people involved have violated the gospel of "hard work and thrift."
> Therefore society should not do too much for them because such extra help "weakens the character" of the recipients. (Lynd and Lynd, 1937, p. 103)

This was the attitude that permeated the philosophy of Middletown America in the 1930s, and it most likely represented Whittier, California, as well. This was the attitude Richard Nixon held through his youth and into his political career. Despite the fact that one of the measures introduced as part of the New Deal provided funds to pay needy college students and thus had made available the money he was paid to do research for Dean Horack, Nixon was to be an outspoken critic of government welfare.

★   ★   ★

By the age of 24, Nixon had completed his formal education. From elementary school through law school he had distinguished himself as a student and as a debater. By high school he showed signs of being a politician. We can only suppose he thought well of himself in this period. He was no longer just his father's son, but a man in his own right. With his drive, his energy, his ambition, he had grown into a person of considerable promise. Unlike his father, whose life had been strewn with failures, Richard had succeeded in almost everything he tried. In the limited arenas the school system provided he repeatedly won deference and respect from others. Whatever fears and anxieties drove him to have his mother smell his breath before he went to high school must have subsided by now, and it is likely that he presented the picture of a confident, articulate young man.

With such an image of himself it is not surprising that he chose to apply to the prestigious firms of Wall Street for his first job. In

December 1936 he and two other students from Duke made inquiries at a number of New York companies; but while William Perdue and Harlan Leathers were fortunate in securing positions, Nixon received only vague, inconclusive replies. Henry Spalding quotes him as saying in 1958:

> As I look back I think I was impressed more by the thick, luxuriant carpets and fine oak paneling of Sullivan and Cromwell's reception room, than by the possibility of being a minor associate of [John Foster] Dulles. I'm sure I would have been there today if they had given me the job; a corporation lawyer instead of Vice President. (p. 103)

But he didn't get the job, and so, in a second attempt to secure a position before his graduation from Duke, he applied to the FBI. This was not just an idle inquiry, for he took the written examinations and asked Dean Horack for a letter of recommendation. However, there was no immediate response, and Nixon did not pursue the matter after graduation.

What factors could have led an ambitious young man who had unsuccessfully applied for positions at Wall Street law firms to turn his attention to the Federal Bureau of Investigation? Images of Wall Street had, of course, permeated his childhood. Wall Street was where the action was, the arena where prowess was tested, where the mighty flourished and the weak were driven out by the competitive struggle. Like the football field, Wall Street was an arena of mortal combat. By the time Nixon was actually looking for his first job, another kind of romantic imagery was emerging on the American scene. Through the '20s, the routine crime of the decade had been violations of the 18th Amendment. Gangsters were for the most part bootleggers, operating in the milieu of big cities, servicing illegitimate bourgeois desires. With the hard times of the Depression, the nature of routine crime changed. Loosely organized mobs of armed bank robbers began to terrorize the countryside, and crime was no longer just an urban problem. Furthermore, the automobile had introduced a new element into the game of cops and robbers, and old jurisdictional boundaries put the agents of law enforcement at a disadvantage. Thus, in 1932, Congress began to establish laws defining various "federal offenses," and ultimately just about any type of crime that involved crossing a state line became so defined. To enforce the new laws, the FBI was transformed from an obscure branch of the Justice Department into a powerful independent agency. In a few short years the G-man emerged as a heroic figure in American life. The young J. Edgar Hoover, director of the agency since 1924, became the embodiment of the "tough cop" as he strapped on his .45 and led his army of hand-picked agents against such lawbreakers as Bonnie and Clyde and Pretty Boy Floyd. G-men routinely engaged in open gunfire with the gangsters of the day, and their exploits made newspaper headlines as well as movie dramas. When Nixon was looking for a job, the image of the supercop had captured the popular imagination, and tough policemen like Dick Tracy were portrayed gunning down gangsters on the funny pages of the daily paper. We can only suppose that, as in his application to Wall Street, in his application to the FBI he was looking for action, and his romantic yearnings were guided by the popular images of the day.

When his youthful yearnings did not materialize, his sober, practical nature took over. With no other prospects in sight, Nixon returned to Whittier. He had not applied to take the California bar examinations, perhaps not anticipating a return to his home state. So Dean Horack wrote a letter to Professor Brenner at Stanford, asking that Nixon be given special consideration. Professor Brenner exempted him from the requirement of being a registered voter; and he passed the bar examination and was duly certified to practice law in the state of California. Then, with the help of his mother, he was introduced to Tom Bewley, one of the prosperous lawyers of Whittier. Bewley's father and Hannah Milhous Nixon's father had been partners in Indiana, before each had migrated west. Well-groomed, well-spoken, ambitious, and bright, Richard made a favorable impression. Bewley agreed to take him on as a partner to replace his partner then retiring. So in 1937, just out of law school, young Nixon was to become established in one of Whittier's oldest and best known law firms.

But Whittier was still a small, provincial town, and the status of his firm in the community had little correspondence to the status of the work he would do—he dealt mostly with divorces, drunk cases, and a variety of traffic violations. But business was brisk, and soon Nixon opened a branch office in the neighboring community of La Habra. According to one biographer (Mazo, 1959), he also made a trip to Cuba during this time, inquiring about the possibility of opening an office in Havana. In addition to his private practice, Bewley was City Attorney for the community of Whittier, and he appointed Dick Nixon his deputy. In this capacity, Nixon had the opportunity to work with the city council drafting ordinances, and an opportunity to plead the prosecution's case in court. Bewley reminisces:

> He was particularly conscious of his clothing. When he tried
> a lawsuit, he had the right stance, and he used the right voice,
> which was low, but which he built up gradually with dramatic
> force. I don't remember that he ever lost a case. (Kornitzer, p. 128)

Regardless of the aspirations he might have harbored before his graduation, Nixon worked hard at being a successful young lawyer in his home town. The same zeal, ambition and energy he had put into school he put into his chosen profession. He maintained the same conscientious attitude toward his grooming, and the same disregard of his nutrition. His secretary of that era recalls:

> He didn't have a regular time to eat. He would send me out
> at all hours for pineapple malts, hamburgers, and sometimes,
> Mexican food. He just about lived on them. (Spalding, p. 115)

In addition to his legal practice, Nixon made his first attempt at being an entrepreneur about this time. The effects of the New Deal were gradually being felt, and it looked as though the country would pull out of the Depression. There would not be a return to full employment until the war effort began, but toward the end of the '30s prospects began to look better than they had for many years. Throughout the era mass marketing in food had progressed, and newspaper advertising had been dominated by the interests of Safeway and Alpha Beta. Food processing was a growing market. With the help of some friends and acquaintances Nixon raised $10,000 and established himself as the president of the Citra Frost Company. The Citra Frost Company intended to market frozen orange juice. Surplus oranges could be bought cheaply in the local area. There was no problem in squeezing and freezing the juice. However, the company was unable to find a suitable container in which to market the commodity and so, after eighteen months, the Citra Frost Company went bankrupt, unable to meet its payroll. Regardless of the success he had already demonstrated in the legal profession, as a businessman Nixon was clearly a failure.

The pattern of success that had dominated his career had become flecked with moments of failure. These were not material failures because, by any overall assessment, his achievements were great. When he left Whittier, he was a grocer's son; when he returned, he was an established professional man. Social mobility had been his. Rather, his failures thus far were failures of romantic aspiration: failure to be at the top, failure to be where the action is. How much his failure to be a football hero, his failure to get a job on Wall Street, his failure to be a G-man, his failure to make a million in the fast-food business affected him is hard to assess, for they were always offset by clear success. Perhaps at most they introduced the possibility of doubt—the possibility that he might not make it, even though he generally did.

The Depression had not diminished American idealization of success, but it had changed the way it was reckoned. In the '20s stories that circulated in mass magazines like *The Saturday Evening Post* defined success in terms of upward social mobility. In the '30s the proportion of stories dealing with themes of success had increased. But now success was defined in terms of recognition and deference from others (Johns-Heine and Gerth, 1957). Thus by the time Nixon graduated from law school it was not enough to do better than your father had done. The world—or at least some part of it—must be cognizant and approving of your achievement. If you didn't make it big, you really didn't make it at all.

The Depression had flattened the hedonism of the jazz age, but it did not arrest the patterns of social change that had been going on through the previous decades. The movies, first introduced in Nixon's boyhood, were to dominate the mentality of his manhood. Even under conditions of unemployment, people continued to go to the movies, just as they continued to drive their automobiles. In gangster films like *Little Caeser* and *Scarface* the daily headlines were dramatized. In the romantic male lead—Clark Gable, Tyrone Power, Errol Flynn—masculine prowess was exaggerated and idealized. Walt Disney introduced new possibilities in the visualization of fantasy. *Snow White and the Seven Dwarfs* broke all previous attendance records. A feature-length cartoon, it dramatized a popular fairy tale that extolled the cheery virtue of hard work for little men and promised every maiden a Prince Charming.

By the end of the '30s union organization began to push for a five-day week, and with shorter work hours there was more time for leisure. Movies and the radio were relatively cheap forms of entertainment, and so through the decade the influence of popular culture grew. Before the First World War there had been no really common culture that linked the urban community on the East Coast with the rural hamlet of the Midwest. By the time of the Second World War there would be an elaborate mass media network disseminating a unified message throughout the country. As the mass media grew, the number of local daily and weekly newspapers diminished. Whatever forces there were supporting the old regional order continued to crumble.

In the '30s the broadcast media came into their own. The simple crystal set introduced two decades before had been transformed into an upright, push-button model that stood majestically in the living room of all but the most impoverished American families. Two decades later the radio was replaced by the television set; but in its own time the radio dominated conventional life. Through the years of the Depression President Roosevelt's fireside chats directly from the set to the citizen reassured the nation in its bleakest hours. Millions also listened to the voice of Father Coughlin, whose anticommunist, anti-Roosevelt, antisemitic broadcasts continued through the decade. Father Coughlin's broadcasts were finally curtailed by public protest, although not before they had influenced an entire generation in how to interpret the meaning of the world in terms of sinister forces of evil.

The music programming that once had dominated the airwaves gave way to comedy and drama: *Amos and Andy* and *Gangbusters* were popular fare throughout the country. So attuned to the radio were its listeners that when Orson Wells broadcast a dramatization simulating an invasion from Mars, many truly feared that Armageddon had come and fled their homes for safety. The power of the airwaves was manifest, and everyday life would never be the same.

By the end of the '30s the standards of living that had dropped so drastically began gradually to rise again. The ebullience of the '20s seemed gone for good, but despair was passing also. The new order seemed to be coming into maturity. The image of the salesman and the booster began to fade from prominence, leaving in their wake the modest, respectable citizen. This was the climate in which Dick Nixon began the adult phase of his life. In addition to his legal and business interests, he began to establish himself in the local community, as he had established himself in the school system in his youth. He became a member of the Junior Chamber of Commerce and was appointed a trustee at Whittier College. He became active in church affairs again, something he had ignored while at law school. When Wendell Willkie ran against Roosevelt, Nixon made a few campaign speeches in Willkie's behalf. When the Whittier Little Theater group conducted tryouts for *The Dark Tower,* he auditioned for the romantic male lead and was introduced to Thelma "Pat" Ryan as his leading lady.

Nixon was now of an age and of a position where by community standards he ought to take a wife. He proposed the first night they met, but Pat Ryan was not as impulsive. It was not until months later, on the cliffs not far from San Clemente, that she finally accepted his offer. The orphaned daughter of Nevada farmers who had migrated to Southern California, she had worked her way through high school and college, selling in department stores, playing bit roles in Hollywood films. She had hoped to find a job in merchandising, but the first opportunity to come her way was teaching business courses at Whittier High School. Unlike the fun-loving Ola Welsh, Pat Ryan was a hard-working, serious young woman. She and Dick Nixon must have seemed the perfect match. Once they were married, they settled down in a little apartment. Dick continued with his law practice; Pat continued to teach school. They lived frugally, saved their money; most likely, they dreamed about the future they would share together.

The nature of that future was to be determined by massive global influences. Through the '30s war clouds had been gathering over Europe. Hitler was a name mentioned frequently in *The Whittier News*. But the nation was divided over what role America should take. The initial attitude of neutrality was supported by a general distrust of all things foreign. The cynical youth of the jazz age were coming into maturity and taking their places as influential citizens. They had been convinced that World War I had been a blunder on the part of their parents' generation, and they did not want to make the same mistake themselves. Despite the fact that Hitler seemed to be the embodiment of evil—the ideal villain to give cause to involvement—it was not until the Japanese attack on Pearl Harbor that the die was cast and popular support for the war emerged as a consuming devotion. This was not a war of idealistic aspiration but a war of defense against aggression. Winning it would not make the world safe for democracy, it would merely stop the enemy. On such pragmatic grounds, American involvement in the war began. Unlike World War I, there was no organized pacifist faction, no objection to appropriations, no resistance to the draft. America had been smitten by a blow from foreign sources, and it seemed the clear duty of every citizen to back the war effort.

As a Quaker, Nixon could have been exempt from the draft. Yet as a red-blooded American male, his duty was clear. In January 1942 he and Pat went to Washington, D.C. to offer their services to the government. Dick began with the Office of Price Administration (OPA), and a few months later, he enlisted in the Navy. As a college graduate, he was given an immediate commission; and after a few years of desk work in the states, he was stationed in the South Pacific as a supply officer. He was respected by the men he commanded and by his commanding officers. In between setting up lines of transportation between supply depots and the battlefield, Nixon managed to open a hamburger and malt stand known as Nixon's Snack Shack. He also learned to play poker and to swear.

Though Quakers are generally committed to pacifism, the doctrine of the inner light means that each must follow the dictates of his own conscience as he sees fit. Thus Nixon would explain, many years later, that even though his mother hated to see him enlist, she knew he must do what was right in his own heart. As a Methodist, his wife was more supportive. She is quoted as saying:

> I would have felt mighty uncomfortable if Dick hadn't done
> his part. Sure, I was unhappy, but so were thousands of other
> young wives. Because of Richard's upbringing he did much
> soul-searching before he made his decision. But once it was
> made, I knew it was for the best. (Kornitzer, pp. 139-140)

However he may have chosen to reckon with his conscience—whether in terms of patriotic duty or in terms of a personal desire for action—once he had made the decision to enlist, he was thrown into a new milieu. The ordinary proprieties appropriate to Whittier, California, were suddenly suspended. War was time out from customary morality. For America's fighting men in the South Pacific, new norms were in order. So "Nick" Nixon fell in with the customary patterns of G.I. language and picked up the habit of gaming in his leisure time.

Poker is a game of fast action and so an ideal way to while away the hours between assignments of duty. It is also a game of profit and loss, and players can measure their success by the extent of their winnings. His war buddies recall Nixon as a conservative player, never betting unless he thought he had his opponents beat at the draw. Employing this strategy, along with bluffing and patience, he became a consistent winner. Biographers differ in the accounts of how much he won at poker in these years. Some say $3,000; others say $10,000. However much it was, along with Pat's savings from her wartime jobs, his winnings provided the Nixons with a postwar bankroll. Whatever the opportunities waiting for the Nixons in the postwar world, they had the cash to capitalize on them. Thus when the offer came to run for Congress, this was the money that supported the growing Nixon

family, and this was the money that paid for routine office expenses
through the course of that first campaign.

★   ★   ★

At the end of the war, Nixon was in his early thirties. He had
a secure position in a growing community to return to, if he so chose.
But then, like the classic moment in a Horatio Alger story, a new,
unexpected opportunity was presented. For years the Republican leaders
in the 12th Congressional District had schemed to defeat the incumbent
Democrat, Jerry Voorhis, who had come into office in 1934 on the
coattails of the New Deal. He had proved to be a popular representative
in the heavily Republican district and had consistently defeated the
Republican opposition in every election thereafter. The Republican
leaders were looking for a candidate to run. They organized a Committee
of 100 and went so far as to put ads in the local papers of the 12th
District:

> WANTED: Congressman candidate with no previous experience
> to defeat a man who has represented the district in the House
> for ten years. Any young man, resident of the district, preferably
> a veteran, fair education, no political strings or obligations,
> and possessed of a few ideas for betterment of country at large,
> may apply for the job. Applicants will be reviewed by 100 interested
> citizens who will guarantee support but will not obligate the
> candidate in any way. (Spalding, p. 148)

Nixon did not read the ad, as he was in Baltimore at the time, engaged
in terminating war contracts. However, the ad proved futile to the
committee, and, in the course of one meeting, Richard Nixon's name
was proposed. Herman Perry was a member of the Committee of 100 and
the president of the Bank of America branch in Whittier. He and
Hannah Nixon knew one another. He had met young Nixon before the
war, when Dick had law offices in the Bank of America building. So
Perry contacted Hannah, who put him in touch with her son. Perry
offered Nixon the opportunity to appear before the committee. Nixon
made a good impression when he said:

> I recognized two lines of thought about America while I was
> abroad. One, advocated by the New Deal, is government control
> regulating our lives. The other calls for individual freedoms
> and all that initiative can produce. I hold the latter viewpoint.

> If the choice of this committee comes to me I will be prepared
> to put on an aggressive campaign on a platform of practical
> liberalism. (Kornitzer, pp. 154-155)

The committee voted to back him as their candidate. They said he would
be a good salesman for the free-enterprise system and introduced him
to Murray Chotiner.

If Nixon had harbored any interest in going into national politics,
there had been no evidence of it thus far. He had been active in
school politics, but when he returned to Whittier he had never been
a precinct worker, never been part of the local party structure. The
speeches he had made in support of Willkie's presidential candidacy
had been part of no organized political involvement, and in fact may have
been motivated as much out of dislike for F.D.R. as from support for
the Republican candidate. But then, quite suddenly, he was both
called and chosen. Henceforth, politics would be his vocation. He
appeared as a dark horse, but he was to be groomed by the king-makers;
and this meant that the Committee of 100 would pay Murray Chotiner
to advise their young candidate on running his campaign. Although
trained as a lawyer, Chotiner had found his forte as a political strategist.
Before encountering Richard Nixon, he had already managed Earl
Warren's victorious campaign for the Senate. In the chaotic world
of California politics, where party affiliation played less of a role than
mass conviction, Chotiner had perfected a system of tough politics.
This was the system he taught Dick Nixon.

Whatever he had gleaned from his involvement in school politics,
from his stint in the carney, from his poker playing in the Navy, Nixon
was prepared to be a receptive student. Chotiner's basic premise was
that, when given the freedom of choice, voters are less likely to vote
for a candidate than they are to vote *against* the opposition:

> We never put out the complete voting record of our candidate,
> vote by vote, in spite of the demands from people within our
> organization. The reason is—even if your candidate has voted
> 99 percent right according to the person who reads the record,
> the 1 percent will often turn the prospect against you. (Costello,
> 1960, p. 46)

To win votes, therefore, it is necessary to conceal the hand of your
candidate. It is also necessary to deflate the opposition, and to do this
you must find the opponent's weak spots. When the vulnerability of the
opposition has been identified, the successful candidate must hammer

away relentlessly. Recognizing that there is a certain toughness, a certain callousness in this strategy, Chotiner counsels:

> There are many people who say we don't want that kind of campaign in our state. They say we want to conduct a constructive campaign and point out the merits of our own candidate. I say to you in all sincerity that if you do not deflate the opposition candidate before your own candidate gets started, the odds are that you are going to be doomed to defeat. (p. 45)

Over the course of their independent careers, Chotiner would codify the principles he introduced Nixon to in 1945. He would argue that at the heart of a democracy the voters want to feel that they are choosing the candidate, and the successful candidate must recognize this. Instead of presenting himself to the people as the party's choice, he must become the people's choice. To do this, the successful candidate must get people talking; he must instigate a network of informal communication that will convince people they want the candidate even before his candidacy has been declared.

Activating involvement at a grassroots level is but part of a successful strategy. In addition, the candidate must establish separate front organizations. Organizations with no connection to the candidate's own party provide a means to capture the interests of those who are not committed to party politics. They provide endorsement for the candidate for those who are dissatisfied with their own party's candidate and, when needed, they can issue unfavorable statements about "their own" candidate.

For Chotiner the essence of democratic campaign strategy was found in dramatization—in particular, in the dramatization of evil. An election must come alive for the voters, and this will not happen if the candidate merely gives voice to cliches, no matter how noble the sentiments they embody. The voters must see the campaign as a fight, a battleground where the goodness of the successful candidate is established by his triumph over the evil opposition. The evil of the opposition candidate is demonstrated in the campaign arena by his defensive posture. If he is to be successful, the candidate must draw the first blood by pointing to the record of the opposition and showing how it can be given a sinister reading. Chotiner notes:

> What is the difference between legitimate attack and smear? It is not a smear, if you please, when you point out the record of your opponent. Of course, it is always a smear, naturally, when it is directed to your own candidate. (Spalding, p. 158)

If the opponent responds by attempting to defend himself against the accusation, new charges must be made to give him yet more to explain. The more he attempts to defend himself, the more he will be seen as cowering before the challenger. And the lower the posture of the opposition sinks, the higher the stature of the successful candidate. In a political campaign, good and evil will always be relative, and the successful candidate starts off by defining the situation for the audience long in advance of the actual encounter. If the opposition rallies to his own defense by making an attack of his own, the successful candidate ignores it. If he does not deign to answer the charges, those charges will appear groundless to the voters, and the stature of the candidate will not be diminished. If the attack of the opposition mounts and grows to such a magnitude that it cannot be ignored, then the successful candidate will answer the charges with a counterattack on the opposition for having launched the charges in the first place.

In addition to cultivating the voters directly, the successful candidate will also cultivate the media. When Chotiner first developed his principles of political strategy, the broadcast media played a relatively small role. Television was yet to become a standard consumer item. Radio had been used to report the outcomes of elections and to disseminate the reassuring voice of the President but the media was not yet the ground of campaign battles. Thus Chotiner's early advice on how to cultivate the media was for the successful candiate to contact the local newspapers, asking about their advertising rates. This show of pecuniary interest would give an advantage to the candidate in successive news stories. Over the year, as the broadcast media grew in influence, techniques for manipulating the media became more sophisticated. But in the early days when Chotiner was first tutoring Dick Nixon, the prescription was simple. It could be accomplished by the successful candidate's wife, sitting in an office with a telephone.

In his own office in Beverly Hills, not far from the growing mecca of commercial imagery, Murray Chotiner had begun to develop an understanding of the world that was based on principles of impression management. In Hollywood all the world was illusion. Vivid, moving images of reality were artfully constructed, and millions were ready to buy whatever fantasy Hollywood had to offer. In addition to the mass marketing of illusion, Hollywood had fostered the celebrity system, in which the personalities of singers and actors were created by manipulating public attitudes about them. In this system the press agent had become a crucial figure, mediating between the buyers and sellers of illusion, ascertaining what the producers of imagery wanted and what the consumers desired, and tutoring clients in how to fulfill the demands of both. What seemed to matter in this system was not so much the facts, but a convincing version of the facts that would sell. In addition to having his office near the seat of impression management, Chotiner had come of age in an era when mass advertising had flourished and principles of consumer psychology had become staples of business acumen. In the 1940s the techniques that had been developed by social scientists working for the government as part of the war effort were being disseminated to the business community. Market research, polling, and opinion surveys were all emergent tools that were useful in capturing a share of the mass market, and Chotiner had a keen sense of their use in politics.

As a professional campaign consultant, Chotiner demanded fees up to $30,000 for his services. What he had to offer was a synthetic vision in which the most sophisticated techniques of Hollywood, Madison Avenue, and social science were melded into a sure-fire strategy for success in politics. Like Bruce Barton before him, he saw the world in terms of simple principles of successful salesmanship.

We do not need to speculate about Murray Chotiner's influence on Richard Nixon's life. Until the time they were introduced in 1945, Nixon had made no close friends. His mother was still influential in his life, and his wife was a helpful companion. But until he met Murray Chotiner Dick Nixon had no boon male companion to share whatever dreams of glory he might harbor, to provide him with guidance and insight. So Chotiner was more than a political adviser. He became Nixon's buddy, and they would remain in close association for many years. Chotiner counseled Nixon on his role in the Hiss case and he managed the 1950 congressional campaign against Helen Gahagan Douglas. Chotiner managed the 1952 campaign for Vice President and masterminded the "Checkers" speech—the television broadcast that saved Nixon's place on the Republican ticket and ultimately assured him of more than a footnote in history. In 1956 Chotiner was called before a Senate investigation committee on charges of influence peddling, though no formal case was made against him. His relationship with Dick Nixon faded from the public eye, but reporters in 1962 noted his association with the ill-fated gubernatorial campaign. Thereafter he again became a regular fixture of Nixon's campaign entourage. Ultimately Chotiner had an office in the White House, not far from the seat of national power, although the Nixon *Memoirs* make no mention of Murray Chotiner after election eve.

Chapter 4
Politics as a Vocation

While other ex-servicemen were going back to the jobs they had before the war, or opening new businesses with government loans, or starting school on the G.I. Bill, Richard Nixon began the postwar period with the opportunity to run for national office. Endorsed by the influential Committee of 100 and advised by the political strategies of Murray Chotiner, Nixon ran against the incumbent Democrat, Jerry Voorhis. Voorhis was a dedicated public official, well respected in his district. But over the years his liberal stance had begun to diverge from his more conservative constituents, who were mainly farmers, ranchers and small homeowners in the suburbs of Los Angeles. By the end of the war Voorhis was ripe for an upset, if only the right candidate could be found.

Nixon began political campaigning in his naval officer's uniform, running ads as Lt. Commander Richard M. Nixon. When he found this presentation alienated enlisted men, he quickly changed to civilian suits and advertised himself as Dick Nixon. He called for rejecting the New Deal philosophy and reasserting the role of individual initiative in economic life. Nevertheless, as the known incumbent, Voorhis made a better showing in the primaries.

The Chotiner strategy for successful political campaigning demanded a dramatization of the race if the tide was to change in Nixon's favor. The method of dramatization would be the attack, and the grounds would be the issue of communism. Since the Russian Revolution, conservative business interests had feared the influence of Marxist doctrine on American voters. Efforts at labor organizing had routinely been labeled as inspired, instigated, and controlled by communist sources and the appellation "red" became the sign of a foreign enemy. The red scare that followed the First World War abated during the prosperous '20s; but with renewed worker organization in the '30s accusations of communism were revived as routine charges in political contests. Through the '40s the war effort had produced nearly full employment and a substantial increase in the real wages of skilled workers. As labor organizing subsided in the face of prosperity and national purpose, charges of communist sympathy faded from the political lexicon. But after the Second World War the issue became salient again. The emergence of the U.S.S.R. as a world power reified the threat of communism to the American way of life, and a postwar survey done by the Republican Party showed a general fear of "the international communist conspiracy" among voters. In terms of the mood of the country, the late '40s were a time when communism could again be reconsidered as a profitable political ploy.

Precedent for making communism an issue was there, and the Nixon-Chotiner opponent could be made vulnerable to an attack on just those charges. Voorhis had been a socialist in the '20s. Over time he had become considerably more conservative, however, and by the time he was elected to office, he was a principled New Deal Democrat. He was also generally popular with organized labor, and the support of organized labor would make him vulnerable to attack. Nixon charged that Voorhis had been endorsed by the Political Action Committee (PAC) of the CIO, and that the PAC-CIO was dominated by organized communist influences. Using the logic of guilt by association, he implied that Voorhis represented communist interests by virtue of the interests of his supporters. A Nixon ad in *The Whittier News* reads: "Citrus Growers Don't Be Fooled Again . . . the CIO-PAC is always pitted against agriculture." Little was said directly about the links between the CIO-PAC and the international communist conspiracy, nor about the links between Jerry Voorhis and the PAC. Rather, the routine use of innuendo, insinuation, and implication left the audience to conclude "the obvious."

As Chotiner predicted, Nixon's attacks on Voorhis's character made the front page of the local papers, and Voorhis's attempts to defend himself were hidden somewhere inside the paper a day or so later. Nixon's challenge to debate Voorhis further served to create a public forum to heighten the drama of the race. Employing his considerable debating skills, Nixon made repeated accusations that Voorhis consistently voted the party line. He would stride across the stage, waving a piece of paper, charging that it contained "evidence" that Voorhis had received the endorsement of communists because he was a sympathizer of their cause. Nixon claimed:

> In the last four years, out of 46 measures sponsored by the CIO and the PAC my opponent has voted against the CIO and the PAC only three times. Whether he wants it now or not, my opponent has the PAC endorsement and he has certainly earned it. (Mazo, 1959, p. 48)

In the five minutes Voorhis had to rebut, he would try to defend his congressional voting record. But the issues were complex. Only Nixon's use of statistics had made them seem simple. Thus in the course of the debates, Voorhis began to take the posture Nixon intended for him. The more he tried to defend and explain, the weaker his argument sounded. The image that began to grow in the 12th Congressional District was that of the incumbent cowering before the charges put to him by his young challenger. Voorhis was destined to spend the rest of the campaign denying he was a fellow traveler.

After his selection by the Committee of 100, Nixon went to meet Norman Chandler, publisher of the *Los Angeles Times*. In 1916 the *Times* building was bombed in the course of a severe labor dispute, and since then the paper had routinely linked the international communist conspiracy with the domestic labor movement. Chandler was sympathetic to Nixon's cause and impressed with him as a person. He said: "This young fellow makes sense. He looks like a comer. He has a lot of fight and fire. Let's support him." (Kornitzer, 1960, pp. 160-161) With the support of the most influential paper in the district and of wealthy Republicans and popular movie stars, Nixon began his career in politics by defeating the incumbent 65,586 to 49,994.

After the campaign it was reported that voters in the district had received anonymous telephone calls saying, "Did you know Jerry Voorhis was a communist?" The Nixon forces denied any involvement in such tactics, but the stories persisted. In conjunction with the aggressive campaign Nixon had waged, such stories engendered a growing force of opposition in the community. For the most part, Whittier had supported Nixon's candidacy, but by the end of the election there were some who were disillusioned. A schoolmate through high school and college told one biographer:

> There was never anything ruthless about Dick when we were growing up. If it was a fair fight anything went . . . but not anything dirty. That's why I could never understand the positions he took in campaigns. I gathered that probably it was a matter of political advice that people gave him. (Mazo, p. 41)

The seeds of disillusionment were to grow, so that by the time he had been elected Vice President, several seniors at his alma mater protested so demonstrably when he was invited to deliver the commencement address that a separate receiving line was provided for those who preferred not to shake Nixon's hand. At the same time, there were many in the community who were impressed with the showing he made and the issues he gave voice to, so along with his critics there was a growing band of loyalists, many of whom remained staunch supporters throughout his political career and long after his fall. Others would become disenchanted over time, as each new political confrontation revealed facets of the man those supporters neither expected nor approved of.

Until his election to Congress, Dick Nixon had been one of millions, an undistinguished lawyer in a provincial town. Whatever aspirations he might have harbored, a career in politics had not been one of them. His wife recalls:

> There was no talk of political life at all in the beginning . . . I didn't feel strongly about it either way . . . I felt that a man had to make up his mind what he wants to do, then after he made it up, the only thing I could do was to help him. But it would not have been the life that I would have chosen. (p. 43)

Regardless of the life Pat Nixon might have chosen, her husband succeeded in his first attempt at public office; and in January 1947 he moved his family from Whittier to Washington, D.C. Suddenly he was one of a select 400. For his wife it was a turning point of sorts:

> It was a turning point, all right, and we went to Washington, where the life of a housewife isn't very much different from life in Pittsburgh or Kansas City. I run a suburban household. (Nixon, 1952, p. 93)

If home life wasn't much different in Washington than it had been in Whittier, Dick's job was pregnant with power. In Whittier he had handled divorces, drunk cases, and traffic violations, worked with the city council on ordinances that had no significance beyond the local community. In Washington he dealt with legislation, investigations, and inspections that affected his nation and, ultimately, the world.

Nixon took to Congress as he had taken to school. As a freshman congressman, he organized a "Chowder and Marching Society" as he had organized the Orthegonians at college. It was an informal association of other freshmen congressmen—including Gerald Ford—who met regularly to exchange information from their various committee appointments and whose collective gathering gave Nixon a power base his novice status did not warrant. As a member of the prestigious Herter committee, he traveled abroad, assessing the postwar world and America's role in it. And as a member of the House Committee on Un-American Activities (HUAC), he was introduced to Father Cronin and a new version of the communist conspiracy.

Father Cronin had come to Washington as a self-styled anticommunist advocate, indignant at the indifference of Congress and the Administration to the communist threat. The version of the communist conspiracy he introduced to Nixon linked communism directly with the American government in the form of espionage agents actively transmitting state secrets to the enemy. During their conversations, the name of Alger Hiss came up for the first time. When it came up again in Whittaker Chambers' testimony before HUAC, Nixon was alert to the opportunity it presented.

Whittaker Chambers was once committed to the communist cause, but he had come to see the error of his ways. He wanted to confess that error, and he wanted others who had been deluded with him to confess as well. Alger Hiss was one of those he implicated in his testimony. Hiss subsequently demanded the right to appear before HUAC and clear his name. Nixon had been sympathetic toward Chambers' account. He found Hiss arrogant and supercilious. As a lawyer, he felt Hiss's careful choice of words—his claim that he had never known a man *named* Whittaker Chambers—too precise, too contrived. He felt it was probably obscuring some real connection. Because Hiss's name had come up in his conversations with Father Cronin, Nixon thought there were grounds for suspicion, even if the other committee members were content to let the matter pass. And Murray Chotiner encouraged him to pursue the matter, since it offered a dramatic opportunity for an aggressive young congressman to make a name for himself. So encouraged, he did.

After agonizing soul-searching, chronicled in both his autobiographical accounts, Nixon transformed the indictment of Alger Hiss into a crusade. He sought out the advice of friends, such as William Rogers. He made repeated visits to Chambers for additional testimony, both on his own and in the company of others whose judgment he trusted. In his zeal and dedication he was spending 18 to 20 hours a day in his office. He writes in *Six Crises:*

> I deliberately refused to take time off for relaxation or "a break" because my experience had been that in preparing to meet a crisis, the more I worked the sharper and quicker my mental reactions became. I began to notice, however, the inevitable symptoms of tension. I was "mean" to live with at home and with my friends. I was quick-tempered with the members of my staff. I lost interest in eating and skipped meals . . . Getting to sleep became more and more difficult. I suppose some might say I was "nervous" but I knew these were simply the evidence of preparing for battle. (Nixon, 1962, pp. 43-44, hereafter referred to as *Six Crises)*

Chambers had merely wanted Hiss and others to confess the error of their ways. When Hiss dared him to repeat his charges in public, Chambers did so on a radio broadcast of *Meet the Press.* Hiss immediately brought suit against him for libel, and in response Chambers revealed microfilm copies of documents he said Hiss had passed to him to pass to the Soviet Union. With such evidence Hiss was indicted for perjury, the statute of limitations on espionage having run out. There would be two trials before he was finally convicted, and for almost two years Nixon's name was on the front pages of the nation's newspapers, clearly linked with the anticommunist cause.

In his accounts of the Hiss case Nixon noted that he had aroused the nation to the domestic threat of the communist conspiracy for the first time. Two years later Joseph McCarthy took up the cause made manifest by Richard Nixon and gave his own name to an era of witch-hunting and red-baiting. But Nixon's youthful autobiographical account makes no connection between his own crusade and the Wisconsin senator's subsequent excesses; neither does the more mature version, written 20 years later. What he does see are the more immediate, more personal ramifications of his action:

> The Hiss case brought me national fame. But it also left a residue of hatred and hostility toward me—not only among the Communists but also among substantial segments of the press and the intellectual community. (p. 74)

In his *Memoirs,* he reiterates this theme and berates those who believed that Hiss was anything less than a threat to the peace and security of America.

The public image that was developing during the Hiss case virtually assured Nixon of reelection to his congressional seat. Soon after Hiss was convicted, Murray Chotiner advised Nixon to run for the Senate. The Committee of 100 had gotten him into office and they wanted him to remain a congressman. Even his old sponsor Herman Perry from the Committee of 100 saw the move as political careerism and not in the best interests of the community. So Nixon lost the collective support of the committee, and with it, the financial backing he had relied on. To counteract this loss, Chotiner began independently soliciting prosperous Republicans, and eventually he established a group of wealthy backers who financed Nixon's bid for the Senate and who were at the heart of the slush-fund charges hurled at Nixon when he subsequently ran for Vice President.

The 1950s were a decade in some ways reminiscent of the 1920s, and in other ways dramatically different. The return to a peacetime economy was never fully realized because of the growing arms race with the Soviet Union. The economic prosperity evident by the end of the war continued into the following decades. Private automobile manufacturing had been abandoned during the war, when factories turned their productive capacity to tanks and trucks. In the '50s cars returned to the market as a popular consumer item. Their size and style became a new arena of fashion, and, as clothing once did, they came to symbolize the status of their owners. Subdividers and contractors offered every couple a home of their own in the suburbs, and the government offered 12 million veterans low-cost loans to subsidize housing. Sales in new houses meant sales in new furniture and household equipment. Ever-increasing numbers of people profited from the upward spiraling economy. New consumer goods came into the market in unprecedented numbers: power mowers, freezers, air-conditioners, television, and so on. But despite the renewed affluence, there were no signs of the widespread hedonism that had characterized the jazz age 30 years before. Above and beyond prosperity hovered the certain knowledge that the nuclear weapons developed during the Second World War could annihilate the entire planet. Those who could afford to built bombshelters in their backyards, and then they debated whether Christians had the right to defend their shelters from encroachment by neighbors in case of attack. School children were routinely subjected to air-raid drills, where they were taught to sit quietly, cover their eyes, and wait for the enemy attack. Such knowledge of the powers of destruction in the postwar world served to dampen whatever high spirits affluence elicited. Despite its economic similarity, the 1950s was a much more subdued decade than the 1920s.

Richard Nixon, who had never been a hedonist, would see nothing amiss with the times. Most likely he found the '50s of his mature years to be the logical continuation of the '20s of his boyhood, with the Depression and the War as merely temporary exceptions to the general rule. The generation reaching maturity at the same time generally thought the same way.

If the mood of the times was sedate, business was as active as it had been before the Depression. The organization of productive forces had been improved through the '30s. The technology that was perfected during the war found its way into domestic life in the form of consumer goods. A whole new market in synthetics developed. With new, more efficient goods to market, the forces of promotion kept up with the forces of production. In the 1920s advertising began to employ principles of psychology and appeals to emotion to motivate consumer spending. In the 1950s motivational research began in earnest, as skills developed by social scientists were put to use by advertising agencies. With techniques such as "depth interviews" and "semantic differentials" marketers were learning how to read consumers' hidden desires. The messages they formulated to tout their wares struck a responsive chord with their audience, for they had found a way to tap the fantasies of the buyer.

In addition, television took over from radio as the dominant broadcast medium. Like the movies, television presented an intense human experience, where viewers could see and hear dramas of various sorts. Most of the early television programming consisted of situation comedies and vaudeville reviews. There were quiz shows and westerns, soap operas and detective fiction, but tales of cops and robbers did not yet dominate the tube. Television also became actively involved in the coverage of political events. The 1952 Republican Convention was the first political convention covered by live television. The Kefauver hearings were also broadcast. In these early years, when television was just becoming a popular consumer item, it seemed that it would serve as a means of enlightenment as well as a source of entertainment. But except for episodic moments enlightenment was always second to its contribution to fantasy, and insignificant compared with its contribution to commerce.

If the arms race had put a damper on the mood of the country, it had also served to heighten fear of the communist menace, for now the conflict of opposing ideologies was backed by the atomic weaponry of superindustrial powers. National figures such as Richard Nixon and Joseph McCarthy gave expression to, and in turn rekindled, the notion that the capitalist system might fall to a foreign foe. At the height of his public power, McCarthy blackened the names of hundreds of persons and ruined the careers of many times more. Yet for three years his conduct went uncensured. In such times images of threat and menace grew, and fear became a routine element of everyday life.

Separated from the ancient feuds of the Old World by thousands of miles of open sea, America was once characterized by a security born of insularity. But the technology of jet airplanes and guided missiles ruptured that sense of security. The U.S.S.R. came to represent a volatile threat to the free world, and with the success of the Chinese Revolution there was even more cause for alarm. The size of the enemy grew: billions of foreign foe, waiting for the opportunity to bury the free enterprise sytem. Protection was called for. The budget for national defense increased.

Richard Nixon made a substantial contribution to the politics of fear. Harping on themes that had been dormant since the days of Father Coughlin's radio broadcasts in the 1930s, he would campaign in California as though the communist conspiracy was the opponent to his office. With his prosecution of Alger Hiss, he began to fan the flames of alarm on a nationwide scale. In 1950 and 1952 Joseph McCarthy campaigned on his behalf, and thus the two were linked as part of a common cause in the eyes of the voters. As Vice President of the nation and so President of the Senate, Nixon was the errand boy who delivered the Senate's ultimate censure to McCarthy. But even after McCarthy had fallen into disgrace, Nixon visited him now and again.

In Nixon's first political campaign Murray Chotiner acted only as an outside adviser. By 1950 Chotiner was named campaign coordinator and manager. His political strategy, implicit in the Voorhis race, was manifest in the contest against Helen Gahagan Douglas, also from the House of Representatives.

Nixon began his campaign for the Senate proclaming:

> The issue is simply the choice between freedom and state
> socialism. They can call it planned economy, the Fair Deal, or
> social welfare—but it is still the same old Socialist baloney
> any way you slice it. (Lurie, 1971, p. 90)

In a station wagon with his wife, an assistant, and a driver, he toured California, making thousands of speeches on this basic theme. In rural hamlets and large cities, at shopping centers and Rotary meetings, he presented himself as the defender of the free enterprise system. While his whistle-stopping went on, campaign literature mailed to Republicans presented Dick Nixon as the party's choice. The literature mailed to Democrats never identified Nixon as a Republican. Rather, it began, "As One Democrat to Another . . ." It noted his war record and his role in the Hiss case as his obvious virtues, thus influencing those who might otherwise vote their own party line. Gradually the tone of his speeches began to change from a statement of the issues to an attack on his opponent. Being careful to distinguish Douglas from the Democratic cause in general, he referred to her as "the actress candidate." He pointed to her congressional voting record, showing how it could be read to demonstrate that she was actually a fellow traveler of the communist way—a red. It was the same tactic he had used with Voorhis, based on the same statistical reasoning. Half a million handbills were printed on pink paper, detailing how Douglas's voting record paralleled that of Vito Marcantonio, a known communist sympathizer. The handbill failed to mention that the majority of Democrats in Congress had voted with Marcantonio on some votes. Chotiner noted, however:

> We only stated the facts. The interpretation of the facts was
> the prerogative of the electorate. (Kornitzer, p. 184)

Caveat emptor was transformed from a maxim of the marketplace to a principle of the political arena. In the last days of the campaign anyone who answered the telephone saying "Vote for Nixon" was offered:

> PRIZES GALORE!!! Electric Clocks. Silex coffeemakers with
> heating units—General Electric automatic toasters—silver salt and
> pepper shakers, sugar and creamer sets, candy and butter dishes,
> etc., etc. WIN WITH NIXON! (Costello, 1960, p. 73)

The link between techniques of merchandising and techniques of electioneering was firmly forged.

In his own home town Nixon's name dominated the front page of the paper. There were fewer paid ads than there had been in 1946, but by now Dick Nixon was somewhat of a celebrity. He opened his campaign before the Republican Women's Club and drew loyal support from various women's clubs in the district. At campaign rallies where long lists of movie stars were noted in attendance, respectable women like Hedda Hopper and Irene Dunne dominated the list. It was almost as though Nixon had actively attempted to muster the forces of her own sex against his opponent. Certainly he cultivated the women's support whenever he could.

There is no mention in *The Whittier News* of any unethical tactics associated with the campaign, nor is there any such mention in the *L.A. Times,* which supported him for senator just as it had supported him for congressman. However, in the local papers of other California communities there was freqent mention of unseemly practices on the part of the Nixon forces. Mention was made of hecklers sent to Douglas rallies to disrupt her speeches; and of a whisper campaign that had been started, accusing Nixon of being antisemitic. The editor of one paper charged that the whisper campaign had been started by the Nixon camp in order to defame Douglas by accusing her of instigating it. They charged Nixon with being Tricky Dick, and the appellation became his albatross ever after. If he had been Gloomy Gus in law school and Nick in the Navy, he was Tricky Dick in politics.

In response to the charges Nixon was making, Douglas began making countercharges of her own. After Senator Joseph McCarthy spoke on Nixon's behalf at a rally in Los Angeles, Douglas stated, "I have nothing but utter scorn for such pipsqueaks as Nixon and McCarthy." (cf. *Memoirs,* p. 77). She insinuated they were fascists. Chotiner cautioned Nixon not to get into a name-calling contest with a woman candidate, so, ostensibly, they let Douglas's attacks pass. But the heat of the battle made repeated headlines, and Nixon's name became more prominent than it would if he had chosen a less aggressive posture to begin with. He won by more than a half-million votes, and even *The Whittier News* expressed surprise at the margin of victory.

There is no mention of the Douglas campaign in Nixon's youthful memoirs. The account written in his mature years portrays Helen Gahagan Douglas as a leftist Hollywood glamor girl, unpopular with the boys in the House of Representatives and unfit for the clublike atmosphere of the Senate. He recounts how even his youthful competitor, Jack Kennedy, was behind Nixon in his battle to defeat her. Nixon describes how Kennedy provided him with a $1,000 contribution for his campaign, "from my father." Parties who could corroborate this little-known secret transaction are now long dead; the only account of it is in the memoirs of an old man recounting the battle he waged for his seat in the Senate, justifying the way he fought it.

In his biographical account of the Douglas campaign, Nixon describes how his opponent, fearing his victory, drew the first blood. Despite the fact that she was a woman, and hence out of place with the boys, she displayed all those characteristics that make a real man: she was tough, ruthless, aggressive, without compassion or pity. Worst of all, she compared Nixon to Hitler and Stalin.

While Nixon ignores the Douglas campaign in *Six Crises,* the supportive biographers of his early career were called upon to provide an account of this momentous juncture in his career, when he was transformed from one in 400 to one in 100. Both Kornitzer and Spalding agree that if anyone is to be held accountable for the style the campaign took, it was Murray Chotiner. Kornitzer notes, for example:

> Nixon's upbringing seems to have had no curbing effect on his instinct to take on a fight when circumstances call for one. And the Senatorial contest was such a case. Murray Chotiner, who master-minded the campaign strategy and was responsible for the "pink sheet," likewise has found no reason for an apology. (p. 183)

Spalding concurs on the nature and extent of Chotiner's influence, but he claims that Nixon was not fully aware of Chotiner's tactics. Both go on to assure the reader that despite the fact that the campaign was "impassioned and tough," it was no different from the ordinary style of California politics. Yet native Californians remembered the Nixon-Douglas campaign as something special in American politics.

Despite such disclaimers on the part of his supporters, when he was interviewed by a British publisher in 1957, Nixon responded to a question about that contest by saying, "I'm sorry about that episode. I was a very young man." (Costello, p. 74) As a point of fact, he was 37 years old. He had been to college and law school. He had been in the war; he had been in Congress. He had been a visiting dignitary abroad. His role in the Hiss case had made him a domestic hero of sorts. He was already a man of considerable stature when he entered the race; he was to come out of it diminished in the eyes of some. As a result of the way he waged his battle against Helen Gahagan Douglas, he would be known as Tricky Dick and his politics would henceforth be suspect to large numbers of voters. Like the Hiss case, the Douglas campaign gave Nixon cause for resentment and anger. In each case he triumphed over the enemy and, just as he did, the number of enemies multiplied.

In January 1951 Richard Nixon was sworn into the office he won as a result of the Douglas campaign. Although his tenure was for six years, his career as a U.S. senator was quickly aborted. In the summer of 1952 he was nominated to run for Vice President, and the following year he took his place in American history as the Vice President of the nation. His rush to power was spectacular.

As a U.S. senator he was pledged to serve the interests of his state in national negotiations. But as Murray Chotiner noted:

> The junior Senator from California doesn't amount to anything. Suppose you are a candidate for Vice President, and we lose. You're still the junior Senator and haven't lost anything. If you win, and are elected Vice President, and at the end of four years, if you become all washed up, you could open a law office in Whittier and have all the business in town. (Boroson, 1958, p. 6)

So despite his wife's expressed desire for a respite from the rigors of campaigning, no sooner was he elected senator than he began more personal negotiations that resulted in his nomination for the second highest political office in the land.

Franklin D. Roosevelt had been in the office of President for fourteen years. For people born during the Depression and raised under the trauma of war, he had been a reassuring symbol of national leaderhip. With his death in 1946 they—as well as others who were older—yearned for someone who would take up the reins of government and assure them there was hope in the postwar years of despair. Dwight D. Eisenhower was the ideal candidate. As a general in the Second World War, he had helped defeat the forces of fascism. As the head of a most powerful industrial nation, he would be able to employ his skills against the forces of communism. So popular was Ike as a symbol that Harry Truman approached him as a possible Democratic nominee in 1948, to substitute for his own, perceptibly weaker, candidacy. Ike declined, saying he did not feel he was suited or prepared for national office. Nonetheless, the groundswell in support of his candidacy continued. Grassroots organizations proclaiming "I like Ike" appeared in local communities throughout the country. Eisenhower's confessions of

ignorance about domestic matters were praised as "humble honesty."
His complex sentences and incoherent thought patterns were labeled
"simple genius." His smile began to win the hearts of the nation, and
it looked as if he could be drafted to run. As a senator on a European
junket, Nixon took the opportunity to pay a personal visit to the general
in Paris. On his return to the States he read a statement in praise of
the man into the *Congressional Record.* For a junior senator this was a
presumptuous act; for an ambitious man, it was a shrewd move.

The leading candidate for the Republican nomination was Robert
Taft, but the titular head of the party, Thomas Dewey, supported
Eisenhower. By most counts the delegate votes for each man were
evenly split, and the vote from one big state, such as California,
would be consequential in giving the nomination to one candidate or the
other. Gradually Nixon let it be known that he personally favored
Eisenhower's nomination, despite the fact that the Republican delegates
from California were pledged to support Earl Warren as their favorite
son.

As the junior senator of an important state, Nixon made himself
available to the media as the spokesman on all sorts of issues. He
made himself available for picnics and mass rallies. On one of these
appearances in New York, he met Thomas Dewey, and Dewey let it
be known that he stood a good chance of being the vice presidential
nominee on a ticket headed by Eisenhower. Dewey, a staunch supporter of
the anticommunist cause, considered Nixon a "white collar McCarthy."

Critical and uncritical biographers alike note the significance of this
encounter between the junior senator from California and the most
influential man in the Republican Party, although there is no mention
of the meeting in his youthful memoirs. It took place long before
the delegates met on the convention floor, and it assured Nixon's place
on the party ticket. Nixon's mature version of his life acknowledges that
he knew in advance that he would not be forgotten if he swung the
Calfornia delegation to the general. Written by a man who had difficulty
remembering the content of conversations about Watergate without the
help of his personal diary, his taped records, or his aide's notes,
Memoirs quotes detailed conversations that took place a quarter of a
century ago and are unrecorded by any instrument except the mind of
the narrator. However, *Memoirs* omits any account of the surprise and
impropriety others saw on the convention floor when Dick Nixon heard
his name put in for nomination as Vice President.

Despite the expressions he feigned on the convention floor, his nomination had been signaled in advance. Through the brief course of his tenure as senator, Nixon had been expressing support of the Eisenhower cause. Soon after Nixon met with Dewey, he began to express reservations about the Taft cause. Pointing to their relative standing on opinion polls, he suggested that an Eisenhower victory would be certain in November, but Taft's chances were problematic. He suggested that Taft had a "loser image." As a part of the California delegation, he was ostensibly committed to the Warren cause, but his loyalties were signaled in advance; on the convention floor he ultimately moved the large California delegation to support Eisenhower's nomination.

The Republican National Convention was a dramatic occasion. The forces of the party were split in their allegiances, assuring a highly contested battle. Television covered the proceedings live, and it was the first time millions of Americans were witness to party politics. It made a great show, and Richard Nixon was one of the stars. Once Ike's nomination was secure, a vice presidential nominee was needed. In terms of power and influence, the Vice President stood in the shadows, but according to the Constitution, he was only a heartbeat away from the head of government. Were anything to happen to the President, the Vice President would automatically succeed. It is expected then, for the welfare of the nation, that some thought should be given to the qualifications of the candidate. However, in the intricacies of party politics, the role of Vice President has yet another meaning: it is a political plum awarded to a party member who can swing votes. Thus American political parties think as much about regional representation of the ticket as they do about personal qualifications for succession. As a westerner, Nixon had an advantage; having already swung his share of the votes on the convention floor, he was due for a reward from those whose cause he supported. Thus when Dewey and the other Republican king-makers began to consider the vice presidential nominee, Nixon's name was among the candidates. In the course of the bargaining and jostling that took place in the back rooms of the convention hotel, that name emerged victorious. The influential members of the Republican party made him an offer an ambitious man could hardly refuse.

Despite the career opportunity the job afforded, Pat did not favor Nixon's accepting the nomination. She resented the demands politics made on their family life. She was open and vocal about her displeasure, and were it not for Murray Chotiner's assurance, Dick might have yielded to her objections. But Murray's reason won out over Pat's passion and Dick became a vice presidential candidate.

If the politics of the Douglas campaign had tarnished his public image, his subsequent conduct would tarnish his image in the world of party politics. In the course of his brief tenure as senator, Nixon made numerous speeches attacking the Truman administration. On at least one occasion he insinuated that Truman was a traitor to the nation because he was "soft on communism." Truman never forgave him for that remark, and later, in his oral biography, he would say:

> . . . All the time I've been in politics there's only two people I hate, and (Nixon's) one. He not only doesn't give a damn about the people; he doesn't know how to tell the truth. I don't think that son of a bitch knows the difference between telling the truth and lying. (Miller, 1973, p. 139)

Truman was also to refer to him as shifty-eyed and vacuous.

In showing himself a dirty out-fighter, Nixon aroused the ire of the opposition. He engendered criticism in his own party by showing himself a dirty in-fighter. Taft was to describe him as "a little man in a big hurry," one who had a mean and vindictive streak when he was frustrated. (Costello, p. 7) Others who expected a display of loyalty and commitment were equally dismayed by his conduct. But there were clearly some who admired his style and were in awe of his success. And this number was to grow.

Once the party ticket was declared, the principals began their separate whistle-stop campaigns across America. In the 1950s campaigning was still conducted on an intimate, face-to-face basis. Candidates toured the country, stopping off in as many local communities as their campaign strategists thought wise. Advance workers preceded the candidate, set up local arrangements, distributed handbills, and assured an enthusiastic audience for the candidate's appearance. Celebrities, food, and music were provided at public rallies, and local citizens were encouraged to come and see the party's choice in person.

Private affairs were held, where the candidate met with special interest groups. Speeches were given, often tailored to the immediate audience. The candidate attempted to convince those assembled of the goals he had for the country and the virtues he embodied. Those assembled had the opportunity to ask questions of the candidate and share their impressions of him with one another. Those who were personally impressed with the merits of the man could tell others who had not attended. In this way a snowballing network of support was generated.

Once media only supplemented this primary mode of campaigning. Both local and national journalists routinely covered the candidate's appearance, writing up their own impression of the candidate and the crowd's response. When advertising began to flourish, candidates began to purchase space in local papers to proclaim their own virtues and objectives. But in 1952 television did not yet dominate American campaign practices. Face-to-face encounters between the candidate and the people—permitting voters an intimate view of those who were running for office—were still the main event in political marketing.

After a trial run in Maine, where speeches and organization were perfected, the Nixon train left from Pomona, California. They anticipated an ordinary campaign. Ike's train would extol the virtues of Home, God, and Motherhood, while Dick cut away at the incumbent administration. Then, quite unexpectedly, rumors began circulating about the existence of a Nixon slush fund. The origins of that fund were the Nixon supporters Chotiner had organized before the campaign for the Senate. They had been convinced to stay on as financial backers during his tenure, to assure his subsequent reelection. The executor of the fund, Dana Smith, said:

> We wanted him to continue to sell effectively to the people of California the economic and political systems which we all believe in. It was immediately apparent to us that this would take money and that Dick himself was not in a position financially to provide it. (Mazo, p. 95)

The origins of knowledge about the fund were stray whispers started at the Republican National Convention by California delegates who were disillusioned by Nixon's betrayal of Warren. The story was eventually picked up by a Los Angeles reporter, who questioned the candidate directly about it. Nixon did not deny the existence of the fund, but referred the reporter to Dana Smith for an accounting of the facts and an interpretation of their meaning. Originally written as a straightforward statement, the story was picked up by the *New York Post,* which ran front page headlines declaring: "Secret Rich Man's Trust Fund Keeps Nixon in Style Far Beyond His Salary." The article noted the large number of real estate and oil interests that were represented among the 76 contributors.

The Nixon-Chotiner strategy was to not respond to the attack. The opposition had drawn the first blood, but an explanation would only put Dick in a defensive posture, and for the sake of political strategy they wished to avoid this. However, while Nixon was committed to his strategy, Eisenhower was waiting to hear an account of the charges against his running mate. And no account was forthcoming.

In the charges that Nixon was supported by a slush fund representing big business interests, the Democrats found a way of answering Nixon's own charges about corruption in the Truman administration. The heat of the campaign mounted, and finally, in a small town in central California, Nixon responded to Democratic hecklers by explaining:

> You folks know the work I did investigating Communists in the United States. Ever since I have done that work the Communists and left-wingers have been fighting me with every possible smear . . . They have tried to say that I had taken $16,000 for my personal use. What they didn't point out is that rather than charging the American taxpayer with the expenses of my office, *which were in excess of the amounts which were allowed under the law,* what I did was to have those expenses paid by the people back home who were interested in seeing that information concerning what was going on in Washington was spread among the people of this state. (*Six Crises,* p. 88; emphasis added)

In that statement Nixon accounted for the origin of the information about the fund and defined the meaning of its existence. If the law limited the amount a senator could receive from public tax funds, there was no reason why private business interests should not make up the deficit. Anyone who thought differently was a red.

But the fund was becoming a national issue, and that simple account was not sufficient. Before the campaign less than half the voters polled knew the name of the Republican vice presidential candidate. Now that figure was considerably higher, and the connotations of the name were not favorable. Furthermore, while charges and countercharges were being made, Ike had been publicly silent, and his silence was not a reassuring sign.

As a matter of fact, Ike had not known Nixon very long. For all intents and purposes, they had been introduced when the party leaders decided to make Nixon Ike's running mate. Witnesses to their first formal meeting observed that the general displayed little warmth toward Dick, although Nixon was clearly eager to please. They noted as well that the general was a bit dismayed at that first meeting, expecting as a running mate someone quite different from the eager young man he was introduced to in the back rooms of the convention, before they first appeared together in front of the television camera. Given such a dubious reception, Ike's present silence seemed ominous. Editorials calling for Nixon's resignation started to appear in newspapers that supported the Republican ticket.

It became clear to the Nixon forces that the opposition included not only their enemy, but their erstwhile supporters as well. It was not enough simply to impugn the character of those who were questioning his honesty and integrity. Some sort of dramatic event was called for to define the situation for the opposition and supporters alike.

"This is politics," Chotiner said. "The prize is the White House." (*Six Crises,* p. 100) He explained how the press was blowing the incident up out of proportion, how they would have to go around the press and address the people directly. He said:

> What we have to do is to get you before the biggest possible audience so that you can talk over the heads of the press to the people. The people, I am convinced, are for you, but the press is killing you.(p. 101)

Nixon's other buddy, William Rogers, concurred with Chotiner's advice, and plans were laid for the greatest show on earth. Sixty million people would sit attentively before their television sets while the vice presidential candidate on the Republican ticket appealed for their affirmation of his right to be there.

In a few short days the Nixon forces had bought prime television time. A foremost objective was an existing audience, and their first choice was the half-hour following the popular comedy "I Love Lucy"; however they settled for the time after the equally popular comedian Milton Berle. They could be assured that when Nixon came on, the audience would be in a good mood. They carefully rehearsed the television production crew, using a local salesman as a stand-in for the candidate, making sure no technical detail was overlooked. When the candidate refers to his wife, the camerman was instructed, pan to the woman sitting on the sidelines.

While the technical forces were being prepared, Nixon was working on the scenario of his lifetime. Once they had decided to broadcast over national radio and television, Nixon had toyed with the press. When reporters asked him what he was going to do, he evaded the issue, hoping to build suspense and hence build an audience. As was his habit during this time, he neither ate nor slept. In *Six Crises* he explains how he thrives on the brink of exhaustion and how exhilarating, how charged the experience is:

> Despite the lack of sleep or even rest over the past six days, despite the abuse to which I had subjected my nerves and body—someway, somehow, in a moment of great crisis a man calls up resources of physical, mental, and emotional power he never realized he had. (p. 120)

So as the pressure mounted, he prepared the lines he would deliver to his captive broadcast audience. Lines that he had used in answering hecklers in his live audiences came to mind, like the remark about Pat's plain cloth coat. Subtle barbs suggested themselves:

> I decided to mention my own dog Checkers. Using the same ploy as FDR would irritate my opponents and delight my friends, I thought. (p. 109)

The organization of his speech took form. He began by defending his financial backers, explaining how he had not violated the law but rather saved the taxpayers money; how he had not used any of the money for his own "personal" benefit, but instead used the funds for "political" expenses. He suggested that the man and the office were distinct entities and what profited one did not necessary profit the other. As documentary proof of this claim, he revealed all of his personal finances, to show that, despite his years in political office, he was still a man of humble means. Since he was not rich, he was not on the take.

In American society personal finances are like sex: one does not talk about them openly. To do so is to bare one's innermost secrets, to stand naked before those whose accounting of people is in terms of dollars and cents. Pat believed that what they owed and what they owned were nobody's business. Dick replied: "I had no choice but to use every possible weapon to assure the success of the broadcast." (p. 110) Those who might question his probity would see, as he revealed his most private self, that there was nothing to hide. His wife would be deeply ashamed of what he had to do in the name of politics and the experience would haunt her ever after.

Once having defended the fund and disclosed his own honesty, Nixon went on the offense, attacking the opposition, showing how they, too, had private financial backers and ways of avoiding the law, demanding that they also make as open and truthful an accounting of their finances as he himself had done.

The period before the broadcast was frantic. There was no expression of support from the party, but rather criticism. Ordinarily Nixon liked to have at least a week to prepare a major speech; now he had only a few days. Encouraged by Chotiner and Rogers, he had persevered even though there were times when he had doubts and reservations. And then, just before he was to leave for the studio, there was a call from Thomas Dewey. Dewey said he had polled the campaign leaders and the majority felt Nixon should use the broadcast time to publicly resign. He did not say specifically what his own feelings were, but it was clear to Nixon in the context of that phone call that even his political backers distrusted him and had reservations about his position on the ticket.

No matter. Since neither Dewey nor the general had given him a direct order, he would go on. The time, the audience, the technology were at his disposal. He would take a chance, run the risk, bet his entire political career on the opportunity to confront 60 million Americans and convince them he was an honest man:

> I knew I had to go for broke. This broadcast must not be just good. It had to be a smash hit—one that really moved people . . . one that would inspire them to enthusiastic, positive support. (p. 108)

It was the performance of a lifetime. Darryl Zanuck, the Hollywood producer, called immediately afterward to congratulate him. Ike described it as "magnificent." Mrs. Eisenhower had been moved to tears while viewing it, as were no doubt millions of other women who were routinely caught up in the raw emotion that television soap operas presented as daily fare.

Like a carney pitchman Nixon had tipped the crowd. In response to his appeal people from the television audience wrote:

> We believe Richard Nixon is thoroughly honest and should be kept on the ticket as Vice-Presidential candidate with Ike.

> There has never been a question in my mind concerning your complete integrity and how anyone who saw and heard you tonight could possibly mistrust you, would seem incredible. I too love my country very much. I am proud of the work you did in regard

> to the Hiss case, and I feel confident that if elected Vice President, you will continue to fight to rid our government of others of his caliber . . . My very kindest regards to your wife and two daughters.
>
> Only a true American could have been frank enough to tell the people all the facts which Richard Nixon did last night in his address to the nation. He will certainly get my vote 100%. He is the kind we need in office! (O'Brian, 1976, pp. 55, 74)

Over a third who wrote in mentioned his honesty and integrity, and almost as many others remarked on his courage and fighting spirit. A few did respond with criticism:

> Senator Nixon appealed to the emotions, not to the intellect, last night. He showed that he needed money to promote himself. He dodged the real question as to legislation he favored at the time.
>
> How do you expect the working man to vote for Nixon? He has accepted gratuities from millionaires; they do not give money for nothing. If a cop on the beat were to accept two bucks, he'd be fired. You should do the same thing to Nixon. (pp. 46, 48)

But the critics were few in number. The overwhelming response was in his favor.

Despite the fact that he had discredited Jerry Voorhis by declaring the "gigantic CIO-PAC slush fund" was behind him, Nixon made little mention of the morality of his own fund. An analysis of the content of the speech done in the sociology department at Whittier College showed that only 8 percent of the broadcast time was spent on the issue of morality, while 34 percent was spent on the topic of Nixon himself. (Jones, 1958) Viewers who saw the revelation of his finances as a revelation of his honesty were left with the conviction that there was nothing wrong with businessmen having a financial interst in a politician. Just as the rich may possess stables of race horses, so too may they possess candidates for public office—groom them and run them to represent their particular beliefs.

The logic behind the revelations worked. Hundreds of thousands of viewers in mortgaged living rooms could identify with the circumstances Nixon described. They would ask, "Why shouldn't this man have an opportunity to run?" In the course of the speech he demonstrated his sincerity, his patriotism, his humility, his devotion to his family. Taxpayers, veterans, young couples, people of modest means, G.I.s, families, working girls, the Irish, dog lovers were all appealed to directly, and many were moved by the pleas he made. In a viewing audience of 60 million, five in every thousand were motivated to respond with a letter, a postcard, or a telegram. The Republican national headquarters was overwhelmed by the mail, which ran 74-1 against his resignation (O'Brian, 1974). Yet professional pollsters were not surprised. What Nixon had evoked was not a random sample of viewer attitudes but the response of a very select segment of the society to an emotional cry for help. Those who communicated their response were those who were positively motivated by his appeals. Most identified themselves as Republicans, and the majority were women. Outside the intelligentsia voters who were embittered critics were localized in California. Few who doubted him made the effort to voice their criticisms, which after all were to be addressed to Republican heaquarters. In the nation at large the association of his name with the anticommunist crusade insured a number of loyal supporters, many of whom had been influenced by the emotional broadcast appeals made by Father Coughlin a generation before. The viewers' response to the party was taken as overwhelming evidence of the attitudes of the people. But the people had not been assayed; only a positive response had been elicited.

Writing his first memoirs nine years later, Nixon noted that the effect of his performance was to make him a national celebrity and to save his career in politics. But he also wrote that it left a residue of ill-will:

> Pat was to go through campaign after campaign as a good trooper, but never again with the same feeling toward political life. She had lost the zest for it. We had both become perhaps overly sensitive . . .
> (*Six Crises*, p. 137)

He reiterates this same theme twenty years later as he writes in his *Memoirs* that thereafter his wife would hate politics and dream of the day her husband would quit.

In addition to his wife's disenchantment, in both autobiographical accounts he writes of how the smears and attacks against him did not end on election day but haunted him ever after: how people accused him of being involved with gambling interests in Havana, of having other financial backers who provided him with other funds, of becoming rich in office, and so on. Despite his displays of prowess, the enemy lingered on.

★   ★   ★

It was Nixon's greatest crisis so far. Forced into the role of a criminal who must defend himself, he portrayed a man who had nothing to fear, and he portrayed that man so convincingly that hundreds of thousands of people were moved to act in his defense. If there is a moment when a person is convinced of the "inner consciousness of power," it must be at that time when he realizes his own will against the overwhelming resistance of others. Against the opposition of powerful members of his own party, against the influence of a hostile press, against whatever forces of evil he believed to be organized against him, Richard Nixon fought for the right to remain on the ticket. And he won.

At what moment did the audacious thought enter his mind that he was more powerful than he might have ever supposed? His mother says he is not a demonstrative person; he does not weep easily. Yet he wept publicly on three occasions during this crisis. The first was early in the scandal, when his mother sent him a telegram stating simply, "Have faith." The second was immediately after his broadcast performance. The third time was on the shoulder of William Knowland, the senior senator from California, after he finally had been assured that Ike would keep him as a running mate. A picture was taken of this last occasion, and in *Six Crises* he writes, "It was that scene that was forever to characterize the fund speech and my reaction to it." (p. 132) Such an important moment in his youthful autobiography, it is completely omitted from the mature account of his life.

Whenever it might have been, if there was a moment of deep conviction in his intrinsic power, the events that surrounded the "Checkers" speech could well have elicited it. Whatever prowess he might have felt as a youth when he tipped the crowd at the Slippery Gulch Rodeo was magnified a thousand times. He had reached the hearts and minds of his countrymen, and they had willingly responded to his cry for help. By his own ability to speak words that were convincing, he had swayed the masses. If a man is ever to consider himself invincible, what better evidence could he ask for? If a man looked for a sign that his inner light of consciousness was aflame, what better evidence could he ask?

At the same time, this crisis of his youthful career created a residue of animosity revived in his *Memoirs* in the following words:

> I regarded what had been done to me as character assassination
> and the experience permanently and powerfully affected my attitude
> toward the press in particular and the news media in general . . .
> The taste for politics soured, but my only recourse—and my instinct
> —was to fight back. I quickly came to feel a kinship with Teddy
> Roosevelt's description of the man in the arena "whose face is
> marred by dust and sweat and blood." (pp. 108-109)

Out of this accute suffering, pain and persecution came many
important lessons. He learned that with the aid of 20th century
technology he could amplify the pathos of his inner being in such a way
that masses of people would be moved to respond to his defense. And he
learned that, with each expansion of his power, embittered, implacable
enemies would nip at his flanks, ready to destroy him for malicious
objectives of their own. He would learn that:

> In politics, most people are your friends only as long as you
> can do something for them or something to them. In this respect
> I don't suppose that politics is much different from other walks
> of life . . . (p. 110)

Chapter 5
Campaigning in America

Reprieved from the disgrace that resignation from the ticket would have brought, Nixon continued campaigning as the vice-presidential candidate. He had become an instant celebrity of considerable note and his public appearances began to draw crowds 20,000 strong. He continued to attack the Truman administration for its inability to deal with communism. He implied that a Democratic victory at the polls would mean the end of the free enterprise system as it was known and loved by all Americans. Eisenhower took up the call, as well, stating:

> What is our battle against communism if it is not a fight between anti-God and a belief in the Almighty? Communists know this. They have to eliminate God from their system. When God comes in, Communism has to go. (Arora and Lasswell, 1969, p. 194)

With this godless international communist conspiracy as the implicit foe of the Republican ticket, the party was victorious in 1952; and a week after his 40th birthday, Richard Nixon was sworn into the office of

Vice President, six years after he first entered politics. In that short period he had gone from obscurity to the second highest office in the land. He was but a heartbeat away from the presidency, and there was no doubt it was within his grasp.

But Chotiner's counsel that the prize was the White House was premature. Despite his formal position, through the next eight years Nixon would languish in the shadow of Eisenhower. There were moments when, as Vice President, he came into his own. Ike's heart attack was one of them; his stroke was another. But, for the most part, Nixon experienced the frustration of rank without power, title without honor. He was conscious of the intrigues that surrounded the highest office in the land, but he was not part of the action. He was not included in Ike's inner circle of confidants and advisers, despite the fact he was heir-apparent.

The men who surrounded Eisenhower were men who had been successful in the business world. They included Charles Wilson, former head of General Motors. As Secretary of Defense, Wilson reformulated the Coolidge doctrine by proclaiming "What is good for General Motors is good for the country." Like the Republican executives before him, Ike governed the country on the assumption that the marketplace was the heart of society, and free enterprise the rule of the market. That his advisers had little understanding of "government" as opposed to "business" seemed to make no difference. As measured by the growth of GNP, the permanent war-time economy assured prosperity. Outspoken critics of the system were restricted to a small number of bearded bohemians who muttered about existential philosophy and extolled progressive jazz. Their disillusionment seemed no great threat.

Through World War II the affairs of the Executive Office had doubled, and Ike began his stewardship by reassigning some of these functions to his Vice President. He made Nixon his liaison with Congress, asked him to sit on the newly formed National Security Council (the position Nixon would later appoint Kissinger to), and requested that he attend many ceremonial functions customarily handled by the President. Thus Dick and Pat Nixon of Whittier, California became active in the formal life of the capital. They were present at occasions of state, met foreign dignitaries, ate imported delicacies, drank fine wine. They were a routine part of the elite society of Washington. Yet their experience with this cosmopolitan lifestyle had little consequence for their personal life. They moved to a more expensive house, befitting their new station, and they now had a full-time maid to help with the housework and child care. But while they themselves were entertained lavishly, they rarely entertained in return. As Vice President, Dick joined no exclusive clubs; Pat eschewed the round of charitable organizations that made up the lives of other Washington wives. William Rogers and Murray Chotiner were still their closest friends.

In addition to his presence at affairs of state, Dick became active in the affairs of his party. During the few short years of his career he had been groomed by party king-makers and endorsed by loyalists, and he had become an eager spokesman in praise of party principles. With no official duty but to preside over the Senate and be informed of the President's health, his involvement in party issues increased. He traveled all over the country to speak to Republicans about Republican concerns. Party members paid thousands of dollars to see him, to eat in his presence at fund-raising dinners. Wealthy backers were moved to contribute considerable amounts to finance party interests, assured by Nixon of the wisdom of their acts. He raised millions of dollars for the Republican coffers; but in his speaking engagements on behalf of Republican candidates he was less successful. Despite the grueling campaign schedule he undertook in the 1954 congressional election—a schedule that covered 48 days, 29,000 miles, and 95 cities—the Republicans lost congressional seats to the opposition party.

Up to this time Nixon had been able to sway voters to the cause he represented by the words he spoke and the logic he articulated. The results of the '54 elections were somewhat of a setback. He had campaigned on the issue of the communist threat, but the power of his imagery no longer evoked the response it once did. Nor did his ability to draw the sympathy of voters on his behalf spread to the candidates he spoke for. If he had a power to move the masses, it was in terms of a most personal cause: his own. At the same time that there was evidence of the limits of his power, there was growing opposition to him as a public figure. Consideration of the next presidential ticket was already underway, and a "Dump Nixon" movement had begun among influential Repubican leaders. In the community his reputation had suffered. Seniors at his alma mater refused to shake his hand at commencement ceremonies. Whittier citizens who proposed to name a street in his honor were overruled by outspoken opponents. The proposal to award him an honorary doctorate was defeated by a vote of the Duke Law School faculty. Sensitive to signs of disrespect, aware of his own limits, he began to talk about resigning from politics. He was

receiving offers of $100,000 jobs in New York law firms, and so there
was an alternative to pubic life—one he had unsuccessfully sought
twenty years earlier. His wife had no passion for politics, and, in fact,
she asked him to put his promise to resign in writing, which he did. But
when party loyalists rose to his support on the rumor he might be
quitting, the resignation he had written for his wife was torn up. He
explained: "Once you get into this great stream of history you can't get
out." (Mazo, 1959, p. 141)

Soured on the experience of public life but committed to remaining
in politics, he found the next few years a difficult period. He devotes
almost a third of *Six Crises* to this period, although by 1978 it is reduced
in significance to one-tenth of his post-Watergate autobiography.
Most consequential was Eisenhower's heart attack, when it appeared
that at any moment Dick Nixon might become President, and the
attention of the entire nation was riveted on him and the sickly
incumbent. A fierce partisan advocate his entire political career, he
had to enact the role of statesman in a time of crisis. Even his bitterest
detractors in the White House could not question his decorum, his
propriety, his concern in the national interest. Nixon writes in 1962:

> I had no desire or intention to seize an iota of presidential power. I
> was the Vice President and could be nothing more. But the problem
> was to guard against what I knew would be easy misinterpretation of
> any mistake, no matter how slight, I might make in public or private
> . . . what I had to do was to provide leadership without *appearing* to
> lead. (*Six Crises*, p. 153; emphasis added)

Both his autobiographical accounts detail the influence of William
Rogers during this period of his career and gloss over the fact that
he lost the active counsel of Murray Chotiner at the same time. In the
course of a Senate committee inquiry into irregularities in war contracts,
Chotiner's name appeared on the books of a uniform manufacturer being
investigated for fraud. Chotiner was called before the committee and
questioned extensively by the committee's counsel—Robert Kennedy—
concerning possible influence peddling. Though no formal case was
made against him, the stigma of accusation blackened his name in
Washington, and his public association with Nixon ceased abruptly.
As Chotiner's influence receded and Rogers' influence grew, a New
Nixon appeared. The brash, aggressive gut fighter was replaced by
the image of a decorous statesman.

Ike's health was deteriorating, but the economy was flourishing.
The Republican ticket that had done so well four years earlier stood

an even better chance the second time around, even though the President's health prohibited an extensive barnstorming campaign. Dick could manage the face-to-face encounters, while television consultants from advertising agencies filled in on the President's behalf. So Batten, Barton, Durstine and Osborn entered the White House to manage the media, and Dick made a whistlestop tour of 33 states, speaking in praise of Ike and the Republican ticket. Together they sold the reelection of an ailing president to the nation.

There was no longer an incumbent opponent to attack, and the controversial issues were gone from his public statements. It appeared that there was indeed a New Nixon, that somewhere along the way a metamorphosis had taken place and the partisan zealot had become a statesman of respectable stature. His loyal supporters extolled the new dimensions of his character, and in 1956 the Republicans defeated the oposition by a margin more substantial than that of 1952. His position in national history assured for another four years, Nixon finally took a break from his grueling work schedule to spend two weeks relaxing in the Florida sun with his friend Bebe Rebozo.

Before the 1956 election Ike had counseled Nixon to chart his own course, suggesting that perhaps a cabinet post would be most suitable for a man of Nixon's ambition. As Vice President, he must perforce be in the shadow of the leader, whereas as a cabinet member he would have an arena of his own expertise to cultivate. Although the offer implied Ike's reluctance to keep him as a running mate, Dick declined the opportunity. After the '56 election Ike encouraged him to make a name for himself in foreign affairs by becoming a roving ambassador, and Nixon took to the assignment abroad as he had taken to campaigning at home. His first trip took 70 days and covered 45,000 miles. He made a 30-day tour of Latin America; a three-week trip through Africa; visits to Rome, England, Russia, Siberia, and Poland. Everywhere he went he enacted the same campaign drama of smiles and handshakes with thousands of people who showed up to see the visiting dignitary from America. In South America his reception was marred by hostile crowds who met him with signs accusing him of being a racist, an imperialist, a warmonger. He and his wife were spat on and cursed. But the hostilities engendered abroad only renewed sympathy for him at home. After suffering abuse and indignity in Venezuela, when the Nixons returned to the States they were met by a crowd of 10,000 and the smiling countenance of Ike himself.

If his treatment in Latin America evoked sympathy from the voters at home, his encounter with Nikita Khrushchev evoked admiration. After years of campaigning against the communist menace, Richard Nixon finally had an opportunity to meet the enemy face to face. And he did not back down. Like the Checkers speech, the "Kitchen Debate" became a historic marker for his career. The front page of the nation's newspapers carried a photograph of Nixon aggressively pointing his finger in the face of the Soviet Premier, while the 70 reporters covering the trip related how he parried and countered the offenses of his opponent and made points of his own. "You don't know everything," he told the leader of world communism as they sipped Pepsi-Cola in a model kitchen at the American National Exhibition in the Soviet Union. Readers at home saw the encounter as a demonstration of Nixon's courage and toughness, and his popularity on the Gallup poll continued to rise. Not everyone was favorably impressed with his performance, however. The Eastern press accused him of taking his campaign for the Republican nomination to the streets of Moscow. But by 1958 the party king-makers had already decided on his role in the 1960 election, and for them the Kitchen Debate was just another dramatic coup.

Nixon had never lost an election since high school, and there was no reason to suppose 1960 would be any different. Throughout the pre-convention period there was the customary factionalism in the party, but in the end he was selected to head the Republican ticket. He was running ahead in the polls, and the campaign strategy focused on how to keep him there until the election. The plan was simple. They would begin at a slow pace, gradually building up to a dramatic crescendo. As for his image, the candidate would run as the New Nixon. The pugnacity of the past was gone; in its stead a thoughtful, experienced statesman appeared. He would tour all 50 states as a dramatic demonstration of his national involvement. He would smile and shake hands with people, make speeches, rally the forces, and, it was anticipated, thoroughly tromp John F. Kennedy, the inexperienced young senator who was running against him.

Nixon had proposed his grand-tour strategy in 1956, but it was rejected on the belief that too vigorous a display on the part of the Vice President could only make the ailing President appear more feeble. But the 1960 race was his own, and he was committed to the idea that the number of hands he shook was roughly proportional to the number of votes he won. So the tour was taken against the counsel of some of his closest advisers, and it proved to be a disaster. The schedule was grueling for both the candidate and his staff. The reporters covering the campaign plane were annoyed at the frenetic pace of the Nixon entourage. And then there was misfortune. A man whose life thus far had been a run of good luck was suddenly dealt a foul blow. Getting out of the car on a stop in Greensboro, North Carolina, he bumped his leg on the door. The leg got infected. It required two weeks' hosptalization, and those two weeks played havoc with the carefully timed schedule the Nixon forces had planned for their successful presidential campaign. In an ill-conceived attempt to make up for lost time, the candidate overexerted himself and drained his health and vitality even further. Tempers started to get short; plans were disorganized; the press became exasperated and their disdain was obvious. The Nixon forces became resentful of the press coverage and the hostilities escalated. They were off to a poor start.

With the growth of mass communications reporters came into their own as the singular conduit between politics and the people. What made public life public was the routine work of the national and local press corps, consisting of newspaper reporters, magazine writers, and radio and television personnel. The presence of this crew was integral to any campaign strategy, and where part of the candidate's forces were deployed to deal with local arrangements, another part were deployed to deal directly with the press. The Kennedy staff maintained an easy, congenial relationship with the media. In return, reporters referred to the candidate as "Jack" and praised his style and grace. Relations between the press and the Nixon staff were not so friendly. Since his entrance into national politics Nixon had been convinced that the press were among his enemies. As a Republican candidate, he could be assured the support of publishers and network managers, but the working press corps was a different breed altogether: Democrats, intellectuals, liberals. Where Kennedy staffers mingled freely and easily with the press, Nixon's stayed aloof. Where Kennedy staffers were helpful and cooperative, the Nixon forces were cool and, in some cases, vindictive. They said things such as:

Stuff the bastards. They're all against Dick anyway. Make them work—we aren't going to hand out prepared remarks; let them get their pencils out and listen and take notes. (White, 1961, p. 377)

In return, the press flaunted their contempt for Nixon more openly. The campaign that had begun with such high hopes began to disintegrate.

It was obvious that Nixon needed some kind of dramatic moment if the gradual deterioration of his campaign was to be arrested. The opportunity came as a proposal that the candidates of the two leading parties debate the issues of the election on national television. There were pros and cons about accepting it. Chotiner advised Nixon not to debate because Kennedy had the built-in advantage of attacking the incumbent administration. Nixon was fearful that his refusal would be taken as an admission of intimidation. Besides, debate was his forte; he had been winning honors and respect by debating since the seventh grade. He had saved himself from much more certain ignominy in 1952 by appearing on television. The combination of the two arguments outweighed Chotiner's objections. So the Kennedy forces and the Nixon forces met with the network forces, ground rules were established, and technical details ironed out. Despite the ravaged health of the candidate, he agreed to appear on television in a series of four broadcasts that became known as "The Great Debates" in television history.

Blindly committed to his convention pledge to visit each one of the 50 states, Nixon continued his basic campaign strategy while arrangements were made for his television appearance. In 1952 Richard Nixon had captured the attention of 60 million viewers. The Great Debates drew 80 million the first night; while subsequent audiences were large, attention dwindled. Poorly prepared but anxious for the encounter, Nixon left for the studio and, getting out of the car, hit his ailing leg on the door once again. It was as though everything were conspiring to contribute to his failure. Disguising the pain, he went on with the show. But it was a miserable performance. The topic for the first debate was domestic affairs, but the expertise Nixon had cultivated as Vice President was foreign affairs. The opponent appeared healthy and relaxed. Nixon was sickly and tense. Where he had triumphed over adversity in 1952, he could not repeat that victory eight years later. In the Checkers speech he had only himself to defend as a person; in the Great Debates he had the entire record of the incumbent administration to contend with. In 1952 he appeared before the camera with only his loving wife present. Now he was hemmed in by a live opponent. Where Dewey had dealt him a psychological blow before his earlier performance, the car door had dealt him a physical blow. He could not cope. He lost sight of the objective of the performance—to reach the hearts and minds of 80 million viewers—and he began to focus on the technicalities of the encounter: a formal debate with John F. Kennedy.

Kennedy formulated his statements with the attention of the viewing audience in mind. But Nixon responded in classic school-boy style, as though more immediate judges were scoring him on formal technique. Through the course of the debates the issues were never clarified. But the images the candidates presented could be compared next to to one another, and Nixon came off the poorer.

The great debater had lost a debate, and it looked as if the relentless campaigner would lose the election. Republican leaders were disappointed with his performance and open in expressing their displeasure. They wanted the old Nixon back, the tough fighter who could win against all odds and any opponent. Nixon was not up to it. He and his opponent were both energetic, ambitious men. But where Kennedy was rich and lucky, Nixon was poor and unfortunate. The outcome was inevitable. Nixon became testy. He began to lose his temper with hecklers in the crowds. He began to express self-pity in his speeches. The reporters showed him no mercy. Instead of the crescendo the Nixon forces had envisioned to climax the campaign, they were forced to contend with disaster. Their candidate began to take on the image of a loser. He began to act like a man on the defensive, a man with something to fear, rather than a ferocious hero.

Retired from public life in defeat, Nixon had time to review his life, to assess his strengths and his liabilities, to make plans for the future. Those plans included running for governor of California, to provide a political base for his second try at the presidency. The assessment of his life involved writing his first autobiography, *Six Crises*. Unlike his second biographical work, *Six Crises* does not begin with his birth and trace out his life in a narrative fashion. Instead, it focuses on a select number of key events in Nixon's career, the number suggested by Ike's work, *Six Challenges*. In reviewing these events, Nixon tries to assess what makes some men strong and powerful and others weak and ineffective. He concludes that the difference lies in their ability to deal with crises. Those who can keep their heads when all around them are losing theirs, those who can envision a plan and stick to it come what may, those with persistence and drive will flourish, while those with lesser talents and abilities will fade away. In *Six Crises* Nixon acknowledges that in every life there is an element of luck, the unexpected opportunity that comes along and opens new possibilities, but he concludes that luck is secondary to pluck. He also concludes that, in facing life's crises,

> . . . the period of greatest danger is . . . in that time immediately afterward, when the body, mind and spirit are totally exhausted and there are still problems to deal with. (p. 433)

No sooner had he formulated these words of insight and understanding than he forgot them. He entrered the California race for governor with the support of wealthy backers and the knowledge that he had never lost an election in his home state. His opponent was Edmund G. Brown, a popular incumbent of New Deal persuasion. Brown campaigned on concrete issues like employment and education; Nixon campaigned on general principles like responsible government. His critics accused him of being opportunistic, of having less interest in state government than in his personal career. So toward the end of the campaign Nixon found himself defending his intentions. In addition, the Brown forces resurrected charges about an unsecured loan of $200,000 that agents of billionaire Howard Hughes made to Nixon's brother Donald when Nixon was Vice President. Accusations of wrongdoing had been made during the 1960 campaign, and, as Attorney General, Robert Kennedy had given serious thought to indicting the Nixon brothers on statutes governing political contributions. As in the Chotiner case, no formal charges were made, but the public renewal of those accusations impugned Nixon's character in the race for governor the following year. So, despite Nixon's optimistic start, the 1962 campaign began to look like a rerun of the previous one. The public seemed unresponsive to his pleas, and the press corps cool and indifferent to his campaigning.

By the time he acknowledged defeat, his anger and disappointment could not be contained. In a bitter diatribe before the television cameras, he accused the press of giving him "the shaft" and went on to make his classic statement:

> I leave you gentlemen now, and you will now write it. You will interpret it. That's your right. But as I leave you I want you to know—just think how much you're going to be missing. You won't have Nixon to kick around any more, because, gentlemen, this is my last press conference. (Witcover, 1970, p. 22)

The emotional flood-out was disaster to his public image. For a man who cultivated the notion that politics was like sports, he had shown himself to be a bad loser—whining, sniveling, vindictive in defeat. Political pundits around the country predicted that this was the end of his public career. But when ABC broadcast a documentary, "The Political Obituary of Richard M. Nixon," they were inundated with 80,000 letters and telegrams protesting the "hatchet-job" they had done on the man. So, despite his obvious failure, it was clear that there was still a constituency in America who supported him, come what may. Such reassurance sustained him through the long years to follow. By the end of the decade he emerged victorious in his second attempt at the presidency. But between his defeat in California and his victory in Washington, the chaos of the '60s intervened.

The 1960s began with a wave of idealism that had not been seen for 50 years. Before the decade was over, the country was rent by violent schisms, and euphoria was replaced by despair. The inauguration of John F. Kennedy was symbolic of the youthful vigor the decade promised at the onset. In place of the ailing old general, drawing his advice from corporate businessmen, here was a youthful intellectual whose counselors came from prestigious universities and whose presence in government gave tentative legitimacy to the intellectual class.

Though America had been a nation conceived in the enlightened vision of 18th century intellectuals, from the time of Andrew Jackson rapid colonization and mass immigration gave supremacy to the values of ordinary folk. By the 20th century these values were epitomized by the small town and the independent businessman. Thus the Kennedy administration signaled a new set of alliances in government and gave encouragement to a youthful urban population who were being college educated in ever-increasing numbers.

Nonetheless, arrayed against the utopian promise of the new administration were smoldering discontents. Despite the abolition of slavery in the last century, black Americans continued to be treated as second-class citizens, denied service and employment, housing and voting rights. With the rise of the Ku Klux Klan, hostility and discrimination escalated through the 1920s, a decade also marked by heightened anti-semitism. In the South lynchings and vigilantes continued through the Depression. Then, with World War II, expanding opportunities for employment encouraged a steady migration out of the South, and by the end of the '40s racial conflict was no longer a regional matter. The Supreme Court decisions on the meaning of equal opportunity did little to change common practice in the 1950s; blacks continued to experience discrimination as a routine part of their lives. By the 1960s their growing discontent found expression in the rise of leaders such as Malcolm X, Martin Luther King, Jr., Stokley Carmichael, and Eldridge Cleaver. The '60s began with nonviolent sit-ins and boycotts. It ended with the burning of ghettos, mass arrests and open gunfights with police.

Whatever hopes and aspirations the new administration inspired, these were soon extinguished by the repeated sounds of assassins' bullets. John Kennedy's death in 1963 was followed by the death of Malcolm X in 1965, and of Martin Luther King, Jr. and Robert Kennedy in 1968. It was an unprecedented spectacle of violence. Idealism was transformed into disenchantment. Students in colleges and universities began to withdraw from the mainstream of culture, to congregate in bohemias like San Francisco's Haight-Ashbury and New York's East Village. Where the beatniks of the '50s posed no serious threat to the estabished order, the hippies of the '60s did. They extolled sexuality and intoxication, eschewed economic success, and in general protested the values of their parents' generation. But while the beats had been recruited from the small numbers of young people born during the Depression, the hippies were recruited from those born during the postwar baby boom. The sheer number of youthful dissenters was overwhelming, and their elders were alarmed.

Where the young people of the middle part of the decade were content to experiment with drugs, sex, and music, by the end of the decade youthful discontent erupted on college campuses throughout the nation. The war in Southeast Asia, begun under Kennedy with an elite corps of special forces, was escalated under Johnson to include massive ground troops. The draft was an ever-present threat to the freedom and liberty of young people already disillusioned with the structure of authority that dictated their lives. Early experience with the civil rights movement in the South was turned toward the conditions of academic life. Confrontations between students and the police became as routine as confrontations between blacks and the police. The fabric of the conventional culture was rent by divisions of race and age, and divisions of sex appeared as well. Dormant for half a century, the women's movement was renewed, just as homosexuals and lesbians demanded equality in the distribution of life's opportunities. By the end of the decade prisoners added their voices to the chorus, and the homogeneous vision of America that had flourished in the 1920s and 1950s fragmented into opposing camps and open hostility.

Eventually the silent majority — the patriotic 100% Americans — found their spokesman in Richard Nixon. The desire to rally their forces against the communist menace was replaced by the desire for domestic law and order. With the enemy identified, victory would assure the silent majority of the unquestioned dominance of values that had flourished through the previous decade, as well as through their own youth. In his inaugural address Nixon cautioned the discontents to lower their voices, but he did not address the conditions that gave rise to their massive disillusionment. Instead, the Nixon administration undertook a systematic program to extinguish the voices that claimed that Ameica represented inequality, injustice, and oppression.

It was in this era of disenchantment and despair that Richard Nixon returned to private life and took up a new career. The transition was a time of resocialization, and the man who knew nothing but how to run for office began to learn something about the business world.

Pat had longed to be out of the public arena ever since the Checkers speech, and her husband did not want for job offers. He was concerned with providing for his family—with building an estate that his heirs could inherit and so start off their lives at an advantage. But money was not the primary consideration. More importantly, Nixon desired to be where the fast action was, and so he turned to the mecca of commerce and trade: New York City. He is quoted as saying:

> New York is very cold and very ruthless and very exciting, and therefore an interesting place to live. It has many great disadvantages but also many advantages. The main thing, it is a place where you can't slow down—a fast track. Any person tends to vegetate unless he is moving on a fast track. New York is a very challenging place to live. You have to bone up to keep alive in the competition here. (Lurie, 1962, p. 273)

In 1960, when it had first looked as if Dick might not continue in politics, the Nixons bought a home in the wealthy Los Angeles suburb of Beverly Hills. After the California defeat they moved to New York City where they bought a cooperative apartment in the same building as Nelson Rockefeller. However, the Nixons did not regularly neighbor with the Rockefellers. Nor did they freely mingle in any of the established social circles of New York society. They invited old friends like industrialists Robert Abplanalp and Elmber Bobst, and financier Bebe Rebozo to quiet evenings at home, and once a year they had a big party for their old political staff. While Dick joined a number of prestigious clubs, ate regularly at exclusive restaurants, and sent his daughters to expensive schools, his personal style seemed no more affected by his new environment than it had when he first moved from Whittier to Washington.

Throughout his life there had been no hobby or pastime that held Nixon's interest outside of work, although over the years he did make an effort to become involved in playing golf, and eventually he cultivated a taste for good wines. If he was not a man involved in the cultural life of his nation, neither was he involved in family life. Although both he and his wife had siblings, his family was not an extended one with frequent gatherings of in-laws and cousins, aunts and uncles. Rather, it was a tight little island gathered against the ever-raging outside world, all of them brought together by ties of loyalty to the embattled head. Beyond Pat and the girls, more and more Bebe Rebozo would become a part of that intimate family circle, and occasionally Rose Mary Woods would be included as well.

Beyond this small group of intimates Nixon had little contact with the outside world. To celebrate family occasions, or to make an occasion of family life, the Nixons sometimes went out to a Mexican restaurant for dinner. But they did not mix socially with other families, nor did they routinely pursue outside activities with one another. Rather, this was a family described by the official White House photographer as eating off TV trays, each separate from the others except for official portraits.

Nixon always speaks of his family very highly, and more will be written of this later. But if we are to assess his values by the allocation of his time and energy, he cannot be considered a family man. Work dominated his life to the exclusion of all other interests. His wife estimated that, while he was Vice President, he was home no more than five or six nights a month; his job in New York was equally demanding. Writing of the presidential years in his *Memoirs,* not until the final crises of Watergate does he describe the members of his family as drawn together, giving advice, solace, and comfort to one another, and, in particular, to him. Before the Watergate crisis, and through most of it, Nixon preferred to spend time by himself in the Lincoln sitting room rather than be with Pat and the girls in the family quarters.

He was a solitary and withdrawn man who could number his intimates on the fingers of one hand. He was distant from humanity at large and isolated from those small social networks accessible to a man of his position. His encounters with other human beings were entirely in the line of work. For the most part, these were formal occasions—a political dinner, a dignitary's reception—or no more than a brisk handshake with the throngs who greeted him at airports and rallies. From social encounters such as these, Richard Nixon gathered his firsthand knowledge of life.

Beyond his immediate social experiences, he also read. For the most part, he read biographies of great men—Disraeli, Churchill, de Gaulle. Once out of college he did not read Dickens or Steinbeck, much less poetry or philosophy. So his indirect knowledge of the world was as limited as his immediate experience. Yet he had a talent, and this talent permitted him to move freely among the power elite, at home as well as abroad, at Bohemian Grove or at the corporate board: he was a consummate salesman, an evangelical huckster with a gifted tongue.

In the first few years in New York, business and commerce dominated his days, and then, gradually, his interest and involvement in politics resumed. With the help of influential friends like Donald Kendall (of Pepsi-Cola) and Elmer Bobst (of Werner-Lambert Pharmaceuticals), he took a job with the Wall Street law firm of Mudge, Rose, Guthrie and Alexander. Through the firm had prestige in the marketplace, it had little power or influence. With the Pepsi-Cola account, Nixon brought the firm into the sphere of multinational corporations, and, in return, he became a partner. In addition to handling accounts such as Pepsi-Cola, he sat on the board of directors of numerous corporations, such as Investors Mutual, Inc. He soon became an active participant in the affairs of high finance in America, in Europe, in the Middle East.

By the time Richard Nixon entered the world of high finance, American business practices had been transformed again by postwar technology. Earlier the introduction of the telephone had permitted tremendous economic growth by speeding up the rate of exchange. The introduction of computer technology did the same, only faster. New synthetics led to cheaper production and hence an increase in potential profits, as long as prices did not go down as the ideology of the open market might predict. These new economic opportunities led to new economic enterprise, but mainly on the part of enormous corporations that struggled for shares of the market just as they developed new products to market. The expansion of corporate growth, inherent in the principles of capitalist production, eventually led to multinational corporations, companies that extended their base of operations beyond their country of origin.

With the growth of multinational corporations, the mutual involvement of business and government expanded. In the 1920s corporate interest in government focused on domestic affairs. By the 1960s corporate interests involved foreign affairs as well. America had moved from isolationism to involvement in the politics of foreign states. The move was justified by philosophical principles of freedom and democracy. It was encouraged by, and supported through, corporate business interests committed to ever-growing rates of profit as the measure of their own success.

Multinational corporations control billions of dollars and millions of lives. They embody principles of corporate organization on a complex scale. They still have labor negotiations at the factory level and still consider customer relations in the market place. But the interests of the people at the top of these structures bear little resemblance to the interests of workers and consumers. For the people who control such corporate enterprise the dominant interest is how to divide up the world on a global level so that (1) their place in the marketplace is assured and (2) profits on transactions increase. Those who manipulate the interests of these businesses are a power elite. They have increasing concern with the legislative process both at home and abroad, since it is the government of a country that controls the conditions of commerce and trade, and thus makes their corporate enterprise possible at all.

From 1963 to 1968 Richard Nixon mingled freely with the power elite. As a self-made man, he was no different from many others whose company he kept. He had made his entry into the world of high finance from Whittier via a dramatic political career. He had shown himself a powerful salesman for the free enterprise system. Although he had not created any financial empire of his own, he had influence and contacts to trade. He had a place in the world of corporate enterprise.

The growth of the free enterprise system meant great riches to some and great losses to others. More and more, the control of everyday life was being divested from the local community and put into the hands of a small number of people with their own particularistic interests at stake. For ever-growing numbers of people the system was not satisfying, but alienating. They might eat and have shelter, entertainment and transportation, but control over the resources of their lives and a voice in the allocation of their energy and attention receded with each advance in the corporate structure. This was the system Richard Nixon sold. He spoke of it in ways that were convincing to millions of ordinary people, who shared the belief in free enterprise but who had no idea of how that principle had developed under postindustrial technology. They embraced the vision he sold of opportunities to increase their own profit. But they could not envision the corporate empires that grew from that principle and ultimately restricted the freedom they cherished and the opportunities they sought.

Richard Nixon was as successful in the world of commerce and trade as he had initially been in politics. He took part in the ongoing round of negotiations by which financial deals were made among business leaders and between businessmen and heads of state. As a representative of corporate enterprise and a former government official, he served to bring parties with common interests together. From time to time his visits with people like de Gaulle, Nasser, and Pope John made news. So at the same time that he traveled in the private world of high finance, he also maintained his celebrity status with the voters.

Furthermore, over the years his harsh, antagonistic public image began to blur. Age mellowed his countenance, and his travels elevated his prominence. The shadows that surrounded his life began to recede, as though it were high noon. He had his loyal devotees, some dating back to the Hiss case, others of more recent conversion. He had the confidence of those whose hopes and fears he articulated. He had the support of those whose interests he represented. He still had his critics, but he was out of public life and no longer fair game for the press. As his power grew, criticism receded.

Most sources agree Nixon intended to try for the White House again as soon as he lost in 1960, but not against Kennedy. The loss of California as a political base in '62 dimmed these early hopes; Kennedy's assassination brightened them. But there was no time to put together a campaign for '64, and there was little support in the party to do so. He had shown himself a two-time loser, and a poor one at that. His supporters deserted him, and the party nominated Barry Goldwater to run on the Republican ticket. Goldwater was considered an extremist and, despite his success at the convention, he received lukewarm support from influential Republicans during his campaign. The exception was Richard Nixon, who campaigned strenuously on Goldwater's behalf and chided other Republicans for not showing similar party solidarity. However loyally he might have campaigned, though, Goldwater's defeat considerably increased Nixon's odds. With no successful spokesman for the party Nixon stood as good a chance as anyone in 1968. So his involvement in party politics was renewed. During the years before the '68 convention he began to campaign as conscientiously for the party at home as he did for Pepsi abroad.

In 1962 it looked as if Nixon's meteoric career in politics had come to an end; by 1968 he had been resurrected. His indefatigable campaigning had won respect and support among party loyalists, although influential members were divided. Many supported him on principle, but he did not have a "win image," and they were hesitant to back a loser. So Nixon took his case to the campaign trail, where his success in the New Hampshire primary was enough to convince the right people to back his nomination for a second chance. The nomination assured, he and his forces began their historic campaign— unlike 1960, it would not be a disaster.

When his chance at the White House came around again, campaigning in America had been radically transformed by the rise of the professional campaign manager and the sophisticated tools of the trade: computers, social research, public opinion polling, television. In the past, paid political advisers had loyalty to one politician or party. Since the fate of the adviser was interdependent with the fate of the candidate, political advisers had a commitment to the two-party system. Now the professional campaign manager sold specialized services to the highest bidder independent of party or person. The fate of the political adviser grew independent of the fate of the political candidate; their relationship became entirely commercial. The only concern the professional campaign manager would have with the political process is that it is the heart of the fast action. Campaign managers say:

> Politics is where the action is. It's the main tent. There are other power elites, society, the military, business, but they are all side shows. (Rosenbloom, 1973, p. 93)

Backstage participants in the political process, such people do not make their reputation among the electorate at large, but rather they vie for prestige in that small group of other professional campaign managers who are their peers. They view one another in terms of how much money each makes, how professional and sophisticated their techniques are, how many successful elections they have managed. Few define their objectives in terms of civic responsibility or the public welfare. They say all that matters is winning. They say, "It's all a big crapshoot" (p. 95). Since firms may work on several campaigns at the same time, though usually not with opposing parties in the same election, whatever losses they experience are cushioned. Unlike the candidates they advise, they are not fully committed to the particular races they manage. Thus contemporary campaign managers bring to the political arena a very special mentality. They define as "amateurs" those whose political involvement is motivated by ideals and principles. As "professionals," they are taken by the game itself.

What the advertising firm of Whittaker and Baxter began in Southern California in the '30s and Murray Chotiner took up in the '40s, hundreds of firms were practicing by the '60s. Their emergence as a social institution transformed the election process. Campaigning for public office became a continual process, with strategies and tactics expensive, time-consuming operations. Equally important, elections in America became a profit-making business. The cost of campaign managers' professional services grew with the complexity of their skills. As more and more candidates hired professional campaign managers, more and more candidates needed their counsel to meet the opposition. So the rate of campaign spending grew. By 1968 it cost $35 million to elect Richard Nixon President, and by 1972 the cost had doubled. The largest single expenditure of each campaign would be spent to control the electronic media. Campaigning techniques guaranteed inflation.

Primed by the precedent already estabished by radio, television grew through the '50s and into the '60s. By the end of the decade 98 percent of all the households in America owned one or more television sets, and those sets were turned on an average of six hours a day. Sets became portable, and color was introduced. New sets dropped in price, and old sets were cheaper still. The experiences offered by television viewing became an entrenched part of all segments of American life. As network broadcasting grew, socializing in the local community dwindled. By 1970 Americans were spending less than half an hour a day "visiting" and more than three hours a day "watching television."

What there was to watch was changing as well. Early television adopted the format established by radio. In the 1950s programming was dominated by comedy shows and variety acts, with an occasional western. By the 1960s the urban crime show began to come into its own. As Nixon was campaigning for law and order, the air waves were dominated by video crime. As programming became more narrow in its focus, the coverage of special events became more refined. War-torn Asian villages and riot-torn black ghettos were covered in close-up detail. Lee Harvey Oswald's assassination was broadcast live, then rebroadcast in slow motion with an identifying arrow to point out the movement of his killer. Viewers could watch their sons and daughters idle on the streets of the Haight-Ashbury or battle on college campuses across the nation. By the end of the decade they could watch the first men land on the moon.

The growth of network broadcasting was aided and abetted by the growth of the advertising industry. To principles of consumer psychology and methods of market research were added the techniques of impression management the electronic media afforded. Claims could be made and illustrated in more immediate, more dramatic ways, and then they could be efficiently transmitted to an enormous audience already captured by the entertainment content of the media. Television provided a new pastime for the nation and a new pathway for promotion. Considerations of the marketplace became infused throughout the day as business interests dominated the nation in leisure as well as at work.

The cathode tube became a canvas upon which vivid images began to represent, and then replace, reality. *Illusion would dominate experience.* In this world of impression management one of the most important elements is name recognition. Thus the ephemeral celebrity system that developed in Hollywood fed into the political process. For example, around 1966 the California firms of Spencer-Roberts and Behavior Science Company took a politically inexperienced Hollywood actor whose name was widely recognized, taught him the necessary political lines, trained him in how to act like a candidate for public office, introduced him to influential Republican leaders, organized "citizen-support groups," and got him elected governor of the most populous state of the union. Through the course of the campaign Ronald Reagan repeatedly accused the incumbent, Edmund Brown, of being a "professional politician," and the accusation was taken as a slur on Brown's integrity, as it was intended. Reagan won by such a substantial majority that serious thought was given to running him for President two years later. What it had taken Richard Nixon a political lifetime to learn, Reagan could accomplish with a crash course—and sufficient cash.

Professional campaign managers make mobility across the top of the elite structure possible. They permit a person who has been successful in one field to go directly to the top of another. They also challenge the party system as the repository of political knowledge and power. When party organization was an effective force in American politics, party bosses moved among the people in their precincts to learn what the voters wanted and exchange services for support where possible. They provided a personal link to the political process. Then changes in the fabric of society began to chip away at the effectiveness of precinct organization. Sheer growth in the total number of voters— although not in the rate of voting—made the system cumbersome and difficult to manage. Growing mobility truncated the personal relationships necessary for the party boss's effectiveness. The bureaucratization of social services like welfare and unemployment took away the tokens of exchange. In short, changes in the organization of society began to erode the precinct system just as the professional campaign manager was emerging as a social institution.

Where precinct organization is a diffuse system, the professional campaign manager is centralized. The power of those who managed American campaigns in mid-century far surpassed the power of political bosses at the turn of the century. With the weakening of the party structure and the centralization of power in the campaign managers, it became easier and easier for specialized interest groups who could afford to buy their services to have a disproportionate influence in the democratic process.

By 1968 the old-style whistle-stop campaign was a relic. Richard Nixon spent one day in Ohio, traveling from community to community, meeting the crowds at the station, talking directly to people. But the objective of the day's activities was not to win the hearts and minds of rural Ohio; it was to provide footage of visual images that Harry Treleaven and his associates could edit and integrate for commercial television broadcasting. The train whistle would add a bit of nostalgia to what would otherwise be an electronic campaign.

Nixon had learned a major lesson from his 1960 defeat. After 150 pages of searching analysis in *Six Crises,* he concludes by writing:

> I spent too much time . . . on substance and too little time on
> appearance; I paid too much attention to what I was gong to say
> and too little on how I would look . . . one bad camera angle on

> television can have far more effect on the election outcome than
> a major mistake in writing a speech which is then picked up and
> criticized by columnists and editorial writers. (p. 457)

It was clear that if the electronic media was to be of use to him, it would have to be controlled. He could not afford to be ruffled by the face-to-face presence of his critics and foes, he could not afford to have his performance interpreted by the press, with their inherent biases. He had to speak directly to the voters, in ways that were convincing to ordinary folks. He had to sell himself.

The Nixon forces organized themselves along two lines. There were the issue men and the image men—those who would counsel him on political strategy and those who would advise him on impression management. To begin with, both forces agreed that Nixon must erase the image of a "bad loser." And so another New Nixon appeared. When he entered politics in the '40s, his public image was that of a brash, aggressive zealot. He was tough, courageous, always ready for a fight, a fierce partisan of ideological causes. He gathered a following of staunch loyalists who liked his style. But he also put off many others, who found his manners barbaric and his motives suspicious. Ike's illness and Nixon's nearness to power in the '50s provided an oppportunity to eliminate the most offensive of his characteristics. Under the tutelage of such men as William Rogers and Robert Finch, an old political associate from California, a New Nixon emerged. This Nixon was more thoughtful, more conscientious, as befitted a man of mature years. He could make claim to being a statesman. But to those who remembered the infamous Kitchen Debate, the New Nixon was still tough. His absence from public life in the '60s gave yet another opportunity to forge a character that would have the widest public appeal.

Researchers on the image staff, employing sensitive linguistic instruments like the "semantic differential," began to tap the fantasy world of voters and elicit the very model of a successful statesman. His advisers wrote memos saying:

> What we have to deal with now is not the facts of history, but an
> image of history. The history we have to be concerned with is not
> what happened, but what's remembered . . . to put it another way,
> the *historical untruth may be a political reality.* (McGinnis, 1970,
> p. 203; emphasis added)

The political reality they chose to construct was an image of Richard Nixon as the leader returning from exile. They satisfied his loyal followers and cultivated all those who remembered his name but whose impressions of his career were fuzzy. The image they projected was calmer, more thoughtful, more compassionate than the image of eight years earlier. The new New Nixon could be respected, if not loved; he was firm but not harsh. Public appearances began to show evenly spaced flashes of warmth. The New Hampshire primary was saturated with carefully organized and edited color film that would create the desired illusion. His advisers wrote:

> New Hampshire: saturation with film, in which candidate can be shown better than he can be shown in person because it can be edited, so only the best moments are shown; then a quick parading of the candidate in the flesh so that the guy they've gotten intimately acquainted with on the screen takes on a living presence—not saying anything, just being seen . . . (p. 198)

This was the main strategy that convinced influential party members to back Nixon's nomination at the convention, and this was the campaign strategy that convinced the electorate to back him at the polls. It was directed by the people who composed the image staff. They devised a theme and created television commercials to fit that theme. They saw that those commercials were produced in a professional fashion and aired on prime viewing time. Programs were made for regional audiences, thus tailoring the basic presentation for maximum viewer effect. There was no longer any question of substance, only the advantage of perspective.

It was clear that Nixon could not take a stand on any of the issues that were dividing the country without alienating large numbers of voters. So instead of addressing war and discrimination, Nixon took up the cause of crime. The country was ripe for a reinterpretation of reality. Armed conflict had become a routine feature of ghetto and campus life. Along with the war in Southeast Asia, these hositilies were covered in full color on the evening news and thereby became a part of every viewer's experience. In addition to the coverage of real-life conflict, television programming was dominated by programs of violence, destruction and harm. Thus the recreational myths American viewers were exposed to reinforced their general apprehension and fear. Something was happening but they didn't know what. Nixon began to capitalize on this sense of anomie. He defined civil unrest as criminal in its intent and nature, thereby bringing it into focus as an enemy to fight against in the cause of righteousness. Nixon's theme for his campaign was law and order. He promised to bring peace to the land, and he said little if anything about his international objectives.

★   ★   ★

John Mitchell and H.R. Haldeman served as the ideologues of the campaign. Murray Chotiner returned to advise on political strategy. Rose Mary Woods, Nixon's secretary since the '50s, was elevated to the inner circle and routinely consulted on strategic matters. To conserve his energy for his rare public appearances and to have him relaxed and healthy looking on the tube, his advisers took the candidate for frequent trips to Key Biscayne, Florida. There they kept him tanned and rested, while they minimized the irritations of everyday life by attending to many of the details of the race themselves.

All was not roses. There were severe differences of opinion between the image men and the issue men, and some of the latter, drawn to the candidate by the cause he represented, resigned. Animosity emerged between Haldeman and Woods, Mitchell and Chotiner, relations that would be carried into the White House and become part of the Nixon administration.

However the dissention among the Nixon forces was not nearly as great as the dissention that racked the opposition party. With the expansion of military involvement in Southeast Asia, the war-resistance movement had grown. Spring and fall mobilizations began to draw increasing numbers of marchers, ultimately culminating in a quarter of a million demonstrators converging on the capital in 1969. Growing more and more fearful of his fate in public appearances, Johnson announced he would not run again, and the field was open for Democratic nominees. The despair at Martin Luther King's assassination a month later was followed by more demonstrations and renewed rioting. The disruptions in the nation's capital led to calling out the military in full battle dress, the first time armed troops had been seen on the steps of Congress since the Civil War. Fear about the present and anxiety about the future grew. If the Democrats were to capture the '68 election, they needed a candidate who could repudiate the policies of the incumbent administration. Then, quite unexpectedly, Robert Kennedy emerged as just such a candidate, one who could convincingly speak for peace abroad and unification at home.

Kennedy's announcement could only be bad news for Nixon, who had calculated his victory on divisions in the opposition party. Kennedy's candidacy offered the possibility of unification. Even worse, for eight years Richard M. Nixon had anticipated a second try at the White House, and suddenly it was like an instant replay of 1960. It looked as if he might have to face a Kennedy again—the rich, confident cosmopolitan against the poor, insecure provincial. But such fears as he might have harbored were short lived. Assassin's bullets put a quick end to Kennedy's aspirations. While the rest of the nation mourned the tragedy, Richard Nixon's immediate nightmare was over. If the opposition forces were divided before, they were in dissarray now. In the ill-fated convention at Chicago the image of the Democratic Party was shattered by its association with violence and civil disruption, and Nixon got to run against a man of origins similar to his own: Hubert H. Humphrey, the son of a midwestern druggist.

Running against an unpopular administration gave Nixon an inherent advantage. Against the televised background of the Democratic convention, his cries for law and order took on new significance, and Nixon started off with a substantial lead, just as he had in 1960. Again the objective of the campaign was to maintain that lead up through the day of the election. In 1960 the strategy had been to visit each state in a demonstration of national interest. Now the candidate would remain aloof, while the media saturated the nation with images of the leader returning from exile, bringing promises of law and order at home and hinting of a secret plan to end the war abroad.

In 1960 the Nixon staff had been petty and vindictive toward the working press; in 1968 they pandered to their comfort. They provided copious handouts and mimeographed statements of the candidate's position on various issues. They provided transportation, photo opportunities, and places to work. But they prohibited the press from face-to-face encounters with the candidate. Reporters could learn little more about the New Nixon then could television viewers, and hence their opportunity to comment and criticize was limited. Unlike the 1960 campaign, the Nixon forces concentrated on controlling the dissemination of information, and so doing they controlled, to their own advantage, the voters' understanding of the world.

Despite the enormous budget and the astute advice of his professional counselors, Nixon just managed to hold his own in the polls, while Humphrey continued to gain. Less sophisticated than the Nixon forces, Humphrey's media advisers had shown him as a human being. Where the Nixon image was always impeccably groomed and framed by a synthetic indoor setting, Humphrey was shown outdoors, sweating and laughing in the open air. Humphrey offered no unifying principles, no decisive leadership. But he appeared as a person and not just a candidate. As the campaign continued, Humphrey began to draw more and more of the uncommitted; it was time for the Nixon forces to go on the offensive. Exploiting the heightened sensitivity that surrounded the Democratic convention, anti-Humphrey commercials were prepared. As a technique of modern campaigning, such tactics were not new. The Johnson forces had used a very effective commercial against Goldwater in 1964. Showing a small child pulling the petals from a daisy, the picture dissolved into that gothic image of the 20th century, the mushroom cloud, while an anonymous male voice-over asked voters to consider what might happen if they voted for the extremist candidate. By implication, Johnson—who did in fact expand the Vietnam War—was the peace candidate. The same logic was employed by the Nixon forces four years later. In the final week of the race a commercial was shown on the popular comedy *Laugh In* that interspersed images of the laughing, gleeful Humphrey with images of rioting, war, and poverty. It was a jarring 60 seconds. It evoked outrage from some who saw it, just as the Johnson commercial had in 1964. Others thought it had been a pro-Humphrey commercial, and still others thought it was just part of that zany *Laugh In* show. In any event, between the anti-Humphrey commercials and a controlled nationwide telethon on election eve, Nixon managed to keep his precious lead. But while he had started out the race as the front runner by a long shot, he won by just seven-tenths of one percent.

Yet he won, and to the victor belong the spoils. In a courtesy gesture, Johnson sent Air Force One to Key Biscayne to pick up the President-elect and arrange for the orderly transition of power. In the company of the associates who had been close to him during the long campaign, Nixon examined the perquisites of the office that would soon be his. As he pushed a button that turned the coffee table into a desk, he said, "It sure beats losing." (Safire, 1975, p. 107)

Chapter 6
Winning and Losing

By a margin of less than one percent of the popular vote, Richard Nixon's personal biography forever merged with the stream of American history, and a new era began. Political commentators predicted a return to normalcy after the turbulent years of the Johnson administration. If there was any rhyme or reason to be found in the vagaries of the electoral process, they argued, then Nixon's victory could be seen only as a popular cry for order and control. He had started in politics with a reputation as a tough aggressive fighter, willing to take on the forces that threatened America from abroad. Now he would focus his attention on the crime and lawlessness that beset the country at home. He would put an end to the discontent and dissent that had inflamed the passions of so many and created a decade of civil strife unknown since the Civil War. Or at least this was the logic attributed to the 63 million American people whose decision to vote in November gave Nixon the fragile mandate to rule the nation for the next four years.

Election day decides which candidate will be vested with the power
and authority of office. But it is not until the inaugural ceremony that
the reality of the candidate's victory is confirmed. Traditionally, the
inaugural ceremony is both a festive and solemn occasion. Balls,
receptions, speeches, and parades reward party loyalists and heighten the
significance of the moment. God is formally invoked to witness the
successful candidate's oath. In his inaugural address the new President
has the opportunity to start a new chapter of national history. Nixon
spoke on the crises of the spirit and the need to put an end to civil
discord, although his inauguration in fact heightened the drama of
dissent. In his *Memoirs* and in the U.S. government's official account
of the occasion, only the traditional formalities are noted. But records
of the National Commission on the Causes and Prevention of Violence
provide a narrative of a different order, for alongside the traditional
ceremonies of the day was a "counterinaugural" as characteristic of the
Nixon adminstration as were the more customary events.

Guerrilla theater and the electronic media both came into their own
in the 1960s. Guerrilla theater transforms ordinary occasions into ironic
commentary, while the electronic media are dependent on what is out of
the ordinary for news. Through the magnification of the television lens,
street theater flourished in the '60s, and the inauguration of the 37th
President provided a stage whereon the contradictions and inequalities
of the prevailing system were heightened and dramatized.

A loose coalition of hippies, yippies, and radical youths had formed
the National Mobilization Committee to End the War. They petitioned
and obtained a permit to hold a demonstration, and 30,000
demonstrators began to converge on Washington at the same time that
those who had come for the traditional inauguration formalities were ar-
riving. By appearance alone, these two groups hardly looked like
members of the same society. Those who came to support the official
ceremonies could have been participants at the Queen's coronation or the
official gathering of the ruling class of any industrial nation. Those who
came to protest the policies of the ruling class could have been cast in the
Three Penny Opera. Their hair was long and uncoiffed. Bearded and
barefoot, they were dressed in Army surplus and Goodwill castoffs. They
appeared as an alien tribe, yet everyone knew these were the children of
the ruling class as well as of the working class and the middle class. They

were not aliens so much as they were alienated from the symbolic markers that spelled respectability in American society.

While the traditional formalities of the inauguration took place, the demonstrators held meetings and seminars to protest the policies that had been guiding the nation for almost a decade. In small bands they gathered at the sites of the official ceremony, shouting "Fascist pig" at reception guests. Wearing chalk-white Nixon masks, they dispersed through the crowds lining the street for the inaugural parade. As the President's limousine passed by, they gave Nazi salutes and cried out obscenities. The President, however, was insulated from such signs of disrespect and from the sentiments of despair that engendered them, for between his limousine and the crowds that had gathered to witness his oath were (1) a line of armed metropolitan police, (2) a line of National Guardsmen in full battle gear, and (3) members of the 82nd Airborne Division without battle gear. Not since Abraham Lincoln's inauguration—when the nation was on the brink of the Civil War—had a United States President been sworn in under armed guard.

Ignored in the official account, this facet of Nixon's inauguration became symbolic of the era ushered in by his ascent to power. Dissent and disruption did not end when he took the oath of office. In the next two years civil strife intensified. Demonstrations that mobilized a million citizens appeared. College students were killed and maimed on campus, black leaders shot in their beds. A judge was executed on the steps of the county courthouse. The chaos and bloodshed that appeared in the nation with the Kennedy assassination reigned well into Nixon's administration.

During Nixon's first term in office, the specter of civil dissent was one of the most serious problems he had to contend with, and some would argue that this was the source of all that followed. Through the course of his administration Nixon attempted to solve the problem of dissent by deploying a visible display of force at the public level and instigating invisible forces whose extra legal powers were a function of their secrecy.

Within two years the apparent face of the nation changed. The show of force that had guaranteed order at the inauguration became a regular feature of the civilian landscape. Ordinary places like banks, courthouses, supermarkets, schools, and airports became places where armed guards and official inspections were routinely found.

At the same time that this visible display of force was manifest, secret forces were also organized. Knowledge of their existence did not come about until the Watergate cover-up began to disintegrate, but they were put in motion long before the break-in of the Democratic National Headquarters. They began with ideas like the Houston plan, which proposed a variety of illegal acts as a way of dealing with domestic dissent. They continued with the Plumbers' operation, which broke the law in an attempt to discredit Daniel Ellsberg, the man who turned the Pentagon Papers over to the press. They involved wiretaps put on the phones of journalists and members of the White House staff, the forging of CIA cables, and other unseemly acts. These operations never involved large numbers of people, and, in the case of the Houston plan, they were authorized but not acted upon. Nevertheless, a clear pattern was emerging. The Nixon administration would not stop at the law in its efforts to uphold the system. Dissent and disagreement, once guaranteed under Constitutional law, came to be defined as a challenge to legitimate authority, and surreptitious means were regularly used to counter the threat they posed.

In the years after Nixon's resignation, those who had been close to the White House described the atmosphere as paranoid. From the Oval Office—through Haldeman and Ehrlichman, through Ron Ziegler, Charles Colson, and Dwight Chapin—there exuded a belief in the existence of embittered enemies who were out to discredit the Nixon administration, the policies it put forth, the people who served it, and, most of all, the man whose person embodied that administration. Similarly, the transcripts of taped conversations convey the mentality of a small number of people under seige from a large hostile force. The President says: "Nobody is a friend of ours. Let's face it." (Nixon, 1974, p. 133)

Nixon did not suddenly adopt this perspective once he was in office. He had been developing it through the course of his career in politics, where he and his colleagues had wheeled and dealed to advance their own interests in the face of competing claims, constantly ready to outfox or outmaneuver the other, and always alert to being outfoxed or outmaneuvered themselves. In this vision of politics government is war. What is at stake is the right to power and authority. Winners and losers, casualties and victors, constitute the outcome of the contest and the objective of all action. With such a definition of the democratic process it is rational to be on guard, ready to take certain advantages, prepared to take certain risks—even if you are the President, the symbol of national unification and the embodiment of Constitutional authority. There is evidence to suggest that Lyndon Johnson was beset by the same attitude, particularly in his last years in office. (Kearns, 1976) So the paranoia manifest in the White House during the Nixon administration was not a unique manifestation of a particular personality. Suspicion and mistrust had become a way of life. If it began among the dissident and the disenfranchised, by the time Nixon took office it had permeated the executive branch of government.

At one time in American history the man who occupied the Oval Office could count on widespread support of the electorate as an expression of patriotic loyalty. This had been the image fostered during Nixon's childhood, and it had been heightened during the Second World War. But that image began to fade as American military involvement continued in wars that grew increasingly unpopular. The armed guard that stood watch over Nixon's inauguration symbolized the crisis of authority that beset the nation. During his time in office Nixon both escalated the war and exacerbated the crises it provoked.

In his campaign he hinted at a secret plan to end the war, but the war did not end with his inauguration. Quite the contrary, it was extended year after year. First it was done in secret, with neither the people nor their representatives informed of the bombing of previously neutral Cambodia. The following spring the further incursion of ground troops was announced on one of the television specials that became characteristic of the administration. In an appeal to the nation to have faith in his insight and wisdom, Nixon justified the escalation of the war as a strategy to end the war. As contradictory as this might appear, many continued to believe the man, although the young did not. In response, their campus demonstrations were treated as though they were armed insurrections, and the White House efforts to stifle dissent were intensified, both in public and in secret.

Vowing that he would not be swayed by the politics of the street, claiming that dissent at home gave aid and comfort to the enemy abroad, promising that he would not be the first American President to lose a war, Nixon continued to intensify the hostilities. He paid lip service to popular sentiment by gradually withdrawing American troop involvement while the technology of destruction was intensified. After the bombing of Cambodia and Laos there was the mining of the harbors in North Vietnam and then the intense carpet-bombing of populated regions during the Christmas season. All this was done in the public name of making peace with honor, although in the inner citadels of the White House it was known as the "mad monk" theory. (See Ehrlichman, 1976; Haldeman, 1978.)

Although criticism of the war grew, criticism of the man who was waging the war was limited. With the exception of the radical and underground presses, newspapers and networks continued to give Nixon credit for attempting to do the best he could with a war he had inherited. When the conventional press finally became disillusioned with the war, they still did not question Nixon's authority to wage it. They assumed that a limited war fought with conventional weapons was still a profitable option in the 20th century. What began under Kennedy as a test of the strategy of limited intervention in global conflict had become a point of national honor under Johnson and Nixon. The war continued to be limited in the sense that nuclear weapons were not used, but American troops and equipment were increasingly deployed to take part in a civil war on another continent.

The justification given for the importance of waging limited war was the domino theory. Based on a version of the international communist conspiracy theory, it proclaimed that if one underdeveloped country fell to communism through civil strife, then another and another would fall, and so on. The domino theory assumed active intervention of established communist regimes in the internal affairs of nonindustrialized nations, and thus justified active American intervention in those same countries to prevent it.

Between the theory of limited war and the domino theory, endless justifications were available to explain why American troops and equipment were in Vietnam and why they could not be removed when it was obvious that there was nothing they could achieve. The government of South Vietnam was a corrupt dictatorship, while the force of the liberation movement from the North had been growing for two decades. Eventually, no one expected victory and everyone demanded peace. But arrayed alongside these pacifist interests were equally strong sentiments of face and right. Even as the nation had become disillusioned with the conflict in Southeast Asia, there had been no general questioning of the moral right of America to intervene actively in affairs of the globe. It was a matter of principle to maintain America's position as a world power. With its abundant natural resources and its highly sophisticated technology, America would defend the right of free enterprise anywhere on earth. To make that claim and not follow through would be to diminish the stature of the nation as a moral leader in world affairs. Peace with honor became a ploy to save face, to end a futile war without ending the right to wage war.

Leaders in government, the media, business, and the military did not question these principles. The churches had provided leadership in questions of moral affairs in the past, but they were slow to grasp the fundamental immorality of the Vietnam War. Voices of dissent could be heard in the schools, and so it became necessary to discredit the intelligentsia's claim to authority and insight. Vice President Spiro Agnew, with the help of eloquent speeches written by the White House staff, acted as hatchet man. Thus, with the exception of some who mobilized on the streets, dissent on the war was not dissent from the system perpetuating that war or a challenge to the authority directing the system.

Yet from Nixon's perspective this is indeed how it must have seemed, for the voices on "the other side" grew in spiraling intensity. Nixon had been elected to bring good news to America, but the news was not good in the spring of 1970. He had come into office to put an end to dissent, but by his very actions he had heightened it. Furthermore, Nixon had an acute sensitivity to the press, whose routine activities served to make the consequences of his actions a part of the public record. Those who knew him well testified that he had a tendency to take all criticism personally and a disposition to overreact. (White, 1973; Safire, 1975) So as the conventional press became more open in its criticism of the war, Nixon became more punitive in his relations with the press. In response to his censure the press became broader in its criticism, and the vicious cycle played out its destiny.

With hindsight it is easy for critics to suggest that, given the fractures and disorders in the body politic that characterized the era, Nixon had no chance to bring the country together. His administration was doomed to failure from the start. But writing in the early years of his administration, critics had neither hindsight nor foresight. All they had was what they knew about the present moment and remnants of history. His traditional detractors were as suspicious of his behavior in office as they had been of his campaign practices. A few were vocal, well placed, and not averse to departing from the party line of their sponsors or the political etiquette of government. But many more who had been skeptical through the course of Nixon's career acceded to the system that gave meaning to his victory. They would moderate their critical judgment in light of the understanding that he was, after all, the President of the United States and a powerful figure in international affairs. So, even though he did not believe it, most of the nation was behind him from the start, willing to give him credit for what he might accomplish. Even though he had won the election by a slender majority of the popular vote; even though he had expanded the war and as a consequence exacerbated the protest and dissent that war had engendered; even though the economy had been steadily deteriorating under his stewardship, by the end of his first term almost two-thirds of the people thought he was doing a good job as President.

Strong public approval was vital to Nixon's objectives, for the success of his political career would ultimately be measured by how he did in the 1972 election.

Why this is so is a function of the accounting of success in America. Success is always relative to: (1) where you start from, and (2) who your competitors are. In a hierarchical world view each success entitles the victor to compete in the next arena. Though limited success brings its own satisfactions, these are pale experiences compared to the ultimate success: to be top dog. With ever-increasing grandeur Nixon had moved from being the grocer's son in Whittier to being the President of the United States of America. So reckoned, his success was enormous. Now the scope would be tested among equally seasoned competitors.

After Roosevelt's alarming success in winning popular elections, Congress resolved to limit the incumbency of the President to two consecutive terms, thereby assuring turnover at the top and a stop rule for the players. Once elected, the most an incumbent could hope for was reelection. This made reelection vital to Nixon's standing among American Presidents and necessary to the accounting of his ultimate success. When judged against his peers, the 36 men who had preceded him and the untold number who might follow, he could not be a one-term President and still consider himself a success.

So, being in office was not much different from running for office. Through the course of his first term, everything he did—or did not do— was assessed by Nixon for its likely effect on his chances in the 1972 race. He staffed his administration with functionaries who had served him well by mapping strategy and commanding personnel in his partisan encounters. What they did on the campaign trail would be done in the Oval Office as well.

For the most part, these were people whose expertise was in the field of advertising, or lawyers with limited experiences, such as zoning or municipal bonds. Their philosophical appreciation of government was nil, and they lacked any understanding of politics that comes from being an elected official or a civil servant. What they did bring to the administration was the tested ability to get their candidate elected; and in terms of how Richard Nixon reckoned success in office, this was all the staff he really needed. His tenure was only a prelude to reelection.

Through Haldeman and Erhlichman, input into the Oval Office was filtered inward and Presidential edicts disseminated outward. John Mitchell managed the 1968 campaign, and he was in charge in 1972 as well. In the interim he took over the Justice Department, thereby establishing the kind of close relationship between President and prosecution that had been characteristic of the Kennedy administration. With the addition of Henry Kissinger the basic organization of the Nixon team was complete. Through Haldeman and Erhlichman in the White House and Mitchell in the Justice Department, the President managed the domestic affairs of the nation, while Kissinger managed his involvement in foreign intrigue.

If winning reelection was one consideration of Nixon's tenure, winning a place in world history was another. Eisenhower's largesse had given Nixon an opportunity to travel the globe and mix with the ruling elite, although, as Vice President, he had neither international nor domestic authority of his own. As President, he was impressed less by the opportunity for domestic leadership than by the opportunity for glory in global politics, for just as Nixon was coming into his own in the stream of American history, the tides of international history were changing and unexpected opportunities appeared that could not have been predicted on the basis of his early career.

Nixon began his political career as a Cold War warrior who subscribed to the image of a free, capitalist world, locked in mortal combat with captive nations enslaved under the iron yoke of communism. He believed in this image before he ever talked with a communist, visited Russia, or studied the writings of Marx and Lenin. But this was not remarkable, for Nixon was a child of his times. The threat communist ideology presented to vested American business interests in the early years of the century had generated the red scare that dominated the imagery of his childhood, while the specter of the international communist conspiracy reappeared as a leitmotif of the Depression. The anticommunist line had never been alien to him, but rather was a part of the world view he grew up with. Through the successes of his own lifetime, he came to believe personally in the unmitigated virtue of free enterprise and individual initiative; and the words of those in authority were sufficient to convince him that the forces of communism menaced his personal self-interests. Those in positions of power and influence had been unsparingly condemnatory of any alternative to the economic system that gavè them their power and permitted them to wield influence. Thus Richard Nixon and the generation of school children growing up after him came to believe in the communist menace with the same conviction Christian children once held about the devil.

Yet compared to the international communist conspiracy, the devil was a mere abstration. As Nixon came into manhood, the Soviet Union emerged as a world power. Added to the ideological threat Marxist principles presented was the military threat of the U.S.S.R.

In the late 1940s and early 1950s some people had begun to argue for a policy of peaceful co-existence among world powers. Others took a tougher stance, and they were initially the more influential. They argued that communism was bent on world domination; that communists were willing to use any means in the quest of their goals; and that even if communists claimed otherwise, Americans could not trust them because they lie. To assure their own freedom, the people of the capitalist world must be ever alert to signs of communist aggression, for the smallest victory on the other side would inflame the enemy's desire for, and commitment to, global control. In this way the logic for maintaining the Cold War was laid down in the postwar years. School teachers who did not define one half of the world as an international aggressor were subject to rebuke, public vilification, and the loss of their jobs. Sociology students who did not respond that Marx was a polemicist and not a theorist did not get passing grades. A unified world view was forged through the educational institutions, bolstered by the media, and proclaimed by public savants. Communism was an aggressive world force that had to be contained at any price, lest the principles that made America a great and moral victor in the battle with fascism be lost forever. The gothic image was in vogue.

While this world view was being forged as an article of faith, newer, more destructive weapons of war were being forged to defend the faith. The concerted effort of the Manhattan project had resulted in the most massive display of force ever let loose by human ingenuity, and arms research continued as a regular budget item of the federal government thereafter. Military allocations for testing and stockpiling weapons increased. While war profiteering was once dependent on the existence of armed conflict, now the rhetoric of "defense" made armaments a profitable venture on a regular basis. The economy grew through the '50s, but it grew by creating an enormous military-industrial complex in which the

military needs for defense generated the demand for industrial, technological, and scientific production. Fear began to direct the economy, and
tools of destruction flooded the marketplace.

The strategists of the Cold War could not foresee the forces they set
in motion. As the techniques of weaponry became ever more refined,
with intercontinental ballistic missiles, atomic warheads, and lethal
biological and chemical substances, the cost of open conflict rose
exponentially. There could never be a definitive military test of the
powers of capitalism against the powers of communism, for there would
be all spoils and no victor. The potential of modern weaponry had made
the image of committed military forces locked in mortal combat obsolete.
If war was to be waged in the modern world, those who waged it would
have to find a new arena.

As Nixon came into power, the postwar situation had finally been
fully understood by those whose self-interest was maintained by control
over the resources and institutions that define national and international
policy. At first they believed that limited war was feasible, but this
proved not to be the case. So an era of detente was necessary lest there
be no future eras. Regardless of what citizens had been told before, this
was a fact of the modern world. A Republican President was an ideal
incumbent to usher in this new era, for the Republican Party traditionally
stood for business interests, and business interests had to be convinced
that co-existence with communism was not the capitulation of free
enterprise. That Nixon had once been a Cold War warrior was of no
consequence. His change in perspective could be attributed to growth
and maturity, and his toughness would reassure those still committed to
the anticommunist movement that he could drive a hard bargain in the
international marketplace.

In 1960 and again in 1968 Nelson Rockefeller and Richard Nixon
had vied for the Republican presidential nomination. Nevertheless,
when Rockefeller's personal adviser in international affairs, Henry
Kissinger, offered himself to Nixon as *his* special adviser on foreign
policy, Nixon had no hesitation about accepting. Ordinarily aloof and
suspicious, ready to see emissaries of the enemy at every juncture, Nixon
was readily open to Kissinger. He provided Kissinger with as free access
to the Oval Office as he provided such tested loyalists as Haldeman and
Erhlichman. No matter that Kissinger was a Jew, a foreigner, a member

of the Eastern Establishment, a Harvard intellectual, a familiar figure in circles that had intimidated Nixon from his early experiences in Washington. Kissinger was necessary to guide Nixon's thinking about foreign affairs and to teach him what he had to know about the reality of global power in an age of nuclear weapons and multinational corporations. They would use one another in a most artful way. Kissinger served as Nixon's intermediary in winding the war down and then winding it around and through Nixon's first administration. On the eve of the 1972 election Kissinger pacified the nation by announcing "Peace is at hand." Although the articles of the negotiated settlement were not ratified until the first days of Nixon's *second* term, the promise sold the nation.

Implicated but not discredited by the Watergate revelations, Kissinger stayed on in Washington to guide Gerry Ford after Nixon's second term was aborted. With Carter's ascendence to office Kissinger faded from public view though not from political influence. He began to make plans to run for political office himself, thereby changing his role from the power behind the throne to the enthroned power.

In the initial days of Nixon's first administration, Kissinger began secret meetings with the People's Republic of China. Years earlier, in his campaign for Vice President, Nixon had vilified Truman for being soft on communism and thus losing 800 million Chinese to the side of the enemy. Nevertheless, without looking back at his own record, Nixon began the complex negotiations that culminated in his historic visit to China on the eve of his renomination. Once Nixon was reelected, Kissinger was rewarded by being named Secretary of State, even at the cost of bumping Nixon's long-time friend William Rogers out of government. As head of the State Department, Kissinger spent little time executing department affairs and more time traveling around the world on the various diplomatic missions that became the hallmark of Nixon's global politics. Between Kissinger's missions and the President's excursions, the Nixon administration earned a reputation for achievement in foreign affairs that even his entrenched critics credited. After he resigned from office in disgrace, this reputation was his trump card. It dominated the televised interviews with David Frost, for which Nixon was nominated for a Grammy award. It was the basis of the Bates College award for international communications made to him in the spring of 1979. The youth who made the presentation of the latter honor was quoted in the newspapers as saying:

> I realize that he violated the Constitution, which I suppose is inexcusable, but that one fact does not negate his other accomplish-

ments. A lot of people have bad feelings about him, but his work
in international communications cannot be denied. (*San Francisco
Chronicle*, March 3, 1979)

Having come into power at an historic juncture, Nixon capitalized
on the opportunities his good fortune made possible. Though he began
his career as a Cold War warrior, he claimed title to peacemaker before
he left office. Dramatic as this transformation from hawk to dove may
appear, no one seemed to notice. Through the course of his career in
public office, he routinely blew with the wind. Richard Nixon had helped
to usher in the McCarthy era with the prosecution of Alger Hiss. When
McCarthy overstepped the boundary of good sense by accusing the Army
of harboring elements that might lead the insurrection against the
free enterprise system, Nixon was the one to carry out the official censure.
Similarly, in his numerous campaigns, one political image after another
was invoked, exploited, and discarded once its usefulness was over.
It was never clear whether Richard Nixon was a principled conservative
or a principled liberal; critics of the right routinely faulted his liberal
tendencies, while critics of the left faulted his conservative moves, and
he openly describes himself as a liberal or a conservative, depending
on the point he wishes to make and the audience he wishes to woo.

If he did in fact act in any principled fashion, it was the principles
of opportunism that guided his conduct. Despite the image of the underdog he cultivated to evoke the sympathy of ordinary folk, his life was
studded with unique opportunities that gave him a competitive advantage
of one sort or another and his response to opportunity was to capitalize
on it whenever he could. Furthermore, he was shrewd enough to create
his own advantage on more than one occasion.

Once the White House was his, new horizons of opportunity opened
up. As chief executive of the nation and commander-in-chief of the
armed forces, he had authority, power, and influence at least equal to
that possessed by those he had been dependent on through his long
career. He was now a man to be reckoned with in his own right, or so he
must have assumed. He had aides and adjuncts and an elaborate communication system that linked him to strategic points all over the world.
He was treated with a kind of deference and respect few ever experience.
He had access to the perquisites of the office, and from them he evolved
an imperial lifestyle at his homes in Florida and California. The costs
of protecting him and caring for his comforts escalated as he took to
traveling from one place on the globe to another, from Key Biscayne to
San Clemente to Washington, D.C.; but few people questioned his right

to put his personal stamp on the office. Beyond social respect and material splendor lay the fact that in his person was vested the authority to set values and priorities at home, and tone and style abroad. In the organizational hierarchy of the United States there was no one superior to him. He was at the pinnacle of the power elite. Where once his opportunities were owed to the largesse of others, now others' opportunities were a function of the decisions he made. Reelected, he would be free to act in ways that were beholden to no one.

Unfettered by any principles other than opportunism, concerned only with establishing his place in world history, Nixon began his drive for reelection by campaigning for Republican candidates in the 1970 congressional race. Like his attempt to assert his influence in 1954, the attempt was a strategic setback. Nixon made "law and order" the theme of his campaign, and a small demonstration in San Jose provided fuel for an impassioned speech in Phoenix. There, in Goldwater country, he gave full vent to his powers of rhetoric. He said:

> Along the campaign trail we have seen and heard demonstrators. But never before in this campaign was there such an atmosphere of *hatred*. As we came out of the hall and entered the motorcade, the *haters* surged past the barricades and began throwing *rocks*. Not small *stones*—large *rocks*, heavy enough to *smash* windows. . . Many who brought their children (to the rally) were *terrified;* others were *incensed* at the *insult* to their elected leaders. All were *repelled* by the atmosphere of *violence* and *hatred* that *marred* the event . . . Some say the *violent* dissent is caused by the *war* in Vietnam. It is about time we branded this line of thinking—this alibi for *violence*, for what it is—pure nonsense. There is no greater *hypocrisy* than a man carrying a banner that says "peace" in one hand while hurling a *rock* or a *bomb* with the other. (Safire, 1975, pp. 329-330; emphasis added)

Many who were witnesses to the San Jose incident came away with a different impression from the President's. They claimed that the demonstrators were few, the number and size of the missiles insignificant, and that the President himself had provoked the outburst by making his classic gesture of victory before entering his limousine.

Regardless of the facts—whether Nixon incited the crowd or the crowd attacked the President—Nixon's version of what happened was used as his election eve telecast in support of Republican candidates. By professional advertising standards, the film of the Phoenix speech made poor media. It was in black and white, and the editing was unprofessional. Nevertheless, Nixon believed the speech embodied the sentiments he wished to project and none of his underlings wanted to accept the responsibility of saying no to the boss. Nixon's performance provided a harsh contrast with the temperate statements of Edmund Muskie, broadcast in full color on the part of the Democratic Party. Political commentators made note of the contrast, and the outcomes at the polls confirmed what the pundits proclaimed. Nixon believed that a tough stance would sell the cause of the President's party. The mid-term campaign disconfirmed that belief, and he spent the next two years cultivating another image.

Image and illusion had been part of Nixon's administration from the beginning. The 1968 campaign was organized in terms of issues and images, and the men who ran the race brought the same perspective into the White House. There, policy and pageantry were interwoven into an image of effective government, and that image was routinely broadcast to the nation. When scandal began to mar the public image of the administration, it was treated as a cosmetic problem and not a moral crime, for the world view of the men responsible for that scandal was rooted in illusion from the very beginning.

The things that were done for the sake of illusion were as vital to the administration as they had been in the campaign, for in a basic sense there was never any distinction between the two. The world view Nixon had been introduced to in Southern California was the world view that had come to dominate the airwaves, the marketplace, and national politics. By mid-century fantasy and illusion were part of the fabric of society, and Nixon had developed a keen appreciation of their role in gaining and maintaining power and authority. The television special became a routine feature of his administration, and the deadlines of broadcast time became an influential factor in policy decisions. The staffing of the cabinet was one example. The search for men with appropriate talents who would be willing to serve as government officials was limited by the deadlines imposed by the historic television special that would announce the President's counselors to the nation. There was no effort to relate the nominee to the area of policy in which he would advise. Instead, like Harding, Nixon selected his cabinet appointments from among his cronies, and it is uncertain just what he learned from the Teapot Dome scandals of his youth.

Like the introduction of his cabinet, the trip to China was governed as much by consideration of pageantry as by considerations of policy. For three decades the United States had refused to recognize the government of mainland China and then, suddenly, on a television spot lasting but 15 minutes, the president announced his pending trip to the People's Republic. The official policy of 30 years was reversed, but no public explanation was given. Instead, the nation was provided with a week of intense television coverage made possible by a special broadcast satellite put into orbit just for the occasion. The arrival of the President's plane in Peking was scheduled in accordance with prime viewing time, not international protocol. Respected reporters described with wonder the mysterious East. The myriad of details was overwhelming, the splendor of the occasion unparalleled. Anyone with access to a television set had access to history in the making. Or at least so it appeared.

The introduction of the cabinet, the trip to China, the trips to Rumania and Moscow, the reception of the astronauts, his daughter's wedding, the visits from chiefs of state all involved the same concern with appearance and effect. In one way or another these occasions provided an opportunity for massive television coverage, and Richard Nixon was seen playing the starring role. He was the man who welcomed back the men from the moon and the man who met Mao. He was the father of the bride and the goodwill ambassador. The interest and attention of millions of people were focused on their television sets, and there the President put his best front forward. His familiar figure and characteristic gestures were routinely associated with the symbols of traditional authority, and, as a consequence, his reputation for embodying traditional authority grew in the public mind.

As the star performer in the pageantry of government, Nixon cut a credible figure. Though he was clearly a mature man, he maintained an aura of youthful vitality. Except for an occasional slip of the tongue, he usually appeared to be in control of his faculties. He moved with apparent ease from one situation to another, although, like everything else associated with his office, this was a function of carefully planned logistics executed by the White House staff.

For example, the "photo opportunity" was a routine part of the White House day, but Haldeman prohibited any photograph that showed Nixon in an embarrassing or compromising position. After Nixon's resignation, aides like Magruder (1975) and Haldeman (1978) and reporters like Woodward and Bernstein (1976) note that, outside the range of the camera, the President's hands frequently shook and under stress he often had difficulty articulating his speech. Yet such information was never part of the public picture reported by the press or seen on television during Nixon's years in power. By managing the images associated with his person, by enhancing the good side and editing the bad, the President subtly controlled peoples' knowledge of him. Seeing one side of the man, they could not grasp that there might be another.

Writing his account of the Nixon administration, Haldeman sees this one-sided view of the President as the only mistake in his zero-defect administration, and he cautions future incumbants to portray a more realistic illusion. Thus Gerry Ford was portrayed making English muffins in the kitchen and his Democratic successor was seen in dungarees, clumping around in the dirt.

★   ★   ★

The 1970 campaign tested the political climate. Where the Nixon forces had believed that a new majority could be created by a strategy of polarization, they now saw the need for unification. The hate monger that had appeared so briefly on election eve was replaced by a model more suitable to the times. In the next two years Nixon cultivated an image of statesman and peacemaker just as he had when he was Vice President and Ike was at death's door. He became again a man above partisan divisions and divisive tactics. Surrogates campaigned on his behalf, speaking lines written by White House speechmakers, while the President remained aloof from party politics. However, at the same time that he cultivated a public image of national unity, he authorized acts of domestic sabotage that had as one of their effects the removal of the front-running Democratic contender from the 1972 race.

The sabotage of the Muskie campaign was one of the first acts in Nixon's drive for reelection. The 1970 congressional race had demonstrated the relative strengths and weaknesses of the two likely contenders. So apprised, the Nixon forces began systematically undermining the opposition to make the challenge easier for their own candidate. A surreptitious campaign of dirty tricks that included forged letters, anonymous telephone calls, hecklers, and spies eventually discredited Edmund Muskie in the public eye, and with him out of the way, Nixon faced a much weaker opponent. With the assassination attempt on George Wallace, Nixon's victory was assured.

At this point in his career, Richard Nixon, like Joseph McCarthy, overstepped the boundaries of good sense. Both claimed to know the enemy that threatened the American way of life, and each was empowered to purge that enemy for the good of the system. But once they began, they found the enemy everywhere. Eventually, each saw the enemy in the very heart of the system. For McCarthy, in the 1950s, the enemy at the heart of the system was the Army. For Nixon, in the 1970s, the enemy was the Democratic Party. Good sense would have dictated to each the futility of identifying such critical institutions as a threat to the system: insofar as each is crucial to maintaining some aspect of the American way of life, neither could be attacked without questioning the way of life they support.

Those who ultimately effected Nixon's fall from power were the same as those who had been instrumental in his ascent. Through the course of his career they had concurred in the enemies he selected and approved of the tactics he employed. But while Nixon's vision had been partisan, the interests his career depended on were bipartisan. The same corporate organizations that made contributions to the Republican campaigns contributed to the Democrats as well, although not as heavily. Customarily, the deficit was made up by contributions from organized labor.

Cash campaign contributions are made for a variety of reasons. In some cases, contributions are made directly to influence policy decisions. More often, those who contribute to the political process want access to ranking government officials, to plead their case directly. Payment is made not for any direct fix but for the right to bypass the official bureaucratic channels. Thus Maurice Stans, raising funds on behalf of Richard Nixon, could promise contributors: "You will not be forgotten." (White, 1975) That was all he needed to say to insure cash contributions of up to $200,000 by responsible officers of corporate giants. No contracts, no receipts. Just a knowing handshake.

However, no matter who was victorious at the polls, corporate interests had nothing to lose. From the standpoint of the organized system of social life the two parties supported, principled differences between them were marginal. Yet both were necessary to maintain the illusion of free choice between competing interests. The ideology of laissez faire capitalism that made possible the growth of corporate oligopoly professed that what makes the American system a great system—as opposed to the totalitarian regimes that characterize communist countries—is that the society is not dominated by one interest group that continues to stay in power and determine policy. Instead, competing interests vie for power, and from this contested struggle, the policy best suited to the nation emerges. In point of fact, the American system is dominated by corporate interest virtually to the exclusion of all other groups. The two major parties—one claiming to represent the interests of business and the other the interests of the workers—merely obscure the basic economic facts of life, and hence perpetuate the myth of democracy.

When Richard Nixon began to treat the Democratic Party as though it were no different from foreign governments, domestic radicals, gangsters, drug pushers, and the like, he began to threaten the structure that held the democratic myth together and protected the interests best served by the existing arrangements. Throughout his administration, in subtle and significant ways, he had moved America toward totalitarianism. As long as this involved stifling the radical voices of dissent, established interest groups engaged in neither organized nor systematic censure. But once he began to tamper with the two-party system, opposition began. With each revelation of the extent to which the Nixon forces had gone to stifle the Democratic Party, that opposition intensified. Once there had only been the underground press claiming Nixon was a criminal. Then the liberal *Washington Post* began printing stories that linked the Nixon White House with the burglary of the Democratic National Committee, the burglary of Ellsberg's psychiatrist, bribery, perjury, blackmail, etc. Gradually the number of conventional newspapers giving play to the stories grew. Ultimately, editorials demanding Nixon's resignation appeared in the conservative press. Similarly, in the Congress at first there were only his routine detractors calling for full disclosure. Then there were renegade party members sitting in official hearings, demanding the facts. Finally, there were loyalists demanding his resignation.

Clearly, he had gone too far.

How far he had actually gone would be revealed through the long, embattled months of Watergate, and even then, not entirely. Once domestic sabotage became part of the Nixon game-plan, a variety of decisions were made as a routine part of the reelection campaign. One of those decisions was the authorization of a quarter-million dollars to finance an espionage plan. In his tenure in the Justice Department John Mitchell had routinely authorized whatever wiretaps the White House thought necessary in its battle against threats to the American way of life. Authorization of the espionage plan Gordon Liddy proposed was just a routine decision in the life of a busy Attorney General.

Wiretapping frequently involves breaking and entering, and when the burglars, financed by the Committee to Re-elect the President (CRP), were discovered in the Watergate complex, documents at the CRP and the White House were destroyed to suppress evidence. In addition, payoffs were made to buy complicity. Jeb Magruder, former White House aide, writes in his autobiography:

> The cover-up . . . was immediate and automatic; no one ever considered that there would *not* be a cover-up. It seemed inconceivable that *with our political power we could not erase this mistake we had made* . . . I went to see Mitchell and he accepted Haldeman's proposal that I return to Washington . . . to take charge of the cover-up. (Magruder, 1975, pp. 260-261; emphasis added)

Thus the Attorney General, the staff at the CRP, and various people at the White House became involved in sabotage against the opposition party and obstruction of justice against the government they represented.

The situation was incredible, and the Nixon forces relied on absurdity as their first line of defense. Who could conceive that the President or his authorized agents would break the law? The President or his authorized agents are the law—or at least they represent it. Deep-seated belief in the reality of this proposition made the charges against the administration seem implausible, and the administration denials appeared to be the more likely truth.

Insulated by the habits of the public mind, the White House used its influence to impede the Justice Department's case against members of the President's various staffs while it used its claims to legitimate authority to issue deadpan denials. Once the administration denied an accusation in bold, unequivocal terms, those who would press the issue further were forced to assert that the government lies. Like asserting that the Emperor has no clothes, it was a difficult statement for many to make, and so the initial cover-up plan succeeded. With the aid of multimillion dollar campaign funds and the assistance of ambitious men willing to do anything for the organization they served, the President's campaign for reelection was a success. His reelection assured, his place in history was secured.

However, reelection did not end Nixon's involvement with criminal malfeasance. On the contrary, it intensified. His very position of power made him vulnerable to pleas for clemency from those who had been willing to take the rap for a while. Those who had abetted the cover-up but had thus far avoided indictment made claims to positions in his new administration, while acts of bribery, blackmail, perjury and obstruction continued.

In his second inaugural speech Nixon asked the nation to "renew our faith in ourselves and in America." This evangelical plea for faith was a recurrent theme through the ensuing months, for just as Richard Nixon was renewing his oath of office, the Watergate cover-up began to unravel. John Sirica, judge of the federal district court jurisdiction in which the crime occurred, was outraged at the implausible explanations the Watergate defendants gave in their attempts to protect their superiors. He used his authority to impose punitive sentences in an attempt to elicit cooperation with the law. One of the defendants broke and, in a letter asking for leniency, James McCord implicated officials at the CRP. Under the instigation of Edward Kennedy, a Senate investigating committee was established to look into the charges of election fraud. The chairman was Senator Sam Ervin, an aging constitutional lawyer. Ervin expressed outrage at the abuses of authority the committee uncovered and at the implications the facts held for the American way of life. Pressure on the White House mounted, and, in response, through the spring of 1973 various members of the White House staff plotted with the President on how to further obstruct due process of law and subvert the constitutional system that gave them their power and authority.

Ironically, while these backstage machinations were going on, the words of the conspirators were being secretly embossed on magnetic tape, part of an elaborate recording system Nixon had installed to document his historical record. The existence of these tapes was not publically known until the following summer, and so for many months Watergate existed in the public mind as the President's word against that of his accuser, John Dean. The charges made in the spring of 1973 were serious charges; but, until the following year, they were hearsay at best.

When the existence of the tapes became known, a protracted battle among the President, the courts, the Congress, and the Justice Department began over who had the right to the information contained in that magnetic record. The President claimed the right to confidentiality as a matter of executive privilege. He argued that unless he could assure his advisers and other top people of the secrecy of their words, they would not speak candidly. The other branches of government claimed access to the record as a function of the investigations they were authorized to undertake. They argued that unless they could hear what the tapes had recorded, they could not evaluate the charges being made.

Ultimately, the Supreme Court was called in to settle the dispute, and it found against the claims of the President. Where Nixon had defied the lower courts, the Senate investigating committee, and the Special Prosecutor, he could not challenge the decision of the highest court in the land and still claim he was acting in accordance with his lawful authority. He acknowledged the Supreme Court decision and relinquished the tapes in question. Four days later, on August 9, 1974, he resigned from office.

★   ★   ★

Like a Greek tragedy played out in real time, the story of Nixon's downfall extended from the summer of 1972 through the summer of 1974. At times it dominated the nation. The Ervin Committee hearings were televised live on three national networks and then rebroadcast at night on public television. Soap operas and game shows were replaced by the spectacle of countless witnesses testifying alternately to the duplicity of the President and to his innocence. Workers brought portable sets to the office, and comedians on late night talk shows made jokes about executive privilege. At times the drama languished, but each new revelation revived popular interest. The Justice Department's charges of bribery and tax evasion against Vice President Spiro Agnew, his heated denial, and then his abrupt resignation—an historic first—passed unnoticed in the highly charged atmosphere of Watergate.

In a strategy called "Operation Candor," Nixon attempted a new version of the old Checkers speech. Denying charges that he had become rich in office by cheating on his income tax, he made his tax returns for the past four years public. But the record they documented contradicted the claims he made, and instead of reassuring the nation of his honesty and integrity, his new revelations only added to the growing suspicion that the President was a crook.

Through public hearings and leaks to newspapers, a myriad of discrediting facts emerged. The existence of the Houston plan and the Plumbers operation became public knowledge. The links between the Plumbers and ITT were revealed, as was the White House enemies list. Donald Segretti's operation to sabotage the Muskie and McGovern campaigns was detailed, and the link between this operation and John Ehrlichman at the White House was established. The involvement of Nixon's two closest aides, as well as Attorney General Kleindienst, led to the resignation of all three, although not to their repudiation.

Numerous examples of illegal campaign contributions were uncovered, and indictments were brought against Maurice Stans, Secretary of the Treasury in Nixon's initial cabinet and the director of finance at the CRP; and John Mitchell, former Attorney General and, until his abrupt resignation for "family reasons," director of the CRP. All of these things happened, but there was little public indignation except on the part of "known Nixon haters." It was not until Nixon fired the Special Prosecutor in an attempt to maintain control over the tapes that any display of public outrage was evinced.

Interest in Watergate had grown, but it was interest in public drama, the spectacle of scandal. When Nixon chose to deny the authority of the Justice Department by discharging the Special Prosecutor, Archibald Cox, two Attorneys General resigned rather than carry out the President's order, and the significance of the drama suddenly became clear. Watergate was no longer "just politics," but in fact a Constitutional crisis in which the power and authority of the President was being tested against the power and authority of the system of justice. In a brief public statement, Cox said:

> Whether ours shall continue to be a government of laws and not of men is now for the Congress and ultimately the American people to decide. (Sussman, 1974, p. 274)

The public responded with a million telegrams and letters, demanding that Nixon's power be curbed.

The Cox firing came to be known as the "Saturday Night Massacre," and the overwhelming public protest it elicited fired the Congress to introduce resolutions of impeachment. Then Secretary of State Kissinger suddenly announced that American forces in the Middle East had been put on nuclear alert; that these were precarious times and it was vital for the American people to rally round the President. Pointing to Nixon's international record—detente, withdrawal, the prospects of peace in the Middle East—Kissinger suggested that the accomplishments of his Administration must offset any role the President might have played in the Watergate scandal.

The definition of the reality of Watergate began to form. There were those who claimed that if the President was in any way involved with the crimes of Watergate, he must be brought to justice. Then there were those who believed than an incumbent President could not be tried in the criminal courts, and thus he must be impeached. There were those who claimed that there was no proof of the President's criminal malfeasance and that, even if he was an accessory after the fact, his leadership was vital to the nation. There were those who claimed that the entire Watergate scandal was a vicious partisan attack on the part of embittered enemies who had been out to get Nixon through his entire career: the communists, the press, the Eastern Establishment.

As attitudes began to polarize, new revelations were assimilated to to preexisting notions. When Nixon finally turned over some of the tapes, a gap of 18½ minutes was discovered in a conversation with Haldeman that had taken place a few days after the arrest of the Watergate burglars. Those suspicious of Nixon saw the erasure as part of a sinister plot, whereas those who were supportive saw it as a simple human error. This polarization was still apparent after his resignation, for not everyone was convinced of Nixon's duplicity. In a poll taken a few months after his fall from office 20 percent of the nation was still behind him. However, he had begun his second administration with almost 70 percent support; in the course of his downfall he had lost half the nation.

He lost them at various points along the way. The firing of the Special Prosecutor was the first significant loss; Operation Candor was a second. When the grand jury finally brought indictments against Haldeman, Ehrlichman, Mitchell, Colson, Strachan, Mardian, and Parkinson, the swell of popular suspicion grew. In a second dramatic attempt to maintain control over his image by maintaining control over the tapes, Nixon made transcripts of the tapes public. This resulted in another significant loss. In a carefully staged television special the President told the nation he was giving them all the facts of Watergate. But even a cursory reading of the record he made public made it clear that this was not the entire story—that the President was still holding back. Furthermore, a close reading of the transcripts revealed a backstage image of the man that some had always suspected and fewer had ever known. The persona Nixon presented to the nation was a pious, principled, law-abiding, altruistic family man; a man always and only acting in dedicated service to the nation. The face that appeared in the edited transcripts was vulgar, self-serving, petty, and mean: he was a man out to get his enemies. Nowhere in the transcripts did Nixon or his various advisers speak of Constitutional oaths, principles of justice, questions of right and wrong. Instead, they made mock of the office they represented, sought to circumvent the law of the land, and guided their actions by the edicts of public relations rather than any principles of moral philosophy.

The publication of the transcripts provoked new, more widespread outrage, but Nixon declared he would not resign. He said, "Let others wallow in Watergate, I am going to do the job I was elected to." (*New York Times* Staff, 1973) As he had in the past, he reiterated: "I'm no quitter." His spokesman, Ron Ziegler, called the Judiciary Committee a kangaroo court and indicted the press in an attempt to redirect the public furor toward Nixon's partisan detractors.

Then, coincident with the loss of popular support the transcripts provoked, the Supreme Court entered into the conflict to decide whether a President can withhold documents that are vital to the system of criminal justice just because he is President.

By the spring of 1974—two years after the Watergate break-in—the forces questioning Nixon's authority began to mount, and it seemed the final act would be seen at any moment. As a matter of fact, the final act would not be seen. The curtain was simply drawn. For three months the Supreme Court deliberated in private while members of the House of Representatives held their hearings on impeachment in public. Toward the end of July the Court unanimously ruled that the President must turn over the tapes to the Court, and the House Judiciary Committee voted 27-11 to recommend impeachment.

With the publication of transcripts of one of the contested tapes, support for Nixon collapsed in the Judiciary Committee, the House of Representatives, and the Senate. His colleagues in the political system had been his last hope. While the people may have voted him into office, only their elected representatives could remove him. As long as this group was loath to act, Nixon had to deal only with the press and the popular mind, both of which were powerless to affect his tenure. Thus far, he had counted on an unspoken understanding that since both he and his colleagues in Congress were participants in the same political process, they would be unlikely to cast the first stone. The strategy had worked for a while. For example, Edward Gurney, a Republican senator from Florida, sat on the Ervin committee and questioned people who were witness to Nixon's affairs. His questions revealed neither chicanery nor duplicity on the part of the administration; then he was indicted on the same charges he had been empowered to investigate in the Senate subcommittee hearings. Senator Herman Talmadge, a Democrat from Georgia, would also face similar charges. So regardless of what other politicians might have personally thought of Nixon and his conduct, their careers were in large measure dependent on unspoken agreements about how to protect one another's interests. Many of the decisions they routinely made had little to do with the interests of the electorate and a great deal to do with their own power and influence in Congress.

But the evidence revealed in the June 23 tape recorded soon after the Watergate break-in made clear beyond any reasonable doubt that Richard Nixon, 37th President of the United States, had conspired to break the law in an attempt to assure his reelection. Those who had been most outspoken in his defense could no longer deny his culpability and maintain their own integrity. And so, in a final broadcast to the nation, Nixon announced that he was resigning from office because he had lost his base of political support.

The curtain came down on Nixon's public career. He retired to his seaside villa in Southern California, and within a few weeks his successor pardoned him for all crimes he did or might have committed. Vital and healthy through five years in office, he was suddenly beset by illness on the eve of the trial of his closest associates. Ron Ziegler announced Nixon was near death's door, and in the routine transition from the Nixon administration to the Ford administration, public sympathy was evoked. Some saw him as a man who had suffered enough, while others believed he had not been brought to justice. Nevertheless, he did not have to give testimony in court, and so his guilt remained moot.

Thirteen years after his first retreat from public life, after having achieved the prize he longed for, Nixon retired from public life once more. In 1962 he had left the public arena under a cloud; 1974 was the same.

The Nixon administration began in a time of turmoil and chaos. The nation was demoralized by an unpopular war, beset by violent confrontations. To many people in the 1960s the world seemed strange and foreboding. Through Nixon's tenure in office, turmoil and chaos intensified, the economy became more erratic, and then, suddenly, the lawlessness of the streets appeared in the executive suites of government. In 1970 the world seemed even stranger. Where only the young had been suspicious of the claims made by traditional authority in the '60s, doubt and suspicion reached epidemic proportions in the '70s. The established institutions that once claimed faith and respect—law, government, business, medicine—went the way of the established church, while more and more converts flocked to evangelical prophets like Billy Graham. Year by year the polls documented failing confidence in the traditional institutions that comprise the established system and, taken together, produce the American way of life.

Despite the erosion of public faith in the institutional order, little changed as a consequence of the Watergate revelations, just as little had changed as a consequence of the Teapot Dome revelations before or Koreagate afterward. The Ervin committee was instrumental in making the machinations of the Nixon administration public, but no proposals for *fundamental* legislative change came out of the public hearings or the committee's deliberations. The Justice Department's case against Nixon's intimates resulted in the conviction of five men who in one way or another had been consequential in making decisions for the nation during the past five years. Others pled guilty, and eventually over 60 people were indicted in the Watergate scandals of the Nixon administration. Yet such massive indictments did not raise the past policies of the administration to a topic of public debate. When the curtain came down on Richard Nixon's career, it simply rose on Gerry Ford's.

With the orderly transition of government, it magically appeared that the system worked. A bad apple was removed from the barrel. A spate of books and articles came out. For the most part they were insiders' accounts: apologies for a weak man in a tough spot. Those who were critical were critical of the person who had occupied the office and not the system that structured the power and influence the incumbent wielded. In the most abnormal of times the image of normalcy was maintained. The nation had learned of monumental infractions of legal and moral codes, the country had been brought to the brink of a Constitutional crisis, the globe had been put on alert for nuclear attack, but things remained pretty much the same.

The electorate had been mere spectators to Nixon's downfall, although they had been vital to his ascent. When the public theater of Watergate ended, the audience was directed elsewhere. In the late 1960s the enemy that focused the attention of the nation and wielded individual sentiments into a unified pattern was crime in the streets. In Nixon's second term it was corruption in government. Once in office, Ford used the authority he inherited to turn the attention of the nation to the economy. Inflation became "Public Enemy Number 1." Employing classic Nixonian techniques, Ford appeared on television to tell the nation, stunned by what they had seen through the last two years, that all America needed was to "Whip Inflation Now." People could send for lapel pins that said "WIN" and display their dedication to a renewed America.

Ford's initial television appearances were clumsy, but he quickly became adept at reading from the teleprompter while maintaining an expression of sincerity. He soon lost his tenseness and hesitancy in face-to-face meetings with the press, and the lines he memorized in briefing sessions were spoken with candor and authority. He replaced some of Nixon's advisers with men of his own choosing. But Kissinger stayed on, and many who were taken out of one office were reassigned to another. Meanwhile, he maintained ongoing communications with his predecessor by telephone and diplomatic courier.

Ford promised the nation an open and forthright administration, but within a fortnight the same pattern of evasion, innuendo, deception, and duplicity that characterized the administration of the 37th American President began to characterize the administration of the 38th. Nothing had changed, even if it appeared to.

A new man was in office, and a new man implied a new regime, even if the new man had been hand-picked by his predecessor. Befitting the weight of the office he would execute, Ford was granted a honeymoon period. People were willing to get behind him because he was the President and he represented America. Yet he was not popular, having started off his tenure by summarily pardoning his predecessor. Not until he let loose a considerable display of military force in the Mayaguez incident did his popularity in the polls show a significant increase. Despite the fact he lost 41 lives and $7 million in equipment in his maneuver to rescue 39 men and $1 million in equipment, he had shown his military muscle. Here was a man America could rally around.

So the end of Nixon's career was not the end of the historical epoch it was part of. Gerald Ford, a man of similar origins who had been subject to the same cultural forces, would guarantee the continuity of a system that had been set into motion around the time of World War I. Then it was an easy transition from Ford to Carter.

·themes·

Chapter 7
Patrons, Buddies, Advisers, and Henchmen

Both the 37th President and the 38th were members of the same generation, and hence they were influenced by a common course of history at the same points in their lives. Although they were dissimilar in style and detail, a family resemblance remains. Gerald Ford's origins were in the Midwest, whereas Nixon began in Southern California, but both were children of petit bourgeois families. Each experienced the economic expansion of the '20s in their boyhoods and thereafter held a vision of America built on a premise of business prosperity. Despite the widespread privation and hardship suffered by many young men through the Depression, both Nixon and Ford attended college. They won scholarships to take them through law school and so began their adult lives in a more advantageous position than their fathers. Moving from petit bourgeois to professional, each affirmed his boyhood faith in free enterprise and individual initiative. Both enlisted in the Second World War as a visible sign of patriotic commitment to the nation that made possible the advantages they had. After the war they began their careers in politics.

Thousands of other young men from the same generation and the same circumstances had similar careers, but not all became President. Cross-cutting the influences that were general to a generation were those that were specific to some people and not others. Assuming that what makes the difference between those who make it to the top and those who don't is whom they know, it is instructive to see how the significant others in Richard Nixon's life contributed to his success.

Patrons

Nixon's political career could never have begun had it not been for a class of patrons: advocates and supporters who served as benefactors. At first the number of patrons were few, but over time they increased in number, wealth and influence.

His first patron was his mother, a woman with ties to the inner circle of the Whittier community. Through his mother's influence, he was introduced to one of the more influential lawyers of the city. When Tom Bewley took him on as a partner in his law firm, Bewley provided Nixon with the opportunity to meet other influential people on his own, and he was no longer dependent on his mother's influence. In his law office in the Bank of America building, he met Hubert Perry, the bank president and an important Republican in the community. Thus his first benefactor provided him with another benefactor, and thereafter the number snowballed.

Nixon had been active in school and community affairs, but he had never expressed any interest in public office. After the war Hubert Perry introduced Nixon to the Committee of 100, which gave him the opportunity to run for national office. Richard Nixon did not become a politician because of any expressed ambition, such as he evinced in childhood about becoming a lawyer. Rather, in classic Horatio Alger fashion, he became a politician because it was his good fortune to have patrons who were willing to support him and further his interests as a way of furthering their own.

What these patrons got for their investment was a salesman. Early in his career, they were outspoken about their objective. When it looked as though the scandal of the senatorial slush fund would abort Nixon's career forever, the administrator of the fund, Dana Smith, said:

Dick Nixon seemed to be the best salesman against socialism
available. That's his gift, really—salesmanship . . . We urged
Nixon to run (for the Senate) for two reasons. He was a Republican
with a chance to win, and he was a proved (sic) believer in free
enterprise . . . Dick did just what we wanted him to. (Donovan,
1952, p. 30)

In fact, Dick did. He proved to be an effective evangelical salesman
for the free enterprise system. He could speak of the advantage of
individual initiative with conviction, finding examples in his own life
and in his wife's life as well. He could portray government as an ever-
expanding elite, imposing unwarranted restrictions on ordinary folks.
Best of all, he could evoke the image of insidious evil, initially in
terms of the international communist conspiracy and later in terms of
crime in the streets. This was perhaps his greatest talent. He was
a man who had a deep inner conviction that forces of evil were loose
in the world and would destroy all that was good unless they were
countered by powers equally ruthless. The dramatic clash of good and
evil resonated in all he said throughout his entire career. This gothic
imagery provided the leitmotif of the world view he propagated, and
ultimately it transformed party politics from thesis and antithesis to
warfare and sabotage.

Early in his career Nixon's patrons saw his potential. In the battle of
opposing world views—the conflict between capitalism and communism—
Nixon could be counted on to support the system that gave his patrons
their power and influence. That he also sold hate and despair, fear and
war, was irrelevant. He could stave off the encroachment of socialism and
thereby protect the interests of the ruling elite, whose class position
was dependent on a widespread, popular belief in "free enterprise."
They, in turn, would subsidize his campaigns for public office. By
means of the massive accumulation of cash and sophisticated techniques
of persuasion, they made "Nixon" a brand name, and his message
became public policy.

The insidious encroachment of communism was a red herring in
the '40s. The Soviet Union, which represented the embodiment of
communist ideology, had emerged as a powerful military force in the
postwar world. But there was little evidence that the working people
of America were on the verge of being seduced or subverted by either
the theoretical or the practical features of Marxism. Interest in communist
ideology had grown during the '30s, but it had grown almost exclusively
among marginal intellectuals and artists of one kind or another. Through

the prosperity of the war years what influence Marxist writing had in the union movement faded as workers' real wages grew. Dissent from the ideological precepts of capitalistic enterprise was not widespread in the postwar years. Rather, what existed was a more or less united cultural front, forged by the war effort and heady with victory. The 1920s had been a time of expanding opportunities and great business prosperity. Through the Depression, the opportunities for citizens to reap the fruits of individual initiative were few, and it looked as though the American Dream was bankrupt. Postwar expansion provided a way of renewing opportunities and hence renewing individual citizens' convictions in the ideology most appropriate to the growth of business profit. Communism became a political ploy. It took the place of fascism in unifying the nation by convincing the public that their interests were threatened by sinister forces. So diverted, citizens did not notice the effects corporate capitalism had on their lives.

Whether the birth of the Cold War mentality was a conspiracy on the part of the ruling class or a consequence of independent decisions made by similar people in similar circumstances, it took root in American soil and flourished. However it came about, it served its makers well for over a decade.

Through his advocacy of free enterprise and his outspoken condemnation of communism, Nixon came to the attention of Norman Chandler, publisher of the *Los Angeles Times*, and the scope and influence of his patrons expanded. In those days before television the patronage of a powerful newspaper publisher could insure a protege widespread, favorable exposure. Nixon's success in the political arena was insured.

Richard Nixon began his political career with the sponsorship of influential patrons. He could be sold to the public as a candidate but he chose to be sold at a higher level than he began. The Committee of 100, his initial patrons, had no particular interest in furthering Nixon's personal ambition, and, when he told them he wanted to run for the Senate, they withdrew their collective support.

Nixon was not without resources, however. Through his good friend Murray Chotiner new backers were cultivated to further his political interests. Those who contributed to the slush fund were men with considerable interests in oil, real estate, movies, and other corporate endeavors. In Richard Nixon they saw a man who would speak out for their interests if he were given the chance. They contributed to his campaign to run for the Senate, and after he won, they continued to contribute to his interests as a way of furthering their own. Through the ensuing years the number of Nixon's patrons grew; each step up the political ladder swelled the ranks. Eventually millions of dollars were contributed to his cause by the largest corporate organizations and the wealthiest families in the nation. Industrialist and financier W. Clement Stone, an ardent Nixon patron, has said:

> Everything is relative. With a family worth in these days better than $450 million, what's a million or two, particularly when you can change the course of history to the principles for which you stand. (Evans and Myers, 1974, p. 89)

To those whose influence and power lie in the shadow of public office, Nixon became the man most suited to rule America. As Vice President he traveled the country, talking to representatives of corporate wealth and others of influence and power, who were impressed by what they saw and heard and what they knew through the grapevine of the ruling class. In turn they made massive contributions to Nixon's campaign and supported his candidacy in a variety of ways. Ultimately they made it possible for him to become President.

Nixon's relation with corporate executives and others of great wealth was an implicit gentleman's agreement. Instructions were never given, details were not worked out, yet each knew what was expected of him. However, Nixon did not participate in the social life that bound the ruling class together beyond their interests in political affairs. So he did not share, or for that matter understand, the larger world view his patrons subscribed to. He remained an outsider to the ruling elite, a pawn. He served their interests, but, in the long run, their interests and his interest were not the same.

In the game of American politics, Nixon had become a pawn with the power of a king. Despite the fact that the system of patronage was fundamental to his power, Nixon was ultimately in a position to betray those he had once been dependent on. The ruling elite eventually recognized the Frankenstein monster they had created, the golem that was, by 1972, destroying the very system they had labored so hard to produce. They withdrew their support, and his political career fell under a cloud. But while he served their interests, they provided the means whereby Richard Nixon, a provincial lawyer, could be President of the United States.

Buddies

Patrons were important to Nixon's political destiny, but they were not sufficient. There were a number of times along the way when he seriously considered quitting, and in addition to resources, he needed encouragement, which was provided by a class of buddies. Buddies offered emotional support, reassurance, and understanding through the long days of embattled conflict. They provided an intimate circle to share the joy of victory and the misery of defeat. Where patrons provided money and influence, buddies provided companionship and solace. They helped take his mind off the problems that besieged him, let him relax and prepare for battle anew.

In some instances Nixon's buddies were drawn from his patrons. Elmer Bobst, who had helped get Nixon his Wall Street job after the '62 defeat, became an intimate of the Nixon family and was known as "Uncle Elmer" to the girls. But in most cases buddies were drawn from his advisers.

Though his patrons grew in numbers, there were never many buddies. Through high school, college, and law school Nixon was typically a "loner." He was active and outgoing in a variety of campus activities, and hence he could be considered a "joiner." However, he did not join for the camaraderie that comes from mutual participation in a collective endeavor but for the sense of personal triumph that comes with victory. So despite the numerous campus organizations he belonged to and the various executive offices he held, he never came close to anyone else at school. H.R. Haldeman put together Nixon's White House staff from men who had joined in common enterprise with Haldeman in school; but no schoolmate of Nixon's joined the administration. He maintained the respect of many he went to school with, and if some were disillusioned along the way, old school chums continued to be his supporters in the community of Whittier. But they were never his comrades. In fact, Murray Chotiner, who began as his first political adviser, became his first buddy.

Chotiner was a few years older than Nixon, but he grew up in the same milieu. His father emigrated from Russia to Pittsburgh and from there to Southern California, where he went into the theatrical business. The movie industry was just beginning, and eventually the Chotiner family owned a string of movie theaters in the Los Angeles area. They were prosperous if not affluent. Both Murray and his brother went to college, became lawyers, and branched out on their own from the entertainment business to law and ultimately politics.

Murray was a precocious youth. He was eager to get a law degree and begin practice with his older brother, who was already experienced in the District Attorney's office. The two brothers, Murray and Arthur, became partners and remained so until Arthur retired in the 1950s. They maintained a general practice and did considerable criminal work, mainly with bookmakers. Gradually they branched out into divorce, and then, in the 1940s, they began to get involved with federal, state, and agency litigation. It was around this time that Murray Chotiner met Richard Nixon.

If law was Chotiner's profession, politics was his passion. As other men might evince a pleasure for gambling, women, money, or art, Chotiner was interested in power. He started at the grassroots level, identifying with the liberal faction of the Republican party. In his early days he was considered a "young Turk." He was drawn to politics by the excitement, the challenge, the battle—the larger-than-life dimensions of the political struggle. He was not seeking fame or recognition in his own right; he would rather be king-maker than king. Thus he was content to keep to the shadows of the political arena, where he mapped strategy, plotted campaigns, and achieved a sense of creating something in the person of a candidate. Eventually, he made a name for himself in Southern California politics, and Richard Nixon's patrons introduced the two.

Chotiner and Nixon first came together in a client-adviser relationship, but they were soon drawn much closer. Chotiner was impressed with the man the Committee of 100 selected. He counseled Nixon at each step of his campaign against Voorhis, and after the battle they shared the heady experience of victory. When Nixon went to Congress, Chotiner continued to advise him. He was supportive in the battle against Hiss where others were critical. He encouraged Nixon to run for the Senate, organized his backers, and managed the Douglas campaign. Again and again they shared the joy of victory.

They made a great pair. Nixon was young and ambitious to be a great man. Chotiner was young and ambitious to make a great man. Their desires were congruent, their objectives compatible. They became close friends. Chotiner continued with his law practice in Southern California, but throughout Nixon's career in Congress and the Senate, and into the Vice Presidency, they remained in constant contact. The Chotiner home was one of the few Nixon visited in Southern California, and Murray was a visitor in Washington, D.C. Telephone calls and letters kept them in contact between visits.

By the time of the Douglas campaign Nixon was 37 and Chotiner 41. Both had considerable experience of varying sorts. Through his father's profession Chotiner learned how illusion is created and how readily it could be marketed in America. In his college studies of political science he learned how power is organized, and he developed a keen, if cynical, appreciation of the democratic process. In his practice as a lawyer he learned the intricacies of criminal and civil law. As a party politico he learned about the prevailing practices of democratic theory. Most of what Chotiner learned he learned from experience, from practical involvement in an ongoing enterprise. He was not a theoretician. The only formal course he took after law school was one in advertising techniques. Nor was he a great reader. For the most part he confined his reading to seven or eight newspapers a day, scanning the political news and learning how reality is constructed in America.

Though he had a family, Chotiner was not a family man. Weekdays and weekends alike he was involved in either law or politics, and when there was a campaign going on he was away from home for long periods of time. He was a bright, energetic man, devoted to the pursuit of power and insightful about how it could be achieved. He had no other commitments in life.

Nixon came to the relationship with somewhat different experiences. Because Nixon was from Anglo-American stock, he was a more likely candidate for public office. There was no conflict over who would be king and who would be king-maker. When the two met, Nixon was just beginning his career and Chotiner already had a noteworthy reputation so in the beginning, at least, there was no conflict over who would give advice and who would take it. Nixon had experience with the carnival, acting, and playing poker. He could see the relevance of the scenarios Chotiner wove and the strategy and tactics he elucidated. They could communicate with one another; and from their communication a style of offensive politics emerged in which the only objective was overcoming the opposition and seizing the power of public office. Through the rest of his career Nixon's politics showed the stamp of his association with Murray Chotiner.

In the mid-'50s Senate subcommittee charges of influence peddling made Chotiner a public liability, and the two went their separate ways for a while. Chotiner felt betrayed by Nixon's public repudiation, since no formal charges ever came out of the committee, but he maintained respect for his friend nonetheless. In times of crisis, Nixon still called him privately, even though he shunned him publicly. Eventually their lives came together again, although they were never as close as they had once been.

In the midst of the Watergate revelations Chotiner died in an auto accident, and Nixon took time out from his own life to attend the funeral, paying respect to the man who originally befriended him. Yet in his *Memoirs* Chotiner's influence in his life is barely mentioned. For a man who continues to lament his brothers' death after 50 years, the untimely death of his oldest buddy is strangely ignored.

In the early years of Nixon's career Murray Chotiner was his only buddy. Eventually, William Rogers became a friend. Like Nixon, Rogers started life from modest beginnings. The son of a New York insurance salesman, he turned to law as a profession. After a few years of private practice he joined the Dewey administration, and then went on to Washington, where he and Nixon met through their joint participation in various congressional committees.

Rogers respected Nixon's legal acumen, his techniques of examination. He saw him as a shy, sensitive intellectual; in the course of their mutual careers he befriended him in various ways.

Nixon's forte was running for office, while Rogers' was administering policy on behalf of the victorious. Under Eisenhower Rogers became Attorney General, and under Nixon, Secretary of State. So as in the relationship with Chotiner, there was no conflict between the objectives each man harbored. Though Rogers had interests in advancing his own career, he was not attracted to the excitement of the campaign trail, and hence he was not a potential competitor. Rather, he was a family man who liked to spend weekends playing basketball with his kids and summers going on trips and excursions.

When Murray Chotiner became a public liability, Nixon turned to Rogers for solace and advice. Where Chotiner had encouraged Nixon's ruthlessness, Rogers encouraged compassion. Particularly in the difficult days of Eisenhower's illness, when it appeared Nixon might be catapulted into executive power, Rogers helped him control his intuitive response to wage a fight and win. With Rogers' advice, Nixon began to cultivate the image of a statesman, and this new image became part of his standard political routine. Nixon was never as close to Rogers as he was to Chotiner, but the span and direction of Rogers' influence was significant in his career.

Around the same time that he grew distant from Chotiner and

dependent on Rogers, Nixon made a third friend. On a brief vacation to Florida a colleague from the Senate introduced Nixon to Bebe Rebozo, and Rebozo became a significant other in Nixon's life. Where Chotiner tutored him in politics and Rogers tutored him in diplomacy, Rebozo taught him high finance.

Bebe Rebozo, son of an immigrant Cuban cigar maker, became a millionaire on his own initiative. When his schoolmates were leaving high school for college and law school, Rebozo took a job as a steward for Pan American Airlines. He was obsequious, industrious, and methodical. Soon he opened a filling station and a tire-recapping business. Under conditions of rationing and wartime shortages, his business flourished. After the war he invested in land, and then in coin-operated laundromats. Eventually he went into the small-loan business. By the time Nixon was elected President, Rebozo had founded a small suburban bank and was one of the largest land speculators in Florida. Quiet, genial and generous, he mixed well with Miami society.

Rebozo cultivated connections with politicians as he cultivated connections with businessmen. He had been a school chum of George Smathers, and when Smathers ran for Congress in 1946, Rebozo was among a group of schoolmates who called themselves "The Goon Squad" and helped Smathers get elected. Smathers and Nixon met as freshmen congressmen, and in 1950 each ran for the Senate on the anticommunist theme. They had a good deal in common. When Smathers introduced Nixon to Rebozo, there was instant rapport.

Rebozo and Nixon were alike in many ways. They were the same age, though Rebozo was a bachelor. Both were methodical, ambitious, hard workers. Each had experienced being an "outsider" to the school crowd in his own way. They were secretive, brooding men and they found comfort in one another's company. Rebozo worshipped Nixon and hated his enemies, and thus he supported Nixon's world view. He was discreet as well as devoted, so Nixon could talk freely with him. He had no political ambitions of his own, so he could be trusted with the secrets of Nixon's ambition. When the pressures of Washington became too great, Nixon would go to Florida to relax, and he sought Rebozo's company for that purpose. They went fishing, walked along the beach, or watched television. Often they were content to sit in silence. In those moments Nixon could withdraw into himself and daydream about glory or revenge.

Nixon customarily visited Rebozo by himself, but Rebozo frequently came to Washington, and gradually he became a regular part of the

First Family. He accompanied the Nixons, their daughters, and their sons-in-law to Camp David, where he had the regular privilege of choosing the movie the family saw. When the Nixons gathered for special occasions, he was usually the only unrelated person present. Were an anthropologist looking at the First Family as though it were an alien tribe, Rebozo might be described as a co-wife.

Rebozo provided more than just solace and companionship. When the two first met, Nixon was a man of modest means. In the Checkers Speech he proclaimed that a cloth coat was all his wife had and all she needed. Once he became President, he became a man of substantial wealth, much of which was gained by speculating in Florida land and hedging on income taxes.

When the Watergate revelations began to destroy the empire Nixon had built, neither Chotiner nor Rogers were implicated. However, Rebozo was accused of holding an illegal $100,000 campaign contribution from Howard Hughes in his Florida bank. There were also accounts of Rebozo's role in "laundering" money from Bahamian gambling casinos so they could be channeled into the Nixon campaign. But as long as Nixon was not formally discredited in the public eye, Rebozo's reputation was safe. He continued to be a loyal friend long after Watergate, as well as an influential man in his own community.

From time to time other men, such as Robert Finch and John Mitchell, entered Nixon's life at significant junctures, and something of a friendship developed. Nevertheless, Chotiner, Rogers, and Rebozo were buddies. They were *old* friends whose intimate association and personal respect were consequential through much of Nixon's political career.

Advisers

Advisers were more numerous than buddies. They were people whose opinions were influential in Nixon's career, but who did not provide emotional support, except in times of crisis. However, since crises were frequent, there is considerable overlap between the two categories. Nevertheless, there is no question that Nixon's key adviser was H.R. Haldeman.

Harry Roberts Haldeman was from the same Southern California milieu that nourished Nixon and Chotiner. Born in 1926, the son of a prosperous merchant, he grew up in the affluent suburb of Beverly Hills. He spent the war years at UCLA, where he majored in business administration and became involved in campus politics through the interfraternity council. After graduation he joined the J. Walter Thompson advertising agency as an account executive. By 1968 he had become office manager and vice-president.

Haldeman did not show any particular promise as a youth. In fact, he had considerable trouble adjusting to the demands of school and the new brand of permissiveness that was becoming a part of public education. So his parents enrolled him in private school where he learned discipline, organization, and respect for authority. By the time he became Nixon's campaign manager, he had developed an impressive array of managerial and administrative skills. He also had a very clear image of the world.

Haldeman saw the good life in America as a society in which everyone knew what to do and went about doing it without question or hesitation. Plans deployed people to their proper place, and those who had power made plans. It was an efficient, pragmatic view of life, consistent with the precepts of Christian Science he learned as a boy. The way to make something happen is to draw up a plan, deploy resources, and let fire. The outcome of action is irrelevant to having a plan for action: if the first plan does not succeed, a second plan is substituted. Ultimately, all that is important in life is to get things done. The things themselves have no intrinsic value; they are only tokens in a game of manipulative strategy.

Haldeman was not a man of vision, although he marketed illusion. He saw himself as an executive secretary, a gatekeeper to power and not genius itself. But he was not without moral sentiments. He despised loose living, inefficiency, and sloth. Most of all he hated permissiveness. Permissiveness was the enemy of a well-ordered society. It was evidence of the breakdown in authority. It resulted in a world where people were given things for nothing or not punished enough.

Though he presented a cool demeanor, he was a man who could muster emotion in support of his sentiments. Thus he was a man who could hate the enemy with as much force and conviction as could Nixon himself. Yet he did not see himself an extremist. Rather, he believed he represented the middle of mainstream American life. If given free choice, every right-thinking person would want the same thing.

Haldeman was attracted to Nixon in the 1940s, when he was in college and Nixon was in pursuit of Alger Hiss. He saw Nixon as a public hero, as well he might, for he came from a long tradition of red-baiting. His grandfather founded an anticommunist organization in Southern

California at the height of the 1919 red scare, and his father was one of the initial contributors to the slush fund that propelled Nixon into the Senate and caused him such misery later. Though Haldeman never took part in party politics at the grassroots level, he did take leave of his job at Thompson to work as an advance man in Nixon's 1956 campaign.

The job of the advance man is not an ordinary one. His objective is to go into a strange community and create support for the candidate. He must get permits and permissions, resources and help, with the immediate goal of creating a crowd when the candidate finally arrives. The creation of a crowd is the singular achievement of the advance man. When crowds gather, emotional contagion is discharged. And when emotional contagion is discharged in the presence of the candidate, the candidate is seen to be a mover of men. The fact that the coincidence of the candidate and the emotion is the work of the advance man's logistics is forgotten in the heat of the moment; what is remembered is how vitally the public responded to the candidate.

For young men on the make being an advance man is an adventure. The heightened atmosphere of the contest, the trials and tribulations of misfortune, the camaraderie of fellow warriors, and, perhaps, the taste of victory—all contribute to its aura. Young men who can afford to take leave of their ordinary jobs at campaign time find it an exciting and profitable alternative to the ordinary workaday world.

Haldeman showed promise as an advance man. His managerial skills made him an effective organizer, and his advertising know-how contributed to the stage he set for the candidate. He did so well that he became chief advance man in 1960, and then campaign manager in 1962. By 1968 the campaign was such an enormous operation that there were any number of managers of one sort or another. But by then Haldeman was Nixon's right-hand man, a person Nixon could trust, a person with whom Nixon could let his guard down.

After the disaster of the 1960 election it was Haldeman who volunteered to stay on and help Nixon do research for *Six Crises.* He was a good listener and an enthusiastic supporter. He helped renew Nixon's power of positive thinking in the dark days after his first defeat. They became close. Along with his ability to organize and order, his ability to reassure Nixon made him a valuable asset.

Haldeman was responsible for most of the staffing of the '68 campaign and afterward the staffing of the White House. He brought in John Ehrlichman, a schoolmate from UCLA; from the advertising agency he brought Lawrence Higby, Dwight Chapin, Ron Ziegler, Kenneth Cole and Bruce Kehrli, who, among themselves, had ties at the University of Southern California. He was responsible for Jeb Magruder's being at the CRP and Charles Colson's being in the Oval Office. Chapin brought his school chums Gordon Strachan and Donald Segretti into the sphere of influence of the presidency; Ehrlichman brought Egil Krogh from his Seattle law office. Krogh was responsible for Segretti's undercover operation and the interlinking chain was complete. The only significant players in the Watergate drama who were not cast by Haldeman were John Mitchell, who came to be an adviser through his association with Nixon in New York, and John Dean and Richard Kleindienst, who came to the White House through the influence of Mitchell (see Figure 2). Through Nixon's years in power distrust and suspicion between Haldeman and Mitchell, combined with the patronage system that staffed the White House, created two hostile camps around the periphery of the Oval Office, and these were the lines of disintegration through the Watergate revelations.

If Rebozo could be described as a co-wife for Nixon's leisure hours, Haldeman was both mother and husband at the office. After the disastrous campaign of 1962 Haldeman realized that if Nixon were to be successful in his run for public office, the public could not see too much of his person. It was not just the persistent remnants of the harsh, aggressive features that characterized Nixon as a young man. As his aggressiveness had been tempered, his irritability grew. Always a person sensitive to criticism, in his mature years he became a person less sure of himself than he had been in youth. The price he paid for public life was that his critics expanded in proportion to his power. If he were to be successful —if he were to achieve the highest office in the land and hold it for as long as possible—he had to be insulated from criticism. So Haldeman began to lay down the rules that governed Nixon's subsequent races and, ultimately, his administration. The most important rule was that the candidate was never to be disturbed emotionally by news of events he could do nothing about. By 1968 journalists began to describe Nixon as a recluse. He had never mingled freely with the press, but now he did not mingle at all. This purposeful isolation from things he could neither accept nor control was carried into the White House as well. Haldeman would husband the President's time as he mothered his psyche. So protected, Nixon was at his best.

Haldeman described his job as protecting the President from trivia so more important thoughts could pass through the Chief Executive's mind. He saw himself as the hatchet man, the one who did the dirty

Figure 2. **Recruitment Routes to the White House**

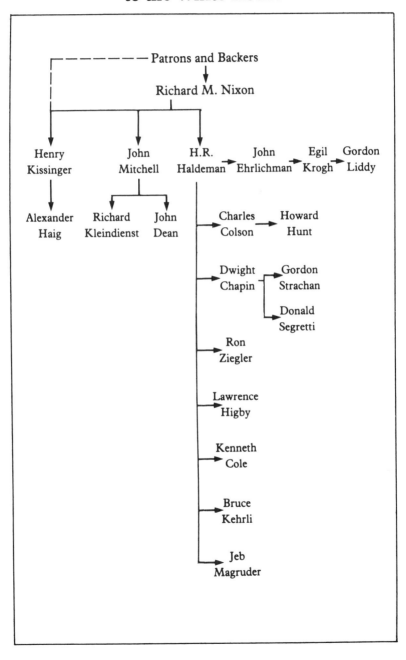

work of punishment and censure—a hard task for Nixon, despite his strong feelings about being tough, the need for punishment, and strict authority. With his keen sense of media and illusion, Haldeman governed the image of the President that was disseminated to the nation, for, as the gatekeeper of the Oval Office, he controlled the flow of information that came to the President and he controlled the output from the President to the nation. His power was second only to one.

To that one he was a highly devoted servant, although after the fall he became the Judas figure for those Nixon loyalists who searched for the locus of evil in the White House. They saw him as a man who became carried away with his own power, a ruthless, arrogant man who ultimately betrayed the one he claimed to serve by installing the electronic taping equipment that was the downfall of the administration.

Despite the aspersions cast by many Nixon supporters, Haldeman remained loyal to his leader. In his book about Watergate, *Ends of Power*, Haldeman writes that he felt betrayed by the attitude Nixon displayed in his televised interviews with talk-show host David Frost. Considering what Haldeman knew about his boss, he did not betray him in return. Rather, he showed considerable restraint in the leaks of backstage information he described.

Haldeman brought peace and quiet to the Oval Office by managing a tightly organized, efficient staff, which he described as a "zero defect system." He also brought influence in the person of John Ehrlichman, a Seattle zoning lawyer who grew up in Southern California and went to UCLA. Only a year older than Haldeman, Ehrlichman went into the service before going to college. The two ultimately became close friends through their interest in campus politics. Like Haldeman, Ehrlichman was a Christian Scientist. Unlike Haldeman, he was not a devoted Nixon fan, and ultimately he was more outspoken than Haldeman in accusing Nixon of betraying the faith and respect that had grown since they first met.

When Haldeman became chief advance man, he invited Ehrlichman to become an advance man too. Ehrlichman did, as a lark. His first assignment involved infiltrating the Rockefeller campaign for purposes of espionage. After Nixon's 1968 nomination, he was assigned as a spy at the Democratic convention, instructed to bring back such intelligence as he thought useful for the Nixon campaign. Despite his graduation from an accredited law school, he had no reservations about his assignment to infiltrate the other side. His understanding was that if something was not explicitly against the law, it was permissible. Furthermore, in the Southern California fraternity system he had learned the politics called "ratfucking": no holds were barred unless something was explicitly illegal, and if a secure cover could be devised, even those limits were open. These were the attitudes Ehrlichman carried from the Nixon campaign into the national arena. Time and time again, in his testimony before the Ervin Committee, he reiterated these principles. The following exchange is typical:

> Q: Well, now as a matter of fact, Mr. Ehrlichman, did you not personally approve in advance a covert entry into the Ellsberg psychiatrist office for the purpose of gaining access to the psychoanalyst's reports?
>
> A: I approved a covert investigation. Now, if a covert entry means a breaking and entering the answer to your question is no. (*New York Times* Staff, 1973, p. 512)

If Ehrlichman's attitude toward the unwritten law was loose, his attitude toward unwritten social codes was strict. He neither drank nor smoked, and he frowned on those who did. He lived a conventional life and believed in similar displays of piety on the part of others. Gambling and women were taboo, drugs unmentionable. He was intolerant of careless mistakes. Only in the profanity of his backstage speech did he flaunt convention, so he could show he was "one of the boys."

These traits he shared with Haldeman, as the two shared religion and boyhood experience. They were close friends. They were tight at work, and along with their respective wives and children they socialized outside work, taking particular pleasure in such homely activities as backyard barbecues. Neither attended the symphony or the opera, museum openings or receptions for distinguished persons or visiting dignitaries, although they had access to such occasions. They did not become part of Washington society, but instead re-created the parochial way of life they had been familiar with in Southern California.

Together, Haldeman and Ehrlichman formed what was called the "Berlin Wall" or sometimes just "the Germans." Reinforcing one another, they maintained a stance of absolute self-righteousness. Despite the indictments and convictions lodged against the pair, neither admitted to wrongdoing or remorse. They continued to subscribe to the belief that the admission of error is a fatal sign of weakness.

Many in the White House came to despise them. They were harsh and punitive in their dealing with subordinates. They demanded unquestioned obedience. As their power grew, dislike for them intensified. Secret Service men joked with one another, saying such things as: "Come the revolution, be sure to save two bullets, one for Haldeman and one for Ehrlichman." (Rather and Gates, 1974, p. 227)

With the introduction of Ehrlichman to the role of Chief of Domestic Affairs, the inner clique of the Oval Office was complete. Haldeman reinforced Nixon, and Ehrlichman supported them both. At any time independent verification was available to check what any two people knew. But the source of that verification was the same pool as the original information. Other points of view were neither solicited nor encouraged. So rather than expanding one another's horizons, the three Southern California heads acted as one. Ehrlichman brought a touch of humor to the proceedings in remarks like: "As the old philosopher once said, facts are nice but slogans sell beer." (Safire, 1975, p. 474) But otherwise there was just grim determination to get the job done, whatever the job might be, and a sense of self-righteousness about the endeavor.

In addition to Haldeman and Ehrlichman, three other men had more or less open access to the Oval Office: Henry Kissinger, John Mitchell, and Charles Colson. Kissinger was never publicly implicated in Watergate, but Mitchell and Colson played central parts.

In the early years of the Nixon administration John Mitchell was known as the second most powerful man in Washington and the President's most trusted adviser. Yet he resigned his position as Chairman of the Committee to Re-elect the President just as the reelection campaign got under way, giving family reasons in justification of his action. No one raised serious questions about why the second most powerful man in the nation and the President's most trusted adviser suddenly abandoned his career to become a loyal and devoted servant to his apparently disturbed wife.

Nixon met Mitchell in 1963, when he went to New York to start a new life. Mitchell was a Wall Street lawyer specializing in municipal bonds. He was a consummate manipulator with a droll, tough exterior. He impressed Nixon with his ability to draft legislation that permitted local and state governments to evade what otherwise might have been their constitutional duty. The two were about the same age; and while their style and experience were widely divergent, they became close during Nixon's years in exile. Mitchell gave Nixon entree into the

Eastern Establishment and became his partner in the practice of law. He tutored him in the ruthless ways of New York City, and Nixon came to trust Mitchell's judgment. In turn, Mitchell was among Nixon's most ardent supporters in his second attempt at the presidency.

Though he had never been involved in party politics, Mitchell was experienced in political battle. Bond issues are routinely hammered out in the back rooms of state and local agencies, while deals and accommodations serve to advance personal interests in these encounters as much as they serve to advance the governmental process. Mitchell was at home in this atmosphere; eventually he would be at home in the arena of national politics.

After Nixon was elected President, Mitchell became Nixon's Attorney General and his chief adviser on all kinds of issues. He stopped by the Oval Office frequently, and through the course of the day there were numerous telephone calls between the White House and the Department of Justice. At his apartment in the Watergate complex, Mitchell had a direct telephone line to the President.

In his role as Attorney General, Mitchell became known as "Mr. Law and Order." Though his prosecution of white collar crime was soft, his prosecution of antiwar demonstrators, students, and blacks was tough. He became the hatchet man for the particular variety of law and order the administration fostered. He suppressed the original grand jury investigation of the Kent State killings, and he suppressed the Justice Department's investigation of the ITT case. He promoted widespread secret wiretapping as an unqualified right of the government. While still in the office of Attorney General, he listened to G. Gordon Liddy's proposal of a million-dollar espionage plan against the Democratic Party. A few months later, officially installed as chairman of the CRP, he authorized funds for a cheaper version of the same endeavor.

Part of Mitchell's job was to define what law and order meant in America during the Nixon years. Equally important was his tough, arrogant image. Taciturn, sarcastic, and unflappable, Mitchell took the brunt of the criticism made by those in opposition to the administration's programs, and hence he insulated the more sensitive President. He could be insulting or charming as the occasion demanded, but whatever his pose, he was a domineering figure. He was always in control, where Nixon's irritability easily broke through the veneer of his toughness. After the news of the break-in of the DNC, Mitchell publicly deplored the incident and categorically denied any involvement of the CRP. Faced with his forceful demeanor and arrogant style, reporters took his statement at face value. When he resigned a few weeks later, "to spend time with his family," his claims were given the same respect. He had stonewalled the nation.

In the early years of the administration, Mitchell's wife was a celebrity in her own right. In an administration that exuded an aura of puritan piety, Martha's outspoken opinions made newspaper copy. As long as she lashed out at the administration's enemies, she was encouraged in her antics. When, in defense of her husband's reputation, she turned her vitriolic tongue on the administration itself, she was summarily silenced. In late-night phone calls to the press, Martha claimed that the Nixon forces were trying to make her husband the scapegoat for what had happened at the DNC, and in the ensuing years it appeared that her claims were well grounded. But at the time they were made—in the summer before Nixon's reelection—great effort was made to make her sound like a raving madwoman and thus support the idea that Mitchell's resignation was motivated by the trials and tribulations of an unstable wife. In his *Memoirs* Nixon identified Martha Mitchell as the fatal flaw whose antics distracted her husband from minding the store.

Although the Nixon forces did in fact conspire to have John Mitchell take the blame for the Watergate burglary, and thereby take the heat off the President, Mitchell refused to play the role of the scapegoat. Yet he remained a Nixon loyalist, and nowhere in the course of the committee hearings or his own criminal trials did he implicate the President as a responsible participant in the crimes he and other Nixon cronies conspired to commit. Instead, he reiterated that he had not told the President about the connections between the CRP and the burglary of the DNC in order to protect his friend from those gothic demons, the "White House horrors" and so reassure the victory of the man Mitchell felt was most suited to rule America.

What Mitchell referred to in testimony as the "White House horrors" were illegal operations such as the break-in of Ellsberg's psychiatrist's office—things which, if they were known, would discredit Nixon's claim to office and honor.

Charles Colson started with the 1968 campaign as an issues man. Though he was originally brought into the White House by Haldeman, their relationship soon fluctuated between cordial and cool. Haldeman respected Colson's political acumen, but he resented his quick ascent into the inner circle.

Colson was a Boston lawyer who hated the Kennedys as much as Nixon did. In many ways his mind worked similar to Chotiner's, and so his proposals for political strategy rang true with Nixon from the start. He quickly became a trusted adviser, usurping some of the power it took Haldeman years to cultivate.

The grand strategic design Colson proposed was the idea of a "new majority" built on the assumption of "ethnic politics." Colson believed that statements on key issues would capture the loyalty of certain ethnic votes. Nixon's stance on abortion could be directed to Catholics, while his statements on Israel would capture the Jewish vote. His position on busing would draw Southerners and blue-collar bigots who might have otherwise been attracted to George Wallace, while themes of free enterprise and individual initiative continued to appeal to business leaders and professionals. New technology made such a fragmented approach to policy feasible. In the old days campaign literature was sent out broadside, the same message going to everyone. Now sophisticated social science techniques made it possible to identify the ethnic composition of an area and send each household literature specifically directed to its special interests. Telephone banks and computer mailings allowed the Nixon forces to circumvent the traditional party structure at the grassroots level and tailor a platform that would harvest the most votes.

Around the White House Colson was known as a "tough operator," and he took pride in this reputation. In his office next to the President's hung a sign saying, "When you've got them by the balls, their hearts and minds will follow." (Rather and Gates, p. 256) Like Chotiner, Nixon, Haldeman, and Ehrlichman, Colson believed that all was fair in love and war, and that politics was war. He would use leaks, plants, lies, and forgeries as routine moves in that game. It was Colson who first proposed the enemies list as a way of getting even with administration's critics. The list was forwarded to John Dean for updating, and Dean wrote:

> This memorandum addresses the matter of how we can maximize the fact of our incumbency in dealing with persons known to be active in their opposition to our administration. Stated a bit more bluntly—how we can use the federal machinery to screw our political enemies. (White, 1975, p. 152)

Dean circulated the original Colson list, and other members of the White House staff checked off prime enemies as well as contributing candidates of their own. The total list came to over 300 names, although the original list Colson started had just 20 names.

It was Colson who first brought Howard Hunt into the White House sphere of influence and it was Colson who began to put pressure on Magruder to use Hunt and Liddy once they had been assigned to the CRP. It was Colson who served as a conduit between Hunt's pleas for clemency and the President. In light of all Colson did in the service of Richard Nixon's career, he felt deeply betrayed when he learned that his conversations with the President were secretely taped and when he learned how the President talked with Haldeman and Ehrlchman behind his back. In the transcripts of the tapes, the President calls Colson an "operator in expedience" and suggests he was a name-dropper and a liability to the team.

Although the indictments against him were numerous, Colson ultimately pled guilty to a single charge and served only six months in prison. Depending on who is judging, the high point or the nadir of his career came when he converted to a fundamentalist Christian sect, cleansed his soul, declared himself a new man, and began converting prisoners to his particular version of Christian ideology.

The men who served Richard Nixon as buddies and advisers had a number of traits in common with each other and with their leader. Many, although not all, grew up in Southern California, and they brought with them a heightened sense of illusion, although a limited sense of vision. Most cultivated a tough demeanor: a ruthless, unyielding manner in which error was the only sin and apology unthinkable. Despite their shrewd, scheming, ambitious natures, they presented themselves as pious, self-righteous men of great virtue and no failing. They were consummate hypocrites. Furthermore, they shared the same experience of getting to the top, and all of them could hate the enemy with an unmitigated passion.

Henchmen

Stretching out through the organizational network of the White House were a host of subordinates whose job was to execute orders without question and to give advice only if asked. The kind of advice they were asked for was how the plans drawn up by the President and his advisers could be put into operation to achieve administrative objectives. They became the henchmen of the administration.

Where buddies were in intimate association with the President and advisers in routine association, subordinates' contacts were episodic and rare. Still, they had considerable power. They were vested with the authority to execute commands in the name of the White House. When they spoke, something happened: personnel and resources were deployed, acts were undertaken.

Subordinates were held responsible for the success or failure of their missions by their superiors, and without a powerful adviser as an ally, those who failed in their missions were fired. Those who had an inhouse patron were encouraged to learn from their mistakes and admonished not to repeat them. Like a small, feudal system, the Nixon administration was run on the basis of patronage and alliances, and young men who sought to advance their careers through government were introduced to this archaic world view.

Ron Ziegler and John Dean were among the host of subordinates whose job was to execute the plans of their superiors. Each in his own way became a key participant in Watergate.

Like Chapin and Segretti, Ziegler was from the University of Southern California. In his youth he developed his facile tongue as a tour guide at Disneyland. After college he came to the attention of H.R. Haldeman, who gave him a job at J. Walter Thompson, in charge of the Disney account. After Nixon's victory at the polls, Haldeman put Ziegler in charge of White House communication. At that time Ziegler was a 29-year-old advertising agent. In terms of influence and authority, he became one of the most powerful men in the administration.

His job at the White House was to run interference between the White House and the press. He was the one to disseminate edicts to the nation in Nixon's name, and he was the one the press questioned in their attempt to get the full picture of what the administration was up to. Ultimately, the structure of national news reporting made Ziegler a key figure in the success or failure of Nixon's enterprises. Figure 3 suggests Ziegler's power.

Every day the news of the nation was disseminated to more than 200 million citizens. But the major part of what the people knew about the state of the Union was known through the words of Ron Ziegler. And he spoke a very strange tongue. His language was the language of obfuscation, in which new terms were routinely coined to explain new situations. When caught in an obvious contradiction, Ziegler would claim to have "misspoken" himself, or he would say to reporters:

> The other statements that were made were based on information
> that was provided prior to these events which have been referred
> to in the President's statement today . . . The way to assess
> the previous comments is to assess them on the basis that they

were made on the information available at the time. The President
refers to the fact that there is new material. Therefore, this is the
operative statement. The others are inoperative. (Walters, 1974,
p. 35)

No matter what he said, however, he had authority behind his words,
and so his words were taken as though they had face value.

Just a subordinate, Ziegler was a most powerful man. When Haldeman and Ehrlichman resigned in April 1973, Ziegler moved in to fill
parts of the role each of them played. Kissinger's top aide, General
Alexander Haig, was given the job of administering the extensive
White House staff. He coordinated the troops. But Ziegler was the idea
man until August 1974.

Figure 3: **Ron Ziegler's Role in America**

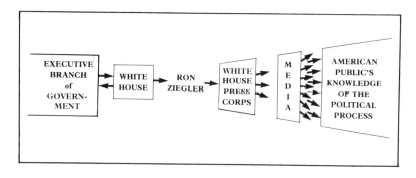

John Dean's power was never as great as Ron Ziegler's. But from
1972 on he was a pivotal figure in the administration.

His roots were in the Midwest, his academic career undistinguished.
Trained as a lawyer, he married a senator's daughter, and in his father-in-
law he found a powerful patron. He was dismissed from his first job
after just six months, accused of unethical conduct. But he was well-
groomed, well-spoken, and well-backed, and so his dismissal did not
abort his fledgling career. He quickly found a position on the staff of
the Republican representative from Ohio, and thereafter found his way
into the interstices of the federal government, where he came to the
attention of John Mitchell. When Ehrlichman moved from Counsel to
the President to Chief of Domestic Affairs, Dean was selected to fill
the vacuum.

As Counsel to the President, his duties were many and varied. He did not manage Nixon's personal affairs. This was the province of Herb Kalmbach, a Southern Californian whose relationship with Nixon went back many years. But anything with legal ramifications that might be relevant to the presidency was the province of John Dean. When the reelection committee was established, he served as a conduit between the White House and the CRP. He was in on the discussion of the original Liddy proposal. During the Watergate revelations Dean claimed he had not considered the discussion of the Liddy plan proper for agents of government. But in the Nixon organization he had no authority to question plans, only the power to execute them. So after the Watergate burglars were discovered, Dean was instrumental in executing the plans for the original cover-up.

Dean was successful in containing the indictments made by the grand jury. At the time of the election Watergate was just the arrest and indictment of seven men, seemingly operating on their own in a bizarre, second-rate burglary. However, by the followng spring it was apparent that the Watergate cover-up tried to cover too much, and it could not be continued by simply manipulating the criminal justice system. The courts and the Senate had opened new fronts, and Dean was faced with the impossible task of controlling the information these investigative bodies had available.

He duly reported all these matters to the President in a series of conversations, which the President secretely taped. But his advice was not taken. Instead of trying to brazen out the original Watergate cover-up by an open admission of culpability on the part of White House staff members, Nixon began to plan the cover-up of the cover-up.

Since Mitchell was not willing to serve as the sacrificial victim to save the administration, Nixon and his key advisers began talking about casting Dean in the role. Internal power plays had characterized life in the Nixon administration from its inception. Now they would be more serious than ever: losing meant a likely criminal conviction and the prospect of jail. With Mitchell squeezed out of the central core, Dean had no ally. Faced with the prospects of a certain loss vis-a-vis Nixon, Haldeman, and Ehrlichman, Dean defected to the prosecution's side and negotiated to become the key witness in the growing case against the President.

Until the discovery of the tapes, Dean was Nixon's only accuser, and in the drama of Watergate that was unfolding he was seen as a central figure. Some accused him of betraying the presidency; others saw him as heroic. Eventually, the President's own words vindicated Dean, and he served a short prison term for his involvement in the criminal obstruction of justice. He was 36 years old on his release, ready to start life anew, which he did as a reporter covering the Bicentennial Republican National Convention for the counterculture newspaper, *Rolling Stone.*

In the heady atmosphere of imperial intrigue that flourished in the White House, subordinates' faithful execution of commands became routine. Orders were not questioned, only implemented, even ones that were patently illegal. In the course of furthering their own career interests, opportunistic young men served to perpetuate the malfeasance conceived by their superiors. Whatever their own ethical principles might have been, in their association with the Nixon administration they became convinced that conscience could be sacrificed to expedience if the price was right.

Volumes will be written on the complexity of the Nixon character. Writers will take some facet of his life to explain, or at least illuminate, who he was, what he did, and why he did it. Some will see his career as a variant of the Horatio Alger myth; others will see it as a story of scandal in high places. Some will say he was defeated by unscrupulous underlings; others will say he was defeated by the very system he claimed to represent. I have suggested that character is a function of broad historical currents and particular significant others. Character is molded by how these forces come together to accentuate or inhibit certain aspects of the person.

Richard Nixon was born as a new historical order was emerging; he came into maturity when the hegemonic version of that way of life was being forged. His personal ambition was instrumental in bringing that new vision into focus in the 1950s, while his ultimate political victory was an attempt to consolidate its fragmenting image in the 1970s. In this sense he is a great man: he will have a place in the books of history, and the tale of his life will be told and retold.

Throughout his life he was supported, encouraged, and assisted by men who shared a world view similar to his and who saw how to advance their own ambitions by advancing those of Richard Nixon. The forces Nixon ultimately brought together in his ascent to power thus consisted of all those elements in the culture and all those characteristics of significant others that were congruent with his own enterprise. In this sense, the Cold War and Ron Ziegler, mass society and Murray Chotiner, were all relevant to the rise of Richard Nixon. The Cold War gave focus to a society in which local culture was disintegrating. Chotiner developed a logic to capitalize on these social changes, and Ziegler developed a vocabulary that could mystify the nation at the same time it purported to be the voice of authority. Others who were significant to Nixon's life in one way or another emphasized, exemplified or exorcised traits in the prevailing culture; and through his association with such people, Nixon became convinced of his own beliefs.

In the last analysis, however, the Nixon era was a product of what a singular man brought to the Oval Office. Significant others in Nixon's life sustained the definitions he acted on, but it was Richard Nixon who brought that collection of people together in the first place. Like Bruce Barton's version of Jesus that was so popular in his boyhhood, Nixon discovered the ability to move people by the words he spoke and the logic he articulated. He became convinced of his mission in life and gathered together a group of undistinguished supporters as disciples of his cause. In turn, his disciples were instrumental in propagating the world view their leader proposed. But it was the world view of the leader that set the tone and style of the Nixon administration, and not underlings betraying their leader by unscrupulous conduct.

Chapter 8
Betrayal as a Way of Life

The enemy gave focus to the Nixon forces. It established a receptive milieu in which the Nixon message resonated as the voice of legitimate authority. It brought together a set of men who acted in the name of that authority.

What made the President's men a team was not any collective vision, no glorified ideology. Other than individual initiative, free enterprise, and opportunism, there was no ideology. There was no philosophical understanding of democracy, no abstract referent for the republican way of life. The law was at best technical rulings written by people who had a vested interest in its wording and nothing like a Mosaic Code sanctioned by some divine force. The Constitution relegated religion to the weekend, and although most of the President's men portrayed themselves as pious and devout, they made a clear distinction between work and church. What governed relations at work was a tough metaphor; on the job compassion, pity and other traditional Christian virtues were considered a weakness rather than a blessing. What drew these men together was their personal loyalty to Richard Nixon and their hatred of the enemy. Permissiveness, the press, the Kennedys, the Eastern Establishment, demonstrators, and Democrats, "nutheads" and "weirdos" embodied the concept of evil, while their leader embodied all that was good. So in this regard they were united as a team and not simply a random collection of opportunistic adventurers.

However, dedication to their leader and hatred of the enemy were the only source of solidarity for the Nixon team. Since each member was dependent on the President for his power and influence, the system of patronage reinforced whatever loyalties individuals had to Nixon as a person. But because the team was only loosely bound together, the elaborate system of in-house patronage divided the team into factions. On the one hand were the men beholden to Haldeman for their jobs and their influence, and on the other were the men beholden to Mitchell. Between Haldeman and Mitchell there was considerable coolness, bordering on animosity.

Haldeman resented Mitchell's influence, and Mitchell resented Haldeman's. Each saw the other as a competitor for the king's ear. Haldeman had the advantage. He had been intimate with Nixon longer and in more situations, and thus he knew the boss better. In addition, his proteges were more numerous. Mitchell's influence with the President came from the fact he was a person to be respected. While both men exemplified the style of arrogant toughness Nixon appreciated, Mitchell was the same age as Nixon and hence a peer, while Haldeman was 13 years younger and hence subordinate. Moreover, Mitchell had proven himself a successful Wall Street lawyer, while Haldeman was at best a West Coast advertising executive, a parvenu in the established social order. So despite the breadth of Haldeman's influence, Mitchell had considerable leverage.

From 1968 on conflict between these two factions was subtle. As the Watergate revelations intensified the opposition to the administration, these factions were the lines along which the team fragmented. (See Figure 4)

The coolness between Haldeman and Mitchell was only one division in the Nixon forces. Although relations between the President and each individual member of the team were cordial, relations between most individual team members were cool. Competition for power and influence resulted in suspicion and distrust among top advisers and second-level subordinates. This general attitude preceded Watergate and was intensified by the events that followed the summer of '72.

Figure 4: Relations Between Selected Members of the Nixon Team

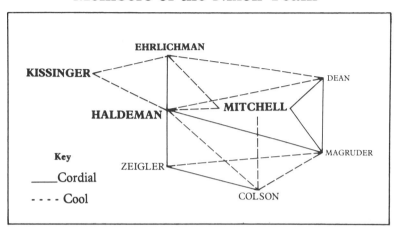

★   ★   ★

In the early years of his first administration Nixon had attempted to consolidate his power as President by a massive reorganization of the executive branch of government. New organizations proliferated, old organizations were absorbed into the new structures or abandoned altogether. Important duties were delegated to staff positions that did not require Senate confirmation, while traditional offices were bypassed altogether. This managerial revolution was not front-page news, but in the process of organizational reorganization, established powers were usurped. Furthermore, the bureaucratic housecleaning that took place in the first administration set the precedent for the reorganization that followed Nixon's reelection. Calling for letters of resignation from the top 2,000 people in the administration, Nixon announced his proposal to eliminate those he thought unnecessary as a move to reduce the size and cost of government while, at the same time, increasing efficiency. From cabinet members to assistants' assistants, Nixon loyalists duly submitted their resignations, and those who were finally to go were so informed by H.R. Haldeman. Those of the top echelon who were dismissed were those who had shown some signs of independence in the past. Melvin Laird was dismissed from the Department of Defense, George Romney from Housing and Urban Development, Robert Finch from Health, Education and Welfare. Eventually Kissinger replaced Rogers as Secretary of State, and all remnants of the soft-line advisers were gone.

The effect of these wholesale dismissals was to undermine the morale of those who were left. It became apparant that past loyalty to Richard Nixon did not ensure his loyalty in return. Thus the ties between the leader and his disciples were weakened just as forces outside the White House were intensifying their opposition. Their sense of loyalty, plus their own guilty knowlege, should have bound subordinates to their superiors. But a pattern of betrayal clearly was evident in Nixon's administration.

After his resignation even apologists were forced to admit that the crime Richard Nixon perpetuated against the nation was betraying the people's faith in constitutional government and the democratic process. For example, Theodore White entitles his treatise on Nixon's downfall *Breach of Faith*. He identifies Nixon's Gethsemane as Watergate, which he explains as an overreaction to the exigencies of the times: the lawlessness of the radical left, the unscrupulous conduct of underlings, the complexity of democratic order in a nuclear world. However, a careful review of Nixon's life suggests that there were numerous times when his actions betrayed the principles he proclaimed and the faith of others was exploited for his personal advantage. In fact, an historical perspective suggests that, for Richard Nixon, betrayal was a way of life.

Let us begin with his youth. People from Whittier and acquaintances from college and law school remember young Nixon as shy, serious, sensitive, determined, diligent, methodical, resourceful, and conscientious. To all outward appearances he was a model boy. Furthermore, there was a close bond between young Nixon and his mother. She taught him about organization, deference, and propriety. She ran interference between her sensitive second son and her domineering, aggressive husband. She helped Richard get his first job after law school and once his own family began, she helped his wife with the children. In many and various ways she provided him with examples of saintly virtue. Despite the principled Quaker devotion of both his mother and his grandmother, however, young Nixon enlisted in the Navy and avidly took part in the war commanding a supply depot behind the lines in the South Pacific. Whatever virtues the Milhous side of his family passed on to him, pacifism was not among them. Despite his mother's gentle faith in him, he came to pride himself in being "the fighting man in the arena." Eventually he dropped the "M" from his signature and, we may presume, thereby severed his ties with the Quaker beliefs the "Milhous" in his name reflected.

This change in his signature did not represent any change in his public posture. He had always proclaimed himself to be a Quaker, despite his considerable involvement with the Methodist Church when he and Pat first went to Washington, and despite his very close ties with Billy Graham, a fundamentalist demagogue whose career parallels Nixon's. For example, as Vice President, Nixon asked Graham to officiate at his mother's funeral and thereby showed considerable insensitivity to his mother's Quaker piety as well as to the community sentiments of his home town. As President, Nixon asked Graham to officiate at private White House services, although these occasions were as much political as they were spiritual. Private religious services at the White House had been suggested by Haldeman as a way of informally communicating with high-ranking members of government and as a way of showing favor or displeasure to subordinates. Since they were "private," not everyone was invited, and those who were excluded could draw their own conclusions. Since they were by invitation, those solicitied could not decline without showing disrespect. Thus the White House church services were evidence not of the spiritual elevation of the administration, but of its methods of day-to-day operation, referred to as "busting arms" and "kicking asses."

Throughout his pubic career Nixon routinely documented his claims of compassion by pointing to his Quaker heritage. In the opening pages of his *Memoirs* he makes frequent reference to his Quaker background, and the reader is given to assume the importance of that influence in his formative years. However, after page 57 there is no further reference to Quakerism but repated references to being a fighter, being a crusader, being tough, being aggressive, and numerous other attributes more fitting the autobiography of a fierce warlord than a gentle Friend. If one searches these memories for recollections of spiritual guidance and advice, it is found only in the person of Billy Graham. In office and out, at various times of crisis—and by his own account, crisis is frequent— Nixon documents his reliance on the fundamentalist world view propogated by Graham and his postwar Christian crusade.

Despite the contrary evidence, Nixon's claim that he was a Quaker always implied he was more than just a gut fighter. Yet if he was ever a Quaker, he clearly betrayed that faith. The only Quaker principle to which he seemed committed was the belief in the self as the ultimate source of all being and knowing. Quakerism, however, proposes much more than just enlightened self-interest. It tempers the powers of the individual by a dedicated compassion to the interests of other human beings. No matter how powerful the inner being may be, a principled Quaker understands he will not employ that power solely in the service of his own interests. Rather, he will look for ways to effect mutual satisfaction between self and others. Principled Quakers can be trusted, for their world view acknowledges an I-thou relation.

Enlightened self-interest is not unique to Quakerism. The cult of positive thinking that began in America around the Civil War rests on the same premise as the Society of Friends (Meyer, 1966). From Mary Baker Eddy through Dale Carnegie and Norman Vincent Peale to est, Scientology, and Mind Control, such sectarian movements have flourished in the nation, supported in large measure by the belief in laissez faire opportunism. Each variant has prosed that the individual, and the powers within him are sufficient to meet the onslaughts of the world. From self-healing to self-aggrandizement, anything can be achieved by the proper frame of mind. All that need be done is to master one's will behind one's desire, and any objective can be realized. The Christian Scientism that Ehrlichman, Haldeman, and many other figures in the advertising industry embraced is a variant of the cult of positive thinking.

Positive thinkers focus on the consciousness of inner experience, but they do not necessarily temper it by acknowledging the validity of others. Positive thinkers do not always see others as comrades on the same road through life. They may see others as competitors, vying for the same objectives, and hence opponents to be overcome by duplicity, chicanery, and guile. Or they may see others as resources, and hence dupes, whose own inner experiences can be manipulated to the advantage of the star performer. Richard Nixon seems to have combined a fundamentalists world view of hellfire and damnation with the manipulative strategy of enlightened self-interest. His very claims betray whatever faith his mother had in her second son.

Nixon's relations with his father were nowhere near as cordial as those with his mother, but he was not a child to rebel. He accepted the harsh authority his father meted out and in various ways tried to please him and elicit praise.

Family accounts attribute his youthful dedication to law as a response to his father's consciousness of Teapot Dome. Twice in his life Frank Nixon, an uneducated, itinerant laborer, came close to striking it rich in oil. Then, suddenly the headlines revealed corruption in high places, associated with oil rights, and the stories chronicled the role lawyers played in the unseemly enterprise. We may hypothesize that Frank said to his boys: "If you know the law, you will not get cheated. If I had known the law, I would be rich." In this way he may have established Richard's positive association between success and law. We do know from his mother's testimony that Nixon committed himself to the law in his boyhood, and he did so by adamantly promising to become "a lawyer who can't be bought by crooks." If that was a promise made to his father as a way of achieving respect in Frank's eyes, he betrayed his father's faith as well as his mother's.

The outlines of betrayal emerge early in Nixon's life. His stint with the carnival was a betrayal of Quaker piety, although it was done with the complicity of his mother and under considerations of life and death.

There is a story of stealing a farmer's latrine while at Whittier College and another story of breaking into the Dean's office to see his grades at Duke. In both cases these bits of biographical lore were considered no more than "schoolboy pranks," expected of anybody in with the in-crowd; they are treated as trivial transgressions. Since the Middle Ages, the norms of the student culture have been much looser than those of civil society, and adults have been tolerant of student mores as long as they do not threaten the established order of everyday life. Even Gloomy Gus was entitled to a prank or two in college. However, while the story of his college excursion into a speakeasy enters the biographical lore in his *Memoirs,* these other two "pranks" are curiously omitted from the same account.

If betrayal in his youth was episodic, the war would change him. It introduced new words into his vocabulary and new games to his repretoire. It taught him about the ultimate conflict of life. War is hell, he learned, and even from his position behind the lines he saw the victims and casualties of all-out conflict. The imagery of war was reinforced when he returned to civilian life, as Hollywood glorified armed conflict, and war heroes were treated with deference and respect. If we can note the moment when Richard Nixon, the sensitive young man from Whittier, became a tough gut fighter, his experiences during the war years seem the most likely time.

Not only did he see the misery and misfortune associated with losing, he experienced the heightened intensity of winning under pressure. Through high school and college Nixon had involved himself in campus politics, and on numerous occasions he experienced the satisfaction of coming out first on the ballot. At the carnival his ability to tip the crowd was a minor victory of sorts, but it did not contribute directly to his own self-interest—his salary as a barker was fixed, and as long as he was not an abject failure, it did not matter how many people he convinced to step up to the Wheel of Fortune. In the Navy it was different. If war was time out from ordinary life, the battle was an intermittent affair. There were times when personnel and supplies were moving swiftly from the supply depot to the front lines and then back again. But there were also times when there was nothing to do except wait until the hostilities resumed. To while away those hours, GIs played cards.

Gaming is frowned on by Quakers. But so is warfare. Wrongs would cancel one another out. Naive and inexperienced when he began, Nixon soon became an astute poker player. He learned strategy and tactics, patience and bluffing. He learned how to calculate his odds vis-a-vis his opponents, and how success meant winning the pot. As a principled Quaker, he could not play cards, for it would involve putting his self-interest above that of the others at the table. In contrast, an enlightened opportunist makes a good game player.

We may hypothesize that between the heightened milieu of armed conflict and the intensity of the poker games that took up his leisure, Richard Nixon came to see the game as a metaphor of life, and to name the game *war*. In the first instance he saw strategy and tactics as basic to any enterprise; in the second he intensified the emotion associated with winning. Losing became slow death.

After the Navy he went directly into politics, and there the metaphor of the game and the imagery of warfare were both reinforced and transformed. The organization of national politics made use of the same language he learned in the South Pacific. Campaigns were waged to win votes and take over strategic positions. Troops were deployed, intelligence gathered. In various ways the political process paralleled what he learned in his years in the service, and apparently he felt right at home.

★   ★   ★

By 1950 Nixon was an experienced politician, with a fair amount of influence, and an astute adviser to manage his affairs. With foresight and care he cultivated power. As a freshman congressman he organized an informal association of powerless representatives, and through their mutual association he won the patronage of senior congressmen. He was appointed to prestigious and powerful committees, and in his association with the House Un-American Activities Committee, he made a name for himself. When he presented his credentials to the original Committee of 100, soliciting their support in his race for the Senate, they refused to go along with his plans. Despite the fact that they had been influential in giving him his political start, he betrayed their interests. Through Murray Chotiner he solicited new patrons, and these new patrons supported him instead.

The treatment of the Committee of 100 is the first clear evidence of betrayal in Nixon's political career. When it appeared that Eisenhower might be nominated by the Republican party and Richard Nixon might have a chance at the Vice Presidency, he betrayed his commitment to Warren and swung the California delegation in support of the general. With each betrayal of others, his own interests advanced.

By this time Nixon began to create a constituency of detractors whose experience with him had resulted in resentment and ill-will. From the very beginning, in the Voorhis and the Douglas campaigns, there were some who were outraged by his studious disregard for the canons of fair play and good sportsmanship. But for the most part his early detractors were localized to Southern California and were powerless in their own right. It was not until his betrayal of Warren that Nixon began to engender distrust and resentment among his peers in the political process.

Resentment and revenge motivated the leaks that came from the Warren delegation and almost destroyed his chances at the Vice Presidency with their implication of influence peddling and corrupt practices. A ritual of intensification began. Betrayal engendered animosity, and animosity engendered betrayal; more betrayal, more animosity. Richard Nixon may have known the source of the information that so menacingly threatened his career, but it is not likely he acknowledged its legitimacy. By now he was entrenched: he was convinced of the importance of his own aspirations and critical of any who questioned his claims. Besides, at least in his own mind, the nomination of Eisenhower was certain eventually; all Nixon did was hasten the moment. So it is doubtful that Nixon saw the part his own conduct played in the trials and tribulations that beset him through the Checkers episode. But it is clear that he sensed the intensity of the opposition on the part of "forces out there."

Those "forces out there" became the enemy in the lexicon of his inner consciousness. Whatever he did, he must not let the enemy get the upper hand, for they would defeat and disgrace him without a moment's hesitation. The press became the most visible and ominous manifestation of the forces that oppressed him; the Kennedys became another. Eventually, everywhere he looked he found opposition, and in the very course of his looking for that opposition, he fostered its emergence.

Eisenhower had little faith in him to start with, so there was little to betray in their relationship. Rather, as in his relations with his father, Nixon sought to cultivate respect and appreciation in the older man's eyes. He tried so hard that, as in his skirmishes in college football, he enthusiastically overstepped the boundaries of fair play. In his very attempt to appease the general, he betrayed the friendshp of Murray Chotiner when Chotiner's reputation came under a cloud. Although he did the hatchetwork for the Eisenhower administration, this did not win him any particular esteem with the general. Eisenhower represented an attitude cultivated in the old order, where gentlemen tempered opportunism by a cultivated deference to Christian piety. Nixon's ruthless, aggressive style did not curry favor, but instead engendered disdain. Thus, throughout his tenure as Vice President, Nixon was dependent on the largesse of a man who had little respect for his protege, the two being bound to one another through a complex network of party loyalties and political alliances.

During the same period, other men of influence and power in both parties began to cultivate a hearty dislike for Dick Nixon. Democratic sentiments could be discredited by assuming partisan motives. The Democrats were his competitors, and in this war that was politics they would attempt to discredit him whenever they saw the possibility of political gain. Certainly he had been willing to defame others to win office; clearly, the opposition felt the same. His detractors within his own party were in some ways similar to his detractors among the Democrats. They, too, had self-serving reasons. Even though all were joined in common endeavor to further the aims of the Republican Party, each was embroiled in a personal endeavor to further ambitions of his own.

Each, Nixon assumed, was motivated by the same searing desire to be top dog as motivated Nixon himself.

The individualism that dominated America from the time of the westward expansion was taken for granted as a part of the political process about the same time. Though the ostensible public commitment of a politician is to the process of government, it is understood that good government will always be weighed against personal advantage. American politicians are—and are expected to be—people of multiple interests. Faith in the system assumes that, in the end, such political individuals, striving to aggrandize their own power, will provide the best possible government. In the competitive struggle for individual advancement, the collectivity will be raised to new heights. Weak forms of government will be passed over; strong forms will survive. Thus Nixon's detractors within the Republican Party could be accounted for by the same logic that explained opposition from the Democratic Party. If the Democrats were competitors for partisan interests, the Republicans were competitors for personal interests.

Although the pattern of political betrayal becomes clear in the early '50s, Nixon's public character underwent a transformation, and the emergent pattern seemingly fades from center stage. During Eisenhower's illness Nixon cultivated a more refined demeanor, as much to curry favor with the general as to insure his own chances in 1960. His past was no liability, however. The men who wielded influence in the Republican Party were men who believed in the tough metaphor. No matter how cultivated and refined you appear on the surface, you must be ruthless if you are to get your own way. The New Nixon simply embodied the best of both views. He manifested the symbolic pretense of the old order —statesmanship—while he advanced more modern notions of the new order—opportunism.

It is difficult to assess the significance of the accusations of illegal voting practices that were associated with the 1960 election. Claiming he did not want to act in any way that would be divisive for the nation, Nixon did not press charges. But what he publicly proclaims and what he actually intends are not always the same thing. More likely it was the case that Nixon believed he was robbed of a victory that was rightfully his but that he failed to find sufficient patrons and backers to take on the awesome Kennedy machine. Years later he wrote in his *Memoirs:*

> I vowed that I would never again enter an election at a disadvantage
> by being vulnerable to them—or anyone—on the level of political
> tactics. (p. 226)

Up to this point in his career, Nixon, as tutored by Chotiner, maintained a preemptory position on what was fair and what was not fair in
a political contest. Writing on how to organize a campaign, Chotiner
(1960) addressed the question of ethics directly. He wrote "truth is the
best weapon we can use" (p. 209) and explained how truth can be distinguished from falsehood by identifying whose interests are served. He
discussed the need to create numerous committees to demonstrate
widespread grassroots involvement with the candidate and make news
when the name of the committee chairman was announced. Other types
of subterfuge were suggested as well. None of them are illegal, but all
of them are at the edge of ordinary understandings about language and law.

This careful pronouncement of ethics is no more than semantic subterfuge, however. In the early Nixon campaigns there was evidence of
practices like whisper campaigns and misleading literature that are bor-
derline at best. They require a particular insensitivity to the niceties of
language and a studious disregard of the spirit of the law to be treated as
acceptable conduct. But assuming that the Nixon forces did have some
self-imposed limits to that point, the charges of illegality that surrounded
the race with Kennedy may have opened Nixon's eyes to possibilities he
had not considered before.

In 1962 the Chotiner strategy almost backfired. By then Nixon had
tutored Haldeman in the principles he had learned from his own mentor.
Chotiner had recommended false-front committees and organizations that
made it appear that factions of one party were in support of the opposition
candidate. In the race against Edmund Brown, the Nixon campaign
committee (which at that time consisted of Herb Klein, Maurice Stans,
Herbert Kalmbach, Haldeman, Ehrlichman, Chapin, and Ziegler) prepared and distributed some 900,000 postcards with the following copy:

> This is not a plea for any candidate. As a Democrat, what do you
> feel we can do to throw off the shackles of this left-wing minority,
> now so powerful it can dictate the course of our party? We can
> break the power of the CDC by refusing to elect their candidates.
> Or we can take acceptable Republicans—if we can find any. What-
> ever we do, in the name of the Democratic Party—Let's Not Deliver
> California to the CDC. (Mankiewicz, 1973, p. 87)

Scripted by the Nixon campaign committee, but addressed to "Fellow
Democrats," the post cards were mailed to Democrats; the printed words

seemed to speak with the authority of the Democratic Party, and the objective was to elicit support for the Republican candidate. Since, *in this case*, the Republican candidate was Dick Nixon, the fraudulent intent of the mailing was obvious. The Democratic Party brought suit, but the case was lengthy and expensive. By 1964, in the belief that Nixon's political career was over, the charges were dropped. So there was never an opportunity for Nixon's conduct or the conduct of his aides and associates to be tested under the law. The legality or illegality of such misrepresentation was never clearly established. It remained moot in the Nixon mentality.

Following the loss in California, Nixon migrated to the East Coast. But he carried with him the provincial world view he had cultivated in the West. Compared to Europe, the East is without traditional roots, without benefit of a culture that emerges from the sifting of the sands of time. Compared to Easterners, Westerners are barbarians. This was the legacy of Nixon's boyhood. Furthermore, most of Nixon's backers were parvenues like himself. Clement Stone, Elmer Bobst, Robert Abplanalp were all self-made men—"two-fisted entrepreneurs," Nixon liked to call them. They brought a barbarian vigor to the marketplace, but their style was not appreciated by the older Eastern Establishment. They became known as "Cowboys" — tough opponents but hardly civilized. They were looked down on by those who had inherited their wealth through the ruthless entrepreneurial expansion of their fathers. In many cases only one generation separated Eastern millionaires from the source of their money, as in the case of the Kennedys. But that single generation was sufficient for the Eastern Elite to make claim to an aristocratic tradition, and hence for them to define the Cowboys as upstarts.

The Rise of Silas Lapham is a classic story in American literature. It portrays the bumbling, suffering experience of the noveau riche in the 19th century, when great wealth was being amassed. Richard Nixon embodies that American myth as he does so many others. It is hard to suppose that a man of acute sensitivity was oblivious to the attitudes of the Easterners who became a part of his daily round. Even though he had made it to the citadel of success, he was looked down on for his manners and style. As in his boyhood experiences in Whittier, he was always just the grocery boy. Furthermore, he never treated criticism of his conduct as a source of information, as feedback about the propriety of his acts; it is likely he mistook the disdain for his manners as rejection of himself as a person. Even if he had "made it" by all objective criteria, inwardly he was still an outsider.

entment grew, and eventually he saw the Eastern Establishment as just another embodiment of the enemy, detractors who were out to get him, deprive him of what was his due. He had worked hard since his days in Whittier to realize the American Dream. But even though he had gone farther than most men, and even though he was supported and encouraged by men who had themselves achieved the American Dream, he felt himself rejected by those whose attitudes counted. His reckoning of his own success was diminished. Certainly Nixon's public behavior shows traces of the hostility, anger, and mistrust that is characteristic of people with deep-seated resentments.

Many years after his exile in New York City, Nixon jotted a few notes while preparing for a news conference, and one of his aides rescued those notes for posterity. He had written:

> Defeat doesn't finish a man. Quit(ting) does. A man is not finished when he's defeated. He's finished when he quits. (Safire, 1975, p. 155)

During the years of his exile, working in alliance with influential patrons in the Republican Party, Nixon curried support anew. Though political pundits declared him dead, he came out of the wings, waged a second battle for the presidency, and he was victorious. But that victory was stained with all manner of disrespect, and the pattern of betrayal that characterized his life in the '50s reemerged in the 1960s.

Some acts of betrayal involved the faith the American people put in his candidacy; others involved important people in his life. The escalation of the war; the punitive measures taken against demonstrators, students, and blacks; detente; and wage and price controls were all betrayals of one group or another. By the time he was inaugurated, the nation had become disenchanted with the war, and Nixon promised to end it. But his promises were soon broken. As President, Nixon swore to support principles of Constitutional justice, but in both public and private edicts he routinely subverted the law. Furthermore, at the same time he subverted the law, he publicly proclaimed his virtue and integrity to the nation. Thus did he doubly betray the faith the voters had placed in him. While he cultivated the support of the right by his anticommunist stance, he betrayed their understanding of his beliefs by making a show of friendship with China and Russia. His economic game plan betrayed the interests of the working class, whom he had cultivated as part of Colson's grand strategy, just as it betrayed the principles of laissez faire capitalism he had claimed to represent from the beginning of his career. In all these ways Richard Nixon acted as a consummate hypocrite. Between his words and his deeds was an unfathomable abyss; one bore no resemblance to the other.

Nixon betrayed the faith that tied citizens to the mythic foundations of American society. He also betrayed the personal faith and loyalty of his associates. Watergate became a contested battle between the Nixon forces and the rest of America. At first, the battle affected the public respect Nixon could muster in support of his administration. Eventually, it affected the very organization that perpetuated his administration and the personal careers of individuals in it, including his own. The lines of conflict and competition drawn in the beginning ultimately divided loyalist from loyalist, and Nixon's own actions separated himself from his followers.

Dissolution of the bonds of loyalty began with the wholesale dismissals that took place after his reelection. For those who had been true in the past, there was doubt and uncertainty. Questions were raised about what could be expected in the future and personal commitments were reassessed. When Patrick Gray, acting head of the FBI, discredited himself at his confirmation hearings, implying there was direction from the White House in the FBI's investigation of Watergate, Nixon withdrew his support of Gray's nomination. The hairline cracks that appeared in the fall of 1972 were fissures by spring of 1973. Those who gave loyalty to the President could see there was no reciprocity.

Through the spring of 1973 the pattern of betrayal was intensified. Nixon tried to maneuver John Mitchell into taking the rap and thereby showed himself less of a friend than Mitchell might have expected. When Ehrlichman and Haldeman came under fire, Nixon promised privately and asserted publicly that he stood behind those who had been loyal to him in the past, that just because charges had been made about their probity he would not dismiss them, as Ike had done to Sherman Adams when Adams' probity was questioned. Yet when pressure from the Justice Department intensified, he asked for their resignations. He promised to take care of his loyal aides financially through the Nixon Foundation, but nothing ever came of this promise either. The only thing he did not promise was executive clemency; that trump card he reserved for himself.

The same pattern is seen again and again. When it was clear that Agnew's misconduct was leading to indictments, criminal trials, and unseemly publicity, Agnew became a liabiity for Nixon's interests. Once Agnew had been praised as forthright and forceful. Now Nixon's henchmen were instrumental in having the Vice President cop a plea, get off light, and, most important of all, sever all association with the administration. William Rogers' faithful service as a friend and adviser was abruptly terminated and Kissinger nominated to take his place as Secretary of State. This betrayal of Rogers' lifelong friendship was passed over with one or two sentences in Nixon's *Memoirs.* The promises Nixon made about looking after John Dean's interests were forgotten as soon as they were made. As the Nixon transcripts show, Henry Peterson from the Criminal Division of the Justice Department was explicity assured confidentiality as he related the prosecution's case against Nixon's top aides. But five minutes later the President reported what Peterson told him to Haldeman and Ehrlichman, who were the object of the Justice Department's investigation. Through the course of the Watergate revelations the Nixon forces solicited surrogates to speak in the President's behalf, using public relations to counter the discrediting information accumulating day by day. Gerry Ford, Hugh Scott, and Barry Goldwater—all influential Republicans—were made dupes in the President's cause. In a convincing display of sincerity, Nixon assured them of his innocence. They, for whatever reason, believed him. They attempted to temper the growing criticism of the Presideent by providing a benign accounting of otherwise sinister facts. Yet Nixon's assurances of his innocence were a line, a strategy, a calculated move in the cover-up of a cover-up. Despite the fact that Republican leaders acted in good faith to support Nixon's reputation, they too were betrayed by what was revealed. Ultimately, Nixon's supporters on the Ervin Committee, as well as those on the Judiciary Committee, were faced with the fact that their leader had lied; and were it not the desire of the nation to get past Watergate as fast as possible, they might have been held accountable for their own duplicity.

Nixon betrayed the faith of his lawyers—Herb Kalmbach, James St. Clair, and Len Garment—men who were dedicated to the task of extricating him from the legal entanglements that characterized his second administration. With straight face and all sincerity, looking honest and earnest, he fed them a line and led them astray. Once the facts finally came out, some of his lawyers were discredited before the bar and others merely appeared foolish. But in one way or another, they experienced the pangs of betrayal.

Finally, Nixon betrayed the wife and family who stood loyally by his side, but who knew no more about his affairs than the rest of the nation.

Not all who were betrayed sought revenge. To his credit as a manipulator, Nixon managed to keep his associates' faith while he sold out their interests.

Ehrlichman's faith was never very deep, and in the course of his court trial he declared himself the innocent victim of chicanery perpetrated by his leader. Haldeman held fast until Nixon's televised appearance on the David Frost show, and then, in his published account of the events of Watergate, he revealed that there was a more sinister Nixon than the man he had permitted the public to see, although he did not go so far as to expose that other Nixon to public view. But Mitchell, Magruder, his lawyers, and his family did not turn on the man who betrayed the loyalty they gave him.

Some would say such devotion was more than Nixon deserved. But his ability to evoke sympathy even when he was most devious was a considerable part of his talent. Just as he promised salvation while he preached hellfire and damnation, so did he elicit compassion for the underdog while he claimed the right to be top dog. He had cultivated the image of a tragic figure, misunderstood and oppressed all his life, and those who were attracted to this posture were not easily turned aside. They saw his fall from power as due to forces outside the man himself, malevolent forces beyond his control, and they could feel sorry for the unfortunate turn his career had taken. After a few months of respectful silence, even those who had finally voted for his impeachment had a few good things to say about him again, and as the years passed more and more former supporters returned to the ranks.

Nixon's ability to manipulate the sentiments of those who were close to him was merely an extension of his ability to manipulate the masses. Throughout his life he dealt in impressions, not facts. The facts of the Voorhis and Douglas campaigns were that his competitors were *not* communists, but liberal Democrats within the mainstream of American tradition. The impression Nixon fostered was otherwise. The fact of his anticommunist stance was not a deep-seated conviction that communism was the embodiment of evil, but only a calculated ploy to advance his own interests. Yet the impression he fostered was otherwise, and many of his most devoted loyalists were drawn to his cause by their belief in this issue. The facts of Watergate were not that Nixon acted to protect the integrity of the presidency and insure national security, but that he acted to further his own ambition to be a two-term president. Yet through the years of revelation that preceded his resignation, he fostered the former impression.

In the end his skill at impression management assured him a government pension and an uncertain reputation. The former supported him in a style more regal than ordinary folks have, while the uncertainty surrounding his career, his years in power, and the circumstances of his resignation permitted him to dream of a second resurrection.

Chapter 9
Impression Management in the Oval Office

Impression management has its roots in theater. Whether we speak of the tribal ceremony of a primitive group or the classic drama of an urban society, the object is to create an illusionary world and thereby evoke a response from those witness to the illusion. Stage, setting, props, and lines are all interwoven to provide an image of reality, and it is this artful creation to which spectators respond. Among primitive people, the participants of tribal ceremonies bedeck themselves in masks and ornate clothing. They take ritual objects from sacred places and on consecretated grounds they enact the dramas that give ordinary life a special meaning. The forms these ceremonials take are believed to be dictated by the gods. Hence the drama is an opportunity for both actors and spectators to reexperience the sacred bond between themselves and the spirits they worship. In the context of such ritual occasions, moral truths are enacted and the moral order is affirmed.

With the development of classical drama in ancient Greece, primitive theater was elevated to an art form, but its moral connotations remained. Greek drama made commentaries on the state of society and observations of the human condition, but it also reminded the spectators, if not the actors, of their links with the gods. By the 17th century the theater had come into its own as a secular institution; its religious basis was gone, its lessons in truth and virtue relegated to the church. The purpose of theater became pleasure, and theatrical production began to focus more and more on refined techniques of impression management. Stage, setting, props, and lines became secular vehicles to proclaim messages of a practical order.

The objective of theater is to heighten awareness, whether sacred or secular. Set apart from ordinary life, it provides an opportunity to see the everyday world in a new perspective. The fact that impression management can alter consciousness was one of the fundamental discoveries of Niccolo Machiavelli. By the end of the 15th century Machiavelli had introduced the principles of impression management into politics. Much like the advice Murray Chotiner gave his own protege 500 years later, Machiavelli counseled his Prince on how to control men's actions by controlling their perceptions. He argued that public life consists largely of deception, lies, and broken promises anyway, and that, in politics, appearances are more important than reality. He claimed that by employing carefully calculated performances, a leader could control his destiny by controlling the impression others had of him.

Techniques of impression management began to diffuse from the theater to public life around the Renaissance. By the 20th century they dominated everyday life in all of its sectors. With the development of movies, radio, and television, varieties of illusion began to monopolize the growing realm of leisure. Business came to depend on image and impression to promote the marketplace as an ever-expanding arena of action, and by mid-century the techniques of impression management developed by the advertising industry joined with those developed by the media, and a new world view emerged. The manipulation of images came to take precedence over the assessment of reality, and new conceptions of truth developed. Truth was what sold.

Sociologists writing in the middle of the 20th century described the appearance of a new personality type to go with the new world view that was coming into focus. David Riesman in *The Lonely Crowd* (1955) introduced the "other-directed person" as an historical figure. He is a person geared less to his own inner feelings than to the assessment others make of his appearance, his line, his status, and his symbols. He is calculating and adaptive. Taken in conjunction with the older American model—the self-made, positive thinker—the new American came to see life as a series of games, encounters where seemly appearances provide an advantage, and principled commitment is irrelevant. In *The Presentation of Self in Everday Life (1959)* Erving Goffman suggested that there were no longer principled truths that served to link the individual with human society directly and thence with the cosmos in general. At best there was a working consensus, a pragmatic definition of the situation that only held for immediate people for the time being. In this modern view life gives testimony to no enduring sacred values. Instead, it is a series of dramatic moments where all that counts is the participant's immediate advantage.

When Goffman's work was first published, his critics disclaimed its overly rational, self-serving portrait. Goffman left no room for the moral order, the sacred spark that set men apart from the beasts on the one hand and the computers on the other. His critics claimed his image of human beings was petty, scheming, ignoble. Such a model might be true for some people in some situations, they argued; but it was not representative of the modern character as a whole. Yet the dramaturgical model took hold in sociology because it seemed to explain so much of contemporary life.

Goffman's critics could not have anticipated the documented talk that took place in the Oval Office during Nixon's administration. In the versions made available to the public by the President himself, his conversations with aides and associates provide a case study in impression management. These examples provide an episodic account of one of Richard Nixon's most concerted efforts to convince the nation of his worth and integrity. The account is episodic in that there were doubtless other times when the topic of Watergate was the object of talk. Thus the public transcripts are not a running narrative. Nor are they just a documented transcript of ongoing conversation.

As the circumstantial case of his criminal liability began to grow, the Judiciary Committee subpoenaed the tapes that had been made secretely in the Prsident' s office the year before. During the spring of '73, the time covered by the subpoena, the elaborate cover-up designed to obstruct the investigation of the burglary at the Democratic National Committee (DNC) began to unravel. To calm the public outrage engendered by his firing of the Special Investigator, Nixon handed over some of the tapes in question. But in response to the Judiciary Committee subpoena for more, Nixon had the tapes transcribed and then he edited out all the material he considered "irrelevant" to the case against him. Thus the transcripts themselves are an object of impression management, having been created to show that there was no impeachable offense.

Having made the documents presentable, Nixon went on television to account for his action. There he explained how he was trying to protect the confidentiality of the presidency and the security of the nation. He said:

> I believe all the American People, as well as their Representatives in Congress, are entitled to have not only the facts but also the evidence that demonstrates those facts. I want there to be no question remaining about the fact that the President has nothing to hide in this matter. (Hearings Before the Committee on the Judiciary, 1974b, p. 85, hereafter referred to as *Hearings*)

He pointed to dozens of bound volumes, piled up like an encyclopedia. He indicated that those volumes contained the true story of Watergate for "anyone who reads his way through this mass of materials." (p. 90) The mountain of evidence seemed imposing, although anyone who sent away for a copy of the edited transcripts received a single volume of some 1,300 double-spaced typescript pages.

Nixon says of these transcripts:

> Never before in the history of the Presidency have records that are so private been made so public. In giving you these records— blemished and all—I am placing my trust in the basic fairness of the American people. (p. 91)

Resting his fate in the hands of the public, he promised "to go forward, to the best of my ability with the work that you elected me to do." (p. 91) However, the Judiciary Committee quickly noted that there were discrepencies between the tapes the President had already handed over and the transcripts he claimed represented those tapes. And there was still no explanation of the 18½ minutes of silence on one of the subpoenaed tapes. Far from reassuring the country of his innocence, his television performance contributed to the suspicion that engulfed him. Editorials in loyal Republican papers began demanding his resignation; his public support was eroding. Yet he did not resign for another four months, when the Supreme Court ordered him to hand over *all* taped documents the Judiciary Committee had subpoenaed.

In the 1950s the revelations of his personal finances was sufficient to quench suspicion that Nixon was a man who had something to hide. As the case against him grew in the '70s, he tried this tactic again

and again. In answer to charges that he had made massive errors in his
income tax, he made public his returns for his four years in office. But
the story they told repulsed many who were more scrupulous in preparing
their own tax returns. Like the revelation of his taxes, the edited
transcripts told more than the President anticipated. They told a story
of a group of men caught up in a network of crime, more concerned with
concocting an alibi than in surrendering to the principles of justice they
were sworn to uphold.

By spring of '73 the President and his men were beset with problems
—facts and revelations that could discredit the line they were trying to
sustain. The line consisted of their unblemished right to power and
authority. The facts involved their criminal liability in the obstruction of
justice. Had the institutions of criminal justice been left to their own
devices the summer before, they probably would have discovered that
Gordon Liddy and Howard Hunt had been hired and paid directly by
the staff at the Committee to Re-elect the President; that they had been
involved in undercover operations of a similar kind in the employ of
the White House; that members of both the CRP and the White House
staff had destroyed evidence linking the Watergate burglars to their own
enterprises; that perjury had been sustained by various officials through
the course of the investigation by the FBI and in the testimony to the
Grand Jury; that data from FBI files had been transmitted to the White
House and directions had come from the White House to the FBI on how
to handle the case. However, the institutions of criminal justice had not
been left to their own devices. As later testimony revealed, there was
no question that, once the burglary had been discovered, a cover-up plan
was put in operation. The objective of that plan was to limit the investigation to low-level functionaries and, by so doing, to protect the
President and his key advisers from criminal liability.

The very organization of the '72 campaign had stressed the separation
of the President from practical concerns. Running as a symbol of the
unification of the nation, Nixon could not be seen involved in partisan
politics. His campaign was not run from the White House but by a
separate organization with a formally independent chain of command.
It was as though the CRP had been created to draft Nixon to run for
office, acting on his behalf but not at his behest. It had no formal ties
with the Republican National Headquarters. It addressed no issue other

than the reelection of the President. As an organization it raised millions of dollars in support of Nixon's candidacy, and it distributed the money for projects to advance his purposes. But while the organization worked on his behalf, the President was not *officially* involved in its affairs. Still, it was obvious that if there were no formal ties between the White House and the CRP, the CRP most intimately represented Nixon's interests. John Mitchell had resigned his cabinet post to take over the management of the committee. Former cabinet member Maurice Stans became CRP Director of Finance. Jeb Magruder, once on the staff of H.R. Haldeman, was made Deputy Director under Mitchell. Various other positions were filled by ambitious young men who had worked at the White House during the first administration and would now work at CRP for the incumbent's reelection. Finally, liaisons were maintained between key men in the two organizations, permitting input and feedback. Had the Justice Department made clear the connections between the burglars and the CRP in the summer of '72, they would have also made evident the connections between CRP and the White House. By hindering their efforts, the various staff functionaries of the two organizations saved Nixon's line about his integrity and thus helped him save face through the election. They did not want to cause Nixon any "personal problems" or "embarrassment;" to protect their President, they engaged in a wide array of criminal offenses.

Criminal liability on the part of high officials in the CRP and the White House was a major problem for the newly elected President. Equally important were the problems posed by exposure of this criminal liability. The operatives in the burglary were *professional* undercover agents. Their superiors could anticipate that they would not be implicated when their hirelings were apprehended. With trust in the immediate loyalty of their subordinates, higher-ups went about systematically destroying documents and sustaining perjury while the Department of Justice was making its case. But the higher-ups did not know for how long and under what conditions their subordinants' silence would be maintained. Liddy, the most professional, would not talk under any circumstances. His loyalty was assured. But the principled dedication of the others was questionable. Concerted efforts to provide the defendants with "fees for their lawyers" and "support for their families" effectively bought their silence through the election. But once Nixon's reelection was certain, the pressures for money mounted. More importantly, there were demands for clemency and pardons. The problems created for the Oval Office escalated. Questions of how the men in the White House could fulfill the demands of the defendants without discrediting the impression they had been fostering became the focal point of long discussions, which culminated in the President's condoning blackmail as a way of silencing Hunt and saving his own face. Like many of the actions taken through the course of his career, this decision entailed considerable risk. But Nixon had gambled and won before, and his power to manipulate the institutions of government seemed at its peak. He and his associates had made it through the campaign, when his access to power rested on the affirmation of his integrity at the polls; they would make it through the ensuing fight with their enemies. Such positive thinking as emanated from the White House gave credibility to the notion that reality could be manipulated to the advantage of the powerful.

Yet revelations that discredited this line continued. The Senate established an investigative committee to look into charges and allegations made during the campaign. Leaks were already appearing in the media from the testimony that had been taken. At his confirmation hearings Patrick Gray disclosed how closely the White House had worked with the FBI during the original investigation of the burglary, and the Senate demanded to hear testimony from John Dean about the meaning of this liaison. After leveling severe sanctions against the silent defendants, Judge Sirica received a letter from James McCord implicating higher-ups at the CRP. Such leaks and revelations resulted in the reconvening of the grand jury, and the problems the Nixon administration faced multiplied exponentially.

In the spring of '73, Richard Nixon might have surrendered to the principles of justice he had sworn to uphold; he could have cooperated fully with the various investigative bodies, or he might have resigned his office in anticipation of the disgrace the actions of his subordinates would bring. But Richard Nixon was not a man to surrender. Seeing himself at his best when engaged in mortal combat, he would fight for his right to remain President. That fight was waged by scripting scenarios to define the nature of reality and thereby legitimize his right to office.

A *scenario* is a plausible story. It establishes an accounting of reality congruent with the image the speakers wish to perpetrate. A major part of the talk in the Oval Office is addressed to scripting scenarios—scenarios of how to deal with the Gray revelations and scenarios of how to deal with the Ervin committee; scenarios of how to deal with the press and scenarios of how to deal with the public. The speakers even develop scenarios for how to deal with one another. For every possible problem there is a script, which, if followed, will foster the illusion of a President whose only interests are national security and the integrity of his office and a staff whose actions were taken solely on behalf of such lofty motives.

Scenarios are interpretive. Nixon's scenarios explain known facts in a way that either negates their sinister meaning or enhances the President's stature.

> NIXON: How do I get credit for getting Magruder to the stand?
>
> EHRLICHMAN: Well, it is very simple. You took Dean off the case . . .
>
> NIXON: Why did I take Dean off? Because he was involved? I did it really because he was involved with Gray.
>
> HALDEMAN: The scenario is that he told you he couldn't write a report so obviously you had to take him off.
>
> NIXON: Right, right. (Nixon, 1974, pp. 821-822, hereafter referred to as *Transcripts.)*

This scenario is indicative of building a *line*. Nixon has been under pressure to show that he is cooperating with the various investigative bodies. His dismissal of Dean will foster just that impression. The public will be convinced of the lengths he is going to to get at the heart of the matter now that undeniable aspersions have been cast on his administration. In fact, ten minutes before the above conversation he has asked John Dean "to continue to help with the PR of the case." (p. 809) This scenario with Haldeman and Ehrlichman has no relevance to the President's actual conduct, but only to the public impression he wishes to foster.

In constructing a scenario, the speakers are concerned not with moral matters, but with the technicalities of engineering an *image*. Thus the difference between a line in a scenario and a lie in fact is often hazy. This distinction is frequently addressed. For instance, the President says to Ehrlichman:

> Have you given any thought to what the line ought to be—*I don't mean a lie—but a line*, on raising the money for these defendants? Because both of you were aware of what was going on you see . . . you were aware of it. (p. 994, emphasis added)

Here the line is clearly a substitute for the truth. It is not a denial of the facts, but an acceptable alternative: a sanitized version. Again, Ehrlichman says to Kleindienst:

> EHRLICHMAN: They'll ask you to whom you've spoken about your testimony and I would appreciate it if you'd say you talked to me in California because at that time I was investigating this thing for the President.
>
> KLEINDIENST: And not now?
>
> EHRLICHMAN: Well, *I wouldn't ask you to lie.*
>
> KLEINDIENST: No, I know.
>
> EHRLICHMAN: But the point is . . . (*New York Times* Staff, 1973, p. 808, emphasis added)

The point is that what is a lie and what is a line is a function of the speaker's perspective. When uttered by the President's team, it is a sound, strategic move. When uttered by the opponent it is devious, disgraceful, and dishonest. Insiders' virtues are seen as outsiders' vices in this relativistic perspective.

The value of the line is found in the innuendo, the ambiguity, the omissions that allow the speaker to evade the truth.

> NIXON: Let's see what he could do. Does Mitchell come in and say, "My memory was faulty. I lied."?
>
> EHRLICHMAN: No, he can't say that. He says . . .
>
> NIXON: "That without intending to I may have been responsible for this and I regret it very much but I did not realize what they were up to. They were—we were—talking about apples and oranges." That's what I think he would say. Don't you agree?
>
> HALDEMAN: I think so. He authorized apples and they bought oranges. (*Transcripts*, p. 347)

Here Mitchell's line exempts him from responsibility of wrongdoing while it still acknowledges his place in the authority structure of the CRP.

The President is not unaware of the costs of being caught in a lie. He repeatedly makes reference to the Hiss case and the fact that Hiss went to jail not because he had been a communist but because he lied about it when questioned under oath. Nixon counsels his aides:

> You can say I don't remember. You can say I can't recall. I can't give any answer to that that I can recall. (p. 235)

> Don't lie to (the FBI) to the extent to say there is no involvement,
> but just say this is a comedy of errors, without getting into it . . .
> (*Washington Post* Staff, 1974, p. 215)

Thus the line must skirt precariously around the truth, never transgressing it, but never revealing it.

The truth as a moral matter is irrelevant. The truth is what sells; what rings true; what the audience will buy. John Dean says:

> If we go that route, Sir, I can give a show we can sell them just
> like we were selling Wheaties on our position. (*Transcripts,* p. 211)

No abstract principle beyond expediency governs these speakers' behavior. Anything that is not an indictable lie can be said in good conscience as an alternative to a discrediting truth. Outright lies can be used if the need is urgent and the lie adequate for the purposes. Through the course of his conversations with Henry Peterson, Nixon repeatedly assures Peterson that the information he is providing will go no further than Nixon's own ears. The President of the United States, he says, needs what Peterson knows to take action in the situation. But once Peterson informs him of the facts pending before the Justice Department with regard to Haldeman and Ehrlichman, Nixon relays that information to his aides, so they can use it as a resource for scripting new scenarios and preparing their own legal defense. Nixon praises Peterson as a loyal soldier, but he betrays his faith and respect nonetheless.

Repeated references to the problem of public relations suggest that facts are seen not as objects to be respected but as symbols to be manipulated. They can be produced or denied, depending on the situation. Activity is of the same order. By late March the public was awash with evidence of misconduct in the Nixon administration. It is clear to the speakers in the Oval Office that "ordinary folks" are anxious for an authoritative interpretation of reality.

> EHRLICHMAN: Symbolically you've got to do something.
>
> NIXON: That's right. Do something so that I am out in front of this . . . They don't think the President is involved but they don't think he is doing enough.
>
> EHRLICHMAN: That's it. That's it . . . Ziegler is not sufficiently credible on this. (p. 373)

Thus the President made a televised statement to the American people assuring them that their best interests were his only interests, that his leadership was forthright and forceful. But his act was not motivated by a dedication to the public welfare. It was a matter of public relations, of cooling the mark out, of telling ordinary folk what they most wanted to hear. The President says to his aides:

> I mean to put the story out (by our) PR people. Here is the story. The true story about Watergate. (p. 151)

What governed Nixon's conduct through the months covered on the transcribed tapes was not what he as a leader owed to his public but what the public was likely to accept when spoken by their leader. He laments: "The problem is what the hell can I say publicly?" (p. 792) More specifically, what can he say that will salvage his image as a decisive and respected leader while at the same time he is immersed in a morass of criminal malfeasance?

Various scenarios are suggested to deal with the problem. Occasionally Ehrlichman or Dean suggest "the modified-limited hang-out road," a more or less open admission of the involvement on the part of his associates. But Nixon rejects this as too costly, depriving him of aid and counsel from his most trusted advisers in his time of greatest need. Not until Peterson made it obvious that the Justice Department had a strong case against Haldeman and Ehrlichman did Nixon agree to cut his losses and accept their resignations. But by then the original cover-up had collapsed. Charges had been made directly against the most powerful men in the CRP and the White House. The only one immune from public indictment was the man all these people had served: Richard Nixon. So while the cover-up unraveled, the techniques of impression management were a success. The President was tinged but not tarnished. New scenarios were scripted to deal with new problems. It took more than a year and the active participation of the Supreme Court before Nixon acknowledged defeat and resigned from office.

Properly scripted, a scenario establishes a credible image. It provides a benign accounting of discrediting facts and reinterprets what appears to be a failing as a virtue. In some cases it is sufficient just to speak to sustain a scenario. When the Senate investigating committee is established, John Dean and Richard Nixon weave a scenario in which Teddy Kennedy—a known Nixon enemy—is behind the Ervin Committee for partisan reasons. Dean says to the President:

> Leak this to the press and the parts and cast become much more apparent. (p. 94)

Quite simply, if the public thinks the Senate committee is motivated by partisan rather than principled reasons, Nixon's refusal to cooperate will be seen in a more benign light.

Some scenarios require more than just a facile tongue, but action is not the favored solution to a problem. Because scenarios must be fluid if they are to be operative and because decisive action sometimes hinders future options, the speakers in the Oval Office prefer to exert control by controlling others' definition of the situation. When carefully thought-out words alone will do this, they are given high priority. In addition, specially selected words are employed to motivate recalcitrant participants. These words are known as *strokes*. Discussing the Ervin Committee, the President asks: "Who is going to be the first witness up there?"

> DEAN: Sloan.
>
> NIXON: Unfortunate.
>
> DEAN: No doubt about it —
>
> NIXON: He's scared?
>
> DEAN: He's scared, he's weak. He has a compulsion to cleanse his soul by confession. We are giving him a lot of *stroking*. (p. 138, emphasis added)

A stroke makes the definition of the situation more palatable. It increases the likelihood that those whose cooperation is sought will come to the proper conclusions.

Strokes are a soft-line approach. Sometimes the speakers have to get tough, and they do this by *pushing*. Like the carrot and the stick, stroking and pushing are two ways to get others to do your bidding. Trying to figure out how the Watergate break-in became "operative," the President asks, "Who pushed?" Dean responds:

> I think Bob (Haldeman) was assuming they had something proper over there, some intelligence gathering operation that Liddy was operating. And through Strachan, who was his tickler, he started *pushing* them to get some information and they—Magruder—took that as a signal to go to Mitchell and say, "They are *pushing* us like crazy for this from the White House." And so Mitchell probably puffed on his pipe and said, "Go ahead," and never really reflected on what it was all about. (p. 179, emphasis added)

By the application of pressure, others are expected to carry out plans on their own initiative. Their superiors are absolved of responsibility for issuing direct commands. But pressure, strokes, and implicit definitions leave considerable room for misunderstandings: eager subordinates may carry out orders that had not been the express intent of their superiors. Discussing Dean's actions in the affair, Haldeman says:

> I can imagine having a discussion: "He ought to leave the country—maybe we ought to deep six (the incriminating documents)" . . . That's interesting that Dean would take that remark and go out and act on it. (pp. 934, 935)

Often, when "orders" come "from the White House," the express person "the White House" represents is never clarified. So subordinates may be getting commands from those who are equal or subordinate to themselves, rather than their superiors. Internal lines of power and authority become blurred; things never intended take place.

Because innuendo and implication can lead to misunderstandings and confusion, the speakers are occasionally called to decisive action. One way the principals may act is by the President's going on television and reading a prepared scenario that takes into account the charges that have been leveled against his administration, makes claim to action of some indeterminate kind, and reassures the public that the well-being of the nation will not suffer. The speakers in the Oval Office scripted a number of scenarios the President could present to the people, and some of these ultimately were issued, either by Nixon himself or by his media stand-in, Ron Ziegler.

Other times public pronouncements alone will not do. Ehrlichman tells the President:

> Well, we got two things. We got a press plan but it rests on some decisions you have to make; on sort of an action plan . . . My action plan would involve your suspension or firing Dean in the course of a historic explanation of your reliance on the Dean report (and) his apparent unreliability. (pp. 987, 989)

But action is not a favored option. Only rarely does the President, on his own initiative, give a direct order to his subordinates, as for example:

> NIXON: For your immediate thing, you've got no choice with Hunt but the hundred and twenty (thousand dollars) or whatever it is. Right?
>
> DEAN: That's right.
>
> NIXON: Would you agree that's the prime thing, that you damn well better get that done?

> DEAN: Obviously he ought to be given some signal anyway.
>
> NIXON: Well (expletive deleted) get it . . . (pp. 236-237)

Examples of such decisive actions are infrequent.

More important than action is the fabrication of documents. Documents stand as the irrefutable facts behind public pronouncements. They substantiate the spoken word. In the summer of '72 Nixon made claim to a documented investigation carried out by John Dean. That report, he said, fully assured the President that no one in the White House was involved in the burglary at the DNC. To plug the mass of leaks and revelations inundating the White House the following spring, Dean's "report" became relevant. It could be given to the Ervin Committee to take the heat off. The President asked Dean to produce the document that he (Nixon) made claim to in August. When Dean could not fake it, the document that had reassured the nation in the summertime became the cause of Dean's dismissal in the spring. The President instructs his counsel:

> NIXON: You've made a complete statement, but make it very incomplete. See, that is what I mean. I don't want too much chapter and verse as you did in your letter. I just want (it) general . . .You see, our own people have to have confidence or they are not going to step up and defend us. You see our problem there, don't you?
>
> DEAN: It is tremendous to have a piece of paper that they can talk from.
>
> NIXON: Pointing out that you are defending the Constitution; responsibility of the separation of powers. We have to do it. (pp. 168-169)

In the preparation of such documents there is no consideration of facts as opposed to impressions of facts. On repeated occasions Nixon instructs his aides to prepare a document, statement, or report in which the content of the statement is the form it takes. He says:

> You could say, "I have this and this is that." Fine. See what I am getting at . . . (p. 167)

> I have said this and that and the other thing and that's that. (p. 736)

> These are my conclusions, chit, chit, chit, chit. (*Hearings,* 1974b, p. 158)

Inconclusive and vague, what counts is the impression fostered: an open and forthright administration willing to answer inquiries and present evidence of its probity when called for. Documents substantiate these claims; they are the props referred to by the lines of the scenario.

In fact, sometimes lines must be carefully constructed lest they infer a document that does not exist. In preparing a public statement for Ron Ziegler to give to the press, the following exchange takes place:

> NIXON: Could we say this?
>
> EHRLICHMAN: No—I wouldn't.
>
> NIXON: Why not? Not true? Too defensive?
>
> EHRLICHMAN: Well, number one—it's defensive—it's self-serving. Number two—it establishes a piece of paper that becomes a focal point for a subpoena and all that kind of thing. (*Transcripts,* p. 389)

For the same reasons documents are not alluded to in all cases, they are destroyed in others. The massive clean-up operation that took place at the White House and the CRP after the burglary was to destroy documents that would have linked the Watergate burglars with heads of state. But documents, once fabricated, take on a legitimate social existence. Rights and obligations are associated with them; they embody the concept of contract. Those who destory them are suspect. William Rogers tells the President:

> You don't expect the head of the FBI to pick up and burn the damn stuff. You can always put it in your safe and say it is unrelated to the investigation. But burn it? Makes you look like a common crook. (p. 1163)

Thus care must be taken in referring to documentation that does not exist and in the way that documentation is handled once its existence becomes discrediting.

Finally, documentation is sometimes added to a line to give it more selling power. In preparing one of his public addresses, Nixon and Haldeman are drafting a statement:

> NIXON: "Four weeks ago we . . ." Why don't we say—shall we set a date? That sounds a hell of a lot stronger if we set a date.
>
> HALDEMAN: All right.
>
> NIXON: "On March 21, I began new inquiries." Strike that. "I ordered an investigation . . ." (p. 1121)

On the basis of documentation as casually fabricated as this Nixon maintained his defense that the first time he heard of misdeeds in the White House was on March 21, when Dean came to him and said: chit, chit, chit.

Not all impression management is teamwork, but the existence of a team adds credible support to the line any individual takes. The speakers in the Oval Office acted as a team, readily colluding with one another to establish an image of a worthy administration. In the context of the transcripts, the members of the White House team included the President as the star performer; Haldeman and Ehrlichman as principal teammates; and Dean, newly recruited to the citadel of power. In addition Ziegler and Mitchell are peripheral members, Rogers and Kleindienst confidants, and Peterson a service specialist co-opted from the Justice Department to help sustain the White House line. Through March and April Dean defects to the Justice Department, the President is stripped of his principal advisers, and Ziegler is promoted to the inner circle. This team—its strengths, its weaknesses, and its likely fate —is given as much attention in the Oval Office as are the scenarios the team will script.

Minor actors come and go through the pages of the transcripts. Among the principals there is constant concern with the loyality of those with whom they have transactions. Exchanges like the following are typical:

> DEAN: Strachan is as tough as nails. He can go in and stonewall, and say, "I don't know anything about what you are talking about." He has already done it twice you know, in interviews.
>
> NIXON: I guess he should, shouldn't he? I suppose we can't call that justice, can we?
>
> DEAN: Well, it is a personal loyalty to him . . . He didn't have to be told. He didn't have to be asked. (p. 146)

Similarly the loyalty of Liddy, Colson, Mitchell, Dean, Peterson, and even Ehrlichman is questioned at one time or another. However, only one member actually defects, and Nixon calls him "the deserter."

When not worring about one another's loyalty, the speakers spend considerable time reassuring one another:

NIXON: I told (Dean) . . . there is no question about people resigning around here. I've got their letters of resignation in hand any time I want them. Wasn't that the proper thing to say to him?

EHRLICHMAN: *That's fine.* (p. 818, emphasis added)

NIXON: Well, I'm not going to talk to (Peterson) any more about that. After all, I'm the President of the country—and I'm going to get on with it and meet Italians and Germans and all these others. You know, really —

ROGERS: *Oh, you do that* . . . (p. 1147, emphasis added)

Strokes are carefully calculated to motivate those who are not team members to take preordained courses of action. Signs of reassurance are more spontaneous attempts to maintain team solidarity by enhancing members' satisfaction and consoling their distress. In the transcripts reassurance most often goes from other team members to Nixon. But members also reassure one another, as when Ehrlichman tells Attorney General Kleindienst, "The enemy is not out to get you." (*New York Times* Staff, 1973, p. 808)

Scripting scenarios and mutual reassurance keep the participants together as a team. But members are not always cooperative. Schisms develop between Mitchell and Rogers, Colson and Dean, Mitchell and Haldeman and Ehrlichman. As leader, Nixon often says one thing to one set of associates and another to a second set, so as not to disrupt the team operation. As in a classic Greek drama, it is clear early in the conversations that someone will have to be sacrificed to satisfy the public demand that justice be seen. Specifically, since it is now known that seven Watergate burglars were not working as an independent organization but as the hirelings of the CRP, someone is going to have to take responsibility for giving them their orders. At first Mitchell seems the logical solution.

NIXON: Mitchell, you see, is never going to go in and admit perjury. I mean he may say he forgot about Hunt, Liddy and all the rest, but he is never going to (admit perjury).

HALDEMAN: They won't give him that convenience . . . unless they figure they are going to get you. He is as high up as they've got.

EHRLICHMAN: He's the big Enchilada. (*Transcripts,* p. 347)

But Mitchell is recalcitrant and uncooperative, so the next likely choice is Dean. The hope is that if Dean is removed from the White House, the public will not clamor for Haldeman and Ehrlichman as well. But Dean balks at being the lone scapegoat and insists that if he goes, the others must go also. When it is clear that he will not get his way, he defects from the White House to join the team at the Justice Department, where a case is being put together against the administration. Haldeman says:

> I think at some point, like you do on anything else, you gotta face up to the fact that the guy is either a friend or a foe—or a neutral. If he's a neutral you don't have to worry about him; if he's a friend you rely on him, and if he's a foe you fight him. This guy (Dean) it seems at this point is a foe. (pp. 1027-1028)

But he is not like any ordinary foe. Having once been a team member, he was privy to many of the secrets of team collusion. The considerable care Dean's removal requires motivates the President to speak:

> The real problem on this damned thing . . . I don't think that kicking Dean out of here is going to do it. Understand, I'm not ruling out kicking him out. But I think you got to figure what the hell does Dean know? *What kind of blackmail does he have?* (p. 992, emphasis added)

As a matter of fact, when he left the White House, Dean took a variety of documents with him: the Houston Plan, involving undercover operations such as firebombing the Brookings Institution; and the enemies list, a roster of people the White House believed were trying to get them. In turn, these documents became some of the most damaging evidence the President had to cope with.

Under the circumstances, the loss of Dean proved to be a considerable setback to the White House. By the end of the month Haldeman Ehrlichman, and Kleindienst resigned as well, and Nixon had to put together a new team to script the scenarios for the cover-up of the cover-up.

While they occupied the White House, Nixon's team was the most powerful in the nation. Representing the highest office in the land, they held the credulity of the American people. Ordinary folk were prepared to accept the President's definition of reality on faith, and the Nixon team counted on this faith as they scripted their scenarios. They also had access to various governmental agencies, giving authenticity to the claims they made. The Justice Department, the FBI, the CIA, and ranking Republicans in the Senate and House were at one time or another all called upon to sustain the line emanating from the White House. Added to this supporting cast were backers and donors willing to make cash contributions as needed. The speakers in the Oval Office did not want for assistance in their monumental endeavor.

In addition, there was unlimited access to the media. Once formulated, their message could be magnified. A staff of 60 persons managed public relations: dealing with the telephone calls of concerned congress-people; answering inquiries made by influential business leaders; drafting statements to be made by Nixon supporters in surrogate appearances; providing handouts and documents to the press. Investigative work on the part of some reporters continued through the spring as it had in fall and winter. But the Washington press corps in general seemed content to let the administration define the facts of life. They accepted their handout or briefing for the day, and the stories they wrote were based on the official statements provided by the Nixon team. The papers also printed every leak and revelation the investigatory bodies uncovered. But they themselves did not weave scenarios to account for the discrediting information. Such speculation was not considered within the province of a "responsible press." Thus the front pages of the papers looked much as they did during the Teapot Dome scandal of the Harding era. There were charges of corruption in high places, and there were denials of those allegations by influential speakers. The relationship of the two was not to be made clear to the readers of the American press for over a year. To some it was never clear.

Even more important than public relations and the newspapers was the medium of television. As President, Nixon had the power to preempt commercial programming on matters of national concern. The speakers in the Oval Office referred to this time when the President went on live television to plead his case directly as "the 9 o'clock news." The technique could not be used too frequently or it lost its dramatic effect. But during his administration, Nixon made use of the 9 o'clock news more frequently than he did the more traditional technique of the presidential press conference. The 9 o'clock news had a distinct advantage for him. He could elude his enemy—the working reporters—while he still got his message across to the American people. He could, in effect, abridge the First Amendment by usurping the critical powers of the press.

By mid-April it was obvious that something decisive had to be done to salvage the credibility of the administration. Nixon's choice was to go on television and make a dramatic pronouncement. As with his triumphant Checkers speech two decades before, he hoped to woo his audience in a reaffirmation of faith. After months of the most devious scheming ever recorded by modern electronic equipment, the President announced to the nation:

> I was determined that we should get to the bottom of the matter, and that the truth should be fully brought out . . . (that) public faith in the integrity of this office would have to take priority over all personal considerations . . . I want the American people . . . to know beyond the shadow of a doubt that during my terms as President, justice will be pursued fairly, fully and impartially, no matter who is involved. (pp. 1297, 1299)

He then announced the resignation of his aides and his Attorney General. With the exception of Dean, he praised them as loyal public servants whose misfortune it was to be tinged by a sordid affair. He located that sordid affair at the CRP, and thereby made claim to virtue on the part of the White House and, by implication, himself. It was a brilliant performance. Set against a bust of Lincoln on one side and a portrait of his family on the other, he played the role of a harried executive whose subordinates' zeal exceeded their judgment. Having admitted to running a loose operation, he would accept the responsibility of tightening up the shop. Then he waxed eloquent about the various noble goals he envisioned for the nation: jobs and opportunity, decency and civility. He took the offensive and demanded that the political process be reformed to rid it of the shoddy practices both sides had been guilty of. He urged the viewers to make these goals their goals. And he ended with a classic cry for help:

> I want these to be the best days in America's history because I love America . . .Tonight, I ask for your prayers to help me in everything that I do throughout the days of my Presidency to be worthy of their hopes and of yours. God bless America and God bless each and every one of you. (pp. 1307-1308)

The similarities between the Checkers speech and his performance in the spring of '73 are striking. In fact, the President and his supporters refer to his spring performance as "doing a Checkers Speech." In both instances Nixon presents himself as a man of integrity, forthright and forthcoming. He pleads to the nation to accept him as an affirmation of faith. But the success of his youth was not repeated. There were many who remained loyal to the bitter end and beyond, but there were many others who, with each new revelation, experienced doubt in the man they thought he was. Many of those saw that he had not answered the charges in his television appearance. And many who had no doubts up to that time had reservations thereafter. Rather than the conclusion of the Watergate affair Nixon hoped for, his spring performance was but a scene in a much larger scenario.

If not the dramatic success he envisioned, his television appearance soothed the nation for the time being. He lost ground in the opinion polls, but it was not until the following fall, with the firing of the Special Prosecutor, that any concerted display of public outrage was seen. So despite the failure of the various scenarios that were scripted in the Oval Office, despite the dissolution of the original Nixon team, despite the steady stream of discrediting information, the techniques of impression management he had used to get through the unraveling of the cover-up kept Nixon in high office for 16 months longer.

Sociologists writing at mid-century had seen the transformation of the moral order. They employed the metaphor of theater to describe its manifest attributes. But the drama they referred to was not linked to the sacred order of abstract principle. Instead it embodied more secular considerations of practical advantage.

It is possible to consider practical advantage a moral principle, as did Benjamin Franklin and other philosophers of the 18th century. But not all enlightened thinkers agreed. Joseph Butler and John Stuart Mill, for example, believed that virtues like prudence, temperance, thrift, and practicality did not constitute moral sentiments in that their immediate referent was the agent and not the community. Morals, they argued, can only come into play when the interests of others are at stake, when benefit ensues to the society, if not (necessarily) to the individual. They made a distinction between prudential and moral truths.(Ossowska, 1970) In contrast to prudential truths, moral truths embody the notion of surrender. To affirm the higher principle, the individual may have to act against personal interest. One example of such principled virtue is found in the medieval code of chivalry. In combat with his peers, a knight who dismounted his opponent dismounted himself, to keep the fight on fair footing. In eschewing his own advantage, the knight gave testimony to his commitment to the code of chilvalry. However, by the 18th century principled consideration for abstract values was no longer seen as the only virtue. It did not disappear completely, but alongside it emerged a version of ethics that embodied prudential truths as values in and of themselves. With the development of commerce and the growth of the middle class, prudence, thrift, self-reliance, practicality, and temperance came to be seen as ethical truths, and the individual who worked for his own advantage could claim to be as moral as anyone else.

As we have seen, the talk in the Oval Office was governed entirely by practical considerations. Occasionally the question of loyalty was raised, but this was loyalty to the immediate team and there was no reference to any community larger than that composed of the speakers themselves. Rather than principled men, these are game players, constantly seeking to win, unfettered by moral sentiments. At the same time, strategic advantage is found in the manipulation of symbols, especially the symbols of moral sentiment. Throughout his statements to the American public Nixon's speech is marked with allusions to integrity, fairness, truth, justice, the democratic process, legal and ethical standards, and so on. These terms evoke the impression the President wishes to convey of his action, but they are not a description of the principles he had in mind when he acted. Such terms become tokens in a game, to be manipulated to the speaker's advantage though not employed in the conduct of his affairs. In fact, the very disparity between his words and his deeds gives testimony to much baser motives of cynicism and hypocrisy.

Cynicism and hypocrisy are manifest in the way the speakers in the White House refer to the law. Although some of his advisers came from advertising, Nixon and other of his key men are trained lawyers. They have gone to accredited, respectable universities and passed the bar exams in their home states. Though their fields of specialization vary, each has been exposed to the philosophy of the law and the ethical principles the law seeks to uphold. Yet nowhere in the speech of these men are those principles reflected. When they are concerned with the law it is in the grossest terms:

> NIXON: They had never bugged Muskie, though, did they?
>
> DEAN: No, they hadn't, but they infiltrated . . . by a secretary.

NIXON: By a secretary?

DEAN: By a secretary and a chauffeur. There is nothing illegal
about that . . . (p. 180)

One of the major problems the '72 campaign faced was the legality of
the tactics the Nixon team used. On numerous occasions the President
and his advisers reflect on what took place, to assess criminal liability
after the fact. Dean gives an account of how the Liddy plan became
operative:

DEAN: So Liddy went back (to the CRP) . . . and tried to come
up with another plan that he could sell. They were talking to him,
telling him that he was putting too much money in it. I don't think
they were discounting the illegal points. Jeb (Magruder) is not
a lawyer. He did not know whether this is the way the game is
played and what it was all about. They came up, apparently, with
another plan, but they couldn't get it approved by anybody over
there. So Liddy and Hunt apparently came to see Chuck Colson and
Chuck Colson picked up the telephone and called Magruder and
said, "You all either fish or cut bait. This is absurd to have
those guys over there and not use them. If you are not going to use
them, I may use them." Things of this nature.

NIXON: Colson, you think, was the person who pushed? (pp.
177-178)

Though Magruder was not a lawyer, Mitchell, his superior, was. And
so were Liddy and Colson. But the legality of appropriate action
is not the question, as Dean suggests when he says: "Mitchell never
really reflected on what it was all about." (p. 179) All that was relevant
was practicality: money, personnel, and technology were available
to do whatever they wanted to do.

The President inquires where the money to finance the Liddy plan
came from. Dean tells him that Herb Kalmbach, Nixon's personal
lawyer, received $1,700,000 left over from the '68 campaign.

DEAN: That (money) came from New York and was placed in a safe
deposit box here . . . Ultimately, the money was taken out to California. He has spent a good deal of this money and accounting for it is
going to be very difficult. For example, he has spent close to $500,000
on private polling . . .

NIXON: Everybody does polling.

DEAN: That's right. There is nothing criminal about it. It's private
polling.

NIXON: People have done private polling all through the years.
There is nothing improper.

> DEAN: That's right. He sent $400,000 . . . somewhere in the South for another candidate. I assume this $400,000 went to Wallace.
>
> NIXON: Wallace?
>
> DEAN: Right. He has maintained a man who I only know by the name of "Tony" who is the fellow who did the Chappaquiddick study.
>
> NIXON: I know about that.
>
> DEAN: And other odd jobs like that. Nothing illegal, but close. I don't know of anything that Herb has done that is illegal . . . Herb's problems are politically embarrassing, but not criminal.
>
> NIXON: There is no illegality in having a surplus in cash after a campaign. (pp. 197-199)

The President is right in his conclusion. There is no statute or law prohibiting a political party from having an excess of funds. Nor is there a statute or law prohibiting "private polling," whatever that may be. Whether one political party can use funds to influence the campaign of an opponent—as was apparently done in the case of Wallace—may be an ambiguous question. But the speakers do not discuss it at any length. Nowhere, in fact, is there a studied consideration of statute and law, a careful reading of the legal codes the President and his official delegates are sworn to enforce. The Attorney General gives no reflection to the "intelligence plan" his hirelings and subordinates propose. The President raises no objections to perjury and blackmail. The law is seen as a mere technicality.

For lawyers to talk this way there must be some grave flaw in their formal education, or there must be a vast hiatus between their formal education and their practical affairs. Nixon and his team did not treat the law as a sacred covenant between free people and their government, but rather as an arbitrary set of regulations that could be eluded or overcome with proper preparation and adequate resources.

Questions of moral truth merely confused the President. He tells Dean:

> I talked to Peterson last night and he made exactly the same point. He said the obstruction (of justice) was morally wrong. No, not morally. He said it may not have been morally wrong and it may not have been legally wrong, but he said from the standpoint of the Presidency, I just can't have it. He seems to think obstruction of justice is a (expletive deleted) hard thing to prove. (p. 796)

There are many who would argue that obstruction of justice is wrong, period. When the personnel at the CRP began to destroy documents, when members of the White House staff began to make overtures to the FBI, when individuals lied to the various investigating bodies, the objective of a just determination of the facts was frustrated. But for Nixon the question is not so obvious. It was not merely that a few papers were shredded, a few hints made to the investigators, a few untruths told under oath. Assessed against these technicalities was the objective of those who had hastily constructed the cover-up: the reelection of Richard Nixon as President of the United States of America. The Nixon team acted in ways that were pragmatic, expedient, and necessary to secure their candidate's reelection. As practical men and consummate game-players, they made use of the advantages their lofty positions, their institutional power, and their surplus cash offered them. In a prudential sense, they could consider themselves as moral as anyone else.

The techniques of impression management Nixon so adroitly employed in furthering his personal career had their roots in ceremonial dramas that once affirmed the moral order. What separates Richard Nixon from the primitive witch doctor are thousands of years of human history, in which the growth of technology repeatedly transformed the objective possibilities of the world, and the shrewd were quick to grasp the advantage. The balance between the sacred and the secular, always precarious, gradually shifted to the side of practical considerations. The abstract principles that once dominated the human mind were transformed into traditional symbols, capable of evoking moral sentiments, but not of motivating moral actions. The heights of civilization envisioned by the ancient Greeks, by the Renaissance, by the Enlightenment, by the 19th century Social Darwinists, and by the 20th century Positivists —all would remain but a dream, in spite of the technological resources that flourished. If there is a lesson to be learned in the backstage talk of the most powerful men in the modern world, it is that abstract principles are worthless when there is material advantage to be gained.

This talk was not the cloistered ravings of the President. It included words spoken on public occasions and to public officials, all of whom were willing to buy the illusionary propositions their leader offered. In this sense Nixon was more like a conman than a shaman. Both the shaman and the conman are concerned with impression management. But the shaman looks out for the well-being of his audience, while the conman looks to take the sucker every time. The power and influence Richard Nixon had access to depended on others affirming his right to office. Unlike hereditary kings whose tenure is secured by monarchical right, Richard Nixon was the President of a country governed by enlightened democratic process. There were rule-governed procedures that gave him access to power, and there were rule-governed procedures that could deny him those rights. But those rule-governed procedures were in turn governed by the disposition of the citizens and their duly elected representatives. And those various bodies were loath to act. They bought the President's line every time. Despite the discrediting facts that began to emerge after the burglary of the DNC, the public reelected Nixon by an overwhelming majority. Despite the revelations that poured forth through the following spring and summer, there was no public outcry until the fall. It was not for another seven months, with the release of the transcripts, that Nixon's public support visibly crumbled. Thus we can only conclude that whatever Richard Nixon's performance implied about his understanding of the world, he shared that understanding with his public. Quite simply, the conman can take the mark only if the mark himself has larceny in his heart. The President could take the citizens only if the citizens themselves were willing to go along with the scenarios he wove. He did not outrage the sense of public decency because the public itself knew that claims of "decency" were a sham. People of influence in the community did not take up the cause of impeachment because they shared the version of the moral order Richard Nixon represented. It was to everyone's advantage to go along with the impression he fostered. Those who dissented were powerless to sway public opinion. So for two years the excesses of Watergate went on, while Richard Nixon made decisions for America in international affairs, and parents taught children virtue at home. When it was all over, people claimed that his resignation was testimony that the system worked. But it was never clear what system they were referring to.

Chapter 10
Metaphor and Innuendo
in Everyday Talk

Talk in the Oval Office is classic backstage talk. With the exception of the President's overriding concern with history, the speakers address no other audience than themselves. They are free to let their hair down and reveal themselves in ways they would conceal if they knew outsiders would be privy to their speech. However, the elaborate electronic equipment Nixon installed and the transcripts he made public transformed that backstage talk into documented evidence. It is possible for "outsiders" to examine systematically the intimate world view of the Nixon administration.

A word of caution is necessary. Because the transcripts are a unique document, it is difficult to assess the significance of their contents. There is no way of telling whether this particular style of talk is unique to Richard Nixon, his aides and associates, or whether the metaphor and innuendo he employed are characteristic of some or all administrations. Throughout the Watergate revelations and in his various public appearances after his fall from office, Nixon maintained that he did nothing any different than any other American president. But the transcriptions of his backstage conversations have no comparison in any other administration, and without comparable records for other presidents there is no way of assessing how unique or how general this style may be.

Accounts of the Kennedy and Johnson administrations suggest that, like Nixon, these men routinely employed a tough metaphor in the company of their intimates. (See, for example: Bradlee, 1975; Kearns, 1976.) So it may be that, like the career of Richard Nixon, the language of the 37th President is in fact a typical representation of a social process—how men come into power in America in the 20th century.

Sociolinguistics is the study of linguistic codes. It seeks to identify the characteristics of speech patterns and, from these, make inferences to the speakers or the speech setting. Using the methods of sociolinguistics, the present chapter investigates the major social institutions represented in the backstage speech of the Oval Office: the presidency, the family, and crime. School, church, law, business, art, music, philosophy or science are of no specific interest to these men. It must be remembered that these transcripts cover only the period when the President and his men conspired to obstruct justice, and so frequent reference to crime can be expected. However, the particular linguistic code these men employed in their discussion of crime is not the juristic code of the lawyer nor the academic code of the sociologist. It is the underworld code of the gangster.

The discovery of gangster talk in the Oval Office led me to look for some social force that supports this particular linguistic code and to look at the consequences it has for decision-making in government. I have called this social force "the male metaphor," and I have addressed it in terms of the administration's image of a "real man" and its style of "men's talk."

The Presidency

Along with the eagle and the flag, the presidency is a visible symbol of American unity. Heterogeneous in its origins, vast in its territory, the entire country is nonetheless represented in the person of the

President. Of all the elected officers of the republic, only the President is selected by voters from every part of the nation. Citizens from sea to sea know his name even when they do not know the name of their local representatives. Thus the country speaks most directly through the President, and he in turn speaks for the country. Furthermore, the wisdom, compassion, and foresight of the person who occupies this office provide reassurance, guidance, and direction to the nation as a whole in troubled times.

As the 37th President, Richard Nixon was the concrete manifestation of these abstract principles from his election in 1968 to his resignation in 1974. He was vocal in articulating domestic priorities and active in negotiating foreign affairs. He regularly and routinely appeared on television to interpret the state of the world to the nation and to attest to his own loyal devotion to duty.

In fact, never had the voters of a free republic had such an intimate view of their leader, spokesman, and titular head. In his frequent television appearances, the 37th President looked the citizens directly in the eye and articulated what stood as the official version of national reality. But over the course of his downfall it became apparent that an intimate view of his countenance was not an inside view of his character; between his public presentations and his backstage machinations there was an abyss of immeasurable proportions. In spite of published revelations, in his resignation speech, Nixon continued to maintain his dedicated loyalty to the nation he represented. Forthright and forceful, he said:

> In all the decisions I have made in my public life, I have always tried to do what was best for the Nation . . . I regret deeply any injuries that may have been done in the course of the events that led to this decision (to resign). I would say only that if some of my judgments were wrong, and some were wrong, they were made in in what I believed at the time to be the best interest of the nation. (*Washington Post* Staff, 1974, pp. xi, xiii)

By then many citizens believed he had betrayed them. But he admitted to no wrongdoing other than poor judgment. He continued to proclaim his basic honesty and integrity and assert his principled dedication to the office he held and the nation he served.

Were such an affirmation a valid description of the man who made it, we would expect to see the importance of the presidency reflected in his private talk as well as in his public proclamations. But such is not the case. The social institution of "the Presidency" is mentioned only occasionally in the transcripts, while the social institution of the family is mentioned frequently. Although Nixon publicly claimed to have the best interests of the nation at heart, when he speaks in private his concerns are about family affairs.

On rare occasions there are flashes of genuine concern about the country he is responsible for. In considering one plausible scenario Nixon says:

> Let's look at the future. How bad would it hurt the country, John, to have the FBI so terribly damaged? (Nixon, 1974, p. 128, hereafter referred to as *Transcripts*)

Dean replies, "I am convinced the FBI isn't everything the public thinks it is" (pp. 128-129), thereby reassuring Nixon that if he has to sacrifice the credibility of the FBI in order to maintain his own credibility as President, it will be no great loss to the country.

As often as the speakers can be found expressing genuine concern about the office of the presidency, they can be found joking and mocking it. These men do not make jokes very often (although they play frequent pranks), so the frequency with which the presidency is a topic of humor is significant. In the following example Ehrlichman weaves a scenario to get Mitchell to take the rap for the Watergate fiasco. He tells Nixon:

> EHRLICHMAN: The President calls Mitchell into his office. He says, "John, you've got to do this. Here are the facts: bing, bing, bing, bing." And you pull this paper out here. "You've got to do this." And Mitchell stonewalls you. He says, "I don't know why you're asking me down here. You can't ask a man to do a thing like that. I need a lawyer. I don't know what I am facing. You just really can't expect me to do this." So the President says, "Well, John, I have no alternative." And with that the President calls the U.S. Attorney and says, "I, the President of the United States of America and leader of the Free World, want to go before the Grand Jury on Monday."
>
> NIXON: I won't even comment on that.
>
> HALDEMAN: That's a silly (scenario). (pp. 438-439)

There is little linguistic evidence to suggest that the President and his men take the symbolic significance of the office seriously, for even in moments when the far-reaching consequences of the office are referred to apologies are appended. The President says:

> You know I was just thinking tonight as I was making up my
> notes for this little talk, you know, what the hell, *it is a little
> melodramatic,* but it is totally true that what happens in this office
> in these next four years will probably determine whether there is
> a chance you could have some sort of an uneasy peace for the
> next 25 years. And that's my—whatever legacy we have, hell, it isn't
> going to be in getting a cesspool for Winnetka, it's going to be there
> (in international affairs). (p. 653; emphasis added)

In this remark the President acknowledges humility with respect to his own pretenses and orders the priorities that command his attention. Whatever the voters of the nation expected when they elected him to office, it was not his purpose to serve their domestic interests but to look after his own reputation in the arena of foreign affairs.

Similarly, in planning how to deal with Watergate as the story breaks through the spring, Nixon considers making a public statement:

> NIXON: (The public statement) isn't going to be done tonight or
> tomorrow night. We can't get it done that fast.
>
> HALDEMAN: I don't think you want to anyway. I think you want
> to end the war and freeze food prices and then (make a statement
> about Watergate). (p. 355)

Again, national priorities are ordered, with foreign affairs first, domestic concerns second, and the facts third—if at all.

For Nixon and his men the sentiments associated with the symbols of the presidency are manipulated as though they were the pawns on a chess board. They are manipulated publicly to convince the nation that the administration is a worthy one, and they are manipulated privately to convince members of that administration to accede to the party line. In trying to get cooperation from Dean, the President invokes "the Country" as a loyalty higher than whatever loyalty his hireling might owe to Nixon personally. Again, when Nixon is assessing the disposition of various members of his team to perjure themselves on his behalf, the following exchange takes place:

> HALDEMAN: I just think (Colson) will do everything he can do
> not to hurt the President.
>
> NIXON: Yeah. That has got to be true of everybody because it
> isn't the man, it's the Office. (p. 483)

Through the course of the Watergate revelations, Nixon occasionally worries about the credibility of the presidency, about tarnishing the image of the office. But in contrast to his strong public reassurances to the nation, his private talk does not demonstrate a deep and abiding concern with the cultural meanings of the office he held.

The Family

Contrary to his public posture, Nixon had little regard for the domestic concerns of the nation. In his private talk with his aides and associates he routinely denegrates the office of the presidency and the principles of unified interest that office symbolizes. In contrast, the domestic concerns of the nuclear family are routinely a topic of talk.

The family is the social institution most frequently referred to by the speakers in the Oval Office and the one held in highest regard. Numerous examples can be given. Nixon makes occasional references to members of his own family—his wife, his daughters, and his "poor, dumb brother." Sometimes he refers to members of his administration as part of the "presidential family" in a metaphorical sense. His aide, Ehrlichman, jokes:

> Our *Brother* Mitchell brings us some knowledge on executive privilege. (p. 277, emphasis added)

With the exception of secretaries, women are referred to only in conjunction with the family, as in the expression "wives and children." Sometimes lower level functionaries in the CRP and the White House are referred to as "kids" or, alternatively, "our little boys." What rare terms of endearment as are exchanged among these men are drawn from family imagery. Ehrlichman's half of the dialogue in a telephone conversation with Attorney General Kleindienst contains the following expressions:

> Yes . . . A list . . . Okay *my boy.* I just wanted you to have a nice time this evening . . . Don't forget, *my tender,* that if there is any way that any of this hearsay of mine I have collected is in any way useful, I would be glad to make it available . . . That is why I am calling you, *my dear* . . . Well you are my favorite law enforcement officer. (p. 635; emphasis added)

The administration's defense of the payments of cash to the Watergate defendants is based on the line that the money went to support the interests of the wives and children of the accused. Ehrlichman says:

> Well, you had defendants who were concerned about their families.
> That's understandable. You had lawyers who were concerned about
> their fees and that's less understandable. (p. 676)

In talking about considerations of clemency, the President says:

> I have a right to say—take a fellow like Hunt (whose wife had died)
> or a Cuban whose wife is sick or something—isn't that right to give
> them clemency for that purpose? (p. 811)

Thus the existence of men's families provides justifications that surpass individual self-interest. As long as the Watergate defendants have families, the money paid to them is not necessarily going to buy their silence, but to support their dependents. As long as families suffer misfortunes of one sort or another, there are other grounds to provide cash than just recognition of loyalty to some common enterprise between the defendants and their supporters.

This principled use of the family and its misfortunes was evinced in the vice presidential confirmation hearings of Nelson Rockefeller as well as in the backstage talk in the Oval Office. When questioned about the enormous gifts and loans he made to various public employees at times in his own career in public service, Rockefeller accounted for the payments by invoking family troubles of one sort or another. One man's wife was sick, another's child had problems. One was nearing the age of retirement and had not yet established a secure estate for his family. The money was provided in deference to the man's domestic responsibilities—as an act of charity—and not in deference to the man's loyalty or support of the Rockefeller cause. This was the line the vice presidential nominee presented in the Senate hearings, and this is the account the senators and the nation accepted.

Although publicly extolled as the basic institution in society, the family is not important because of any intrinsic values it perpetuates. Rather its importance comes from the fact that it is a socially acceptable justification, to be invoked when justifications are called for.

The family is useful for other reasons as well. The speakers in the Oval Office represent a male world, and more will be said of this later. While ties to the domestic circle and the feminine interests the home represents give legitimacy to the men's accounts of benign or altruistic motives, they also establish vulnerabilities. Men's families may be treated as soft spots when it is necessary to apply pressure. Thus one way to evoke compliance is to threaten a man's family interests. Talking about how Strachan was being treated by the Justice Department, Ehrlichman reports to the President:

> He called to get advice. He said they really worked him over, said
> stuff as, "Listen Strachan, you're going to jail; think about your
> wife, think about your baby and how would you like to be disbarred,
> and — " (p. 933)

Women are soft spots for the Nixon team. The cover-up requires
the implicit cooperation of large numbers of people. Some, like secretaries,
are peripheral in terms of their power and influence, but nonetheless
they are privy to consequential information. Hence their importance
to the cover-up far exceeds their ordinary importance in men's affairs.
Secretaries may infiltrate campaigns, provide leaks to media, and break
under questioning, all relevant considerations for the White House men.
They see the secretaries as a potential pool of "stupid human errors,"
and Dean says:

> There are a lot of *weak* individuals and it could be one of those who
> crosses (us) up: the *secretary* to Liddy, the *secretary* to Jeb Magruder.
> Chuck Colson's *secretary,* among others. (pp. 253-254; emphasis
> added)

Similarly in their role as wives, women are potential liabilities.
They are important to maintain men's images of social responsibility,
but they cannot always be trusted to uphold the men's view of the world.
Dean tells the President:

> When I say this is a growing cancer, I say it for reasons like this.
> Bud Krogh, in his testimony before the Grand Jury, was forced to
> perjure himself. He is haunted by it. Bud says, "I have not had a
> pleasant day on my job." He said, "I have told my wife all about
> this. The curtain may ring down one of these days, and I may have
> to face the music, which I am perfectly willing to do."(p. 195)

Although the President responds by saying, "Perjury is an awful hard
rap to prove" (p. 196), the implications of Dean's words are clear. If
wives begin putting pressure on their husbands to surrender to the
principles of justice, the cover-up is likely to unravel.

In repeated and various ways the family is invoked as a relevant
consideration in the transcribed talk. These men may not speak to one
another as though God or the law were relevant to their interests, but
they do talk as though there were no question of a man's loyalty to the
family. The existence of the family gives testimony to interests that
surpass the personal interests of one man alone, and hence it provides
grounds for men to argue the altruistic basis of their actions. When offered
as a public account, family interests constitute legitimate interests;

questioning their sincerity is socially taboo. A man who has a wife and family is by definition a man who acts in interests greater than his own.

Nixon and his associates make rare mention of any interests beyond those of the the domestic circle. Neither the community nor the nation poses relevant considerations that conflict with or supersede those of the nuclear family. In this very limited view of the meaning of altruism, the speakers in the Oval Office evince a pattern similar to that identified as "amoral familism" by Edward Banfield in his study of impoverished peasants in southern Italy (Banfield, 1958).

Amoral familism is a syndrome of thought and action that conceives of the world in terms of hostile and benign forces. Those who stand outside the small circle of the nuclear family are potential competitors and therefore potential enemies. Those who stand within the domestic circle are allies. In this version of the universe all the forces of evil are located outside the family, while goodness consists only in working and sacrificing for the family. As a result of this attitude, the villagers in Banfield's study were unable to cooperate or act together for any objective transcending the material interests of their immediate families. At home they were loyal and devoted, but in community affairs they were hostile and indifferent. The law was disregarded when there was no reason to fear punishment, and in everyday affairs there was no connection between abstract principles and concrete behavior.

Banfield explains this world view of the peasants of Montegrano (a fictional name) by pointing to the impoverished conditions of their material circumstances. The speakers in the Oval Office are neither impoverished nor powerless, but they invoke the same idiom. Although vested with the responsibility for leadership and direction of a powerful industrial nation, the members of the Nixon administration talk as though the only relevant loyalties are those of the immediate family. They talk as though they were amoral familists.

Deference to familial concerns is evident in Nixon's private talk, and again in his *Memoirs*. However, in the conflict between his personal career and his family interests, the latter have routinely suffered. During the first period in New York City, when he was outside the public arena and his daughters were grown but not married, he was most involved in doing homey things. But even then there were trips abroad for Pepsi Cola and trips at home for the Republican Party, and at no time was the family the dominant interest in his life.

Once in the White House, Nixon took many trips to San Clemente and Key Biscayne, sometimes with his wife and sometimes with his married daughters. But in the accounts of these family trips there is little to suggest that this was a family taking mutual pleasure in one another's company. Whether on vacation or in its residences, the members of the Nixon famiy were as likely to spend time alone as they were to spend time with one another. They never mixed socially with other families. When the President desired to relax, to take it easy and enjoy himself, he was more likely to spend time with Bebe Rebozo than with Pat and the girls.

Despite the deference paid to the family as a noble institution in his public and private speech, Nixon's own family was not close except in times of crisis. Yet biographers routinely invoke the term "close" to describe the Nixon family. After writing a favorable, although not flattering, biography, Mazo (1959) concludes that Nixon is "a doting father and a thoughtful husband" (p. 235). The only evidence he presents in support of this contention is that Nixon remembers birthdays and anniversaries, and that occasionally he, his wife, and their daughters concoct surprises for each other. In a more recent family portrait, Safire concludes:

> The Nixons reflect something Americans need, both as symbol and as truth: a close family life . . . A man with a lifelong helpmeet and well-raised kids, who bring in upright in-laws, can't be all bad. (Safire, 1975, pp. 611-612)

Despite this idealized description of Nixon family life, Safire titles his chapter on Pat Nixon "Alone Together." Again, the author brings few examples to suggest this is an intimate family and more to suggest that it is at most a formal family, where the roles of husband, wife, and offspring are stylized performances.

The few glimpses of domesticity Safire provides embody imagery such as the following:

> When the private office in the Executive Office Building was newly decorated, a beige silk ottoman was placed in front of the easy chair. Going over a speech, the President wanted to stretch out; he went to the bathroom, came back with a towel, and spread it over the new silk before putting his feet up, undoubtedly because his wife made him feel guilty about ruining furniture. (p. 611)

Here is a portrait of a man dominated in his rare moments at home and dominating the world beyond the domestic circle. Safire continues:

> In times of stress, he would flatly forbid (Pat) to read the news-
> papers or look at the television news, which she accepted with
> relief. Julie would then tell her what she needed to know. (p. 611)

Similarly, through the course of the Watergate revelations, Nixon denied his family access to the truth with the same thoroughness he denied the facts to the nation. So if this was a close family, that closeness was not predicated on mutual experience nor on shared views and objectives.

However, if they were not sharing time, company, and innermost experiences, members of the Nixon family were bound together by intense ties of loyalty. Nixon's wife and daughters routinely supported his claims to being a devoted husband and father. They regularly rallied to his defense in time of trouble. In an essay published in *Ladies Home Journal* in the spring before his resignation, Tricia wrote:

> Richard Nixon is a man who has never lied, not even a white lie, to
> his family or to the American people. He has told us that he was not
> a part of the Watergate episode . . . His word is his bond . . . Why
> are the accusers doing this cruel thing to my father and the
> country? Is jealousy the name of this dangerous game? . . . I think
> that history will record that Watergate was a politically motivated
> matter . . . These people wanted to be rid once and for all of
> Richard Nixon, to satisfy their own jealousy of a man who by his
> accomplishments reminded them of their own ineptitude and
> failure. (Cox, 1974, pp. 136, 164)

Through the course of the Wategate revelations, Julie was a regular speaker on behalf of her father's cause, and after his resignation she continued to rally behind him, as did his wife. So even in disgrace the members of Nixon's family were bound by intense ties of loyalty. They praised his conduct in foreign affairs and berated his detractors. They insisted he was misunderstood and hence misjudged, and they spoke out publicly in an attempt to set the record straight. If we are to understand the chroniclers' descriptions of the Nixon family as a "close" family, it is in this sense. What tied the Nixons together as a social unit was their devoted loyalty to the head of the family and not the shared experiences of the members.

Those experiences the Nixons did share were shaped by decisions of a patriarchal nature. Despite Pat's express and continued dissatisfaction with public life, and despite her husband's written promises to resign, Nixon continued to pursue public office, and his wife resigned herself to his order of priorities. She reflects in an interview:

> I used to catch myself resenting the fact that Dick's time with
> the family was so limited, but then I would say to myself, his work
> is what's important now—we can wait. (Feldman, 1975, p. 75)

Through a multitude of public engagements she stood by his side, a pleasant if pained expression on her face. At campaign dinners and affairs of state she sat by influential Republicans and foreign dignitaries, making conversation about matters that had no meaning in her life. Throughout her husband's public career she was a devoted helpmeet, and this was the image of solidarity the First Family projected to the nation.

The deference paid to the family by the men of the Nixon administration did not involve respect for the tender values embodied in domestic life. The speakers in the Oval Office did not respect compassion, pity, conciliation, cooperation, or any other so-called feminine virtue. Rather, what makes the family important to these men is that it gives them a respectable image. It was a useful token to deploy on the campaign trail. Its existence could be used to cover activities that might otherwise be maliciously interpreted. If need be, the fate of a man's family could be used as a threat. The family was important in social life because it served men's interests and not because it made an important contribution in its own right.

Similarly, women were important because their existence made the family possible. Though accorded symbolic respect, women have only a peripheral place in the male world. Other than to reassure and support him, the only woman to play an active part in Nixon's public career was his secretary, Rose Mary Woods. In his attempt to save himself from disgrace during the Watergate revelations, she was entrusted the sensitive task of listening to and transcribing the taped talk. But her voice was never documented as a part of those transactions. When the 18½-minute gap was disclosed, she was the one expected to take the blame, although it was clear she never had any part in the backstage machinations of the Nixon administration. When she refused to take the rap, General Alexander Haig was forced to invoke "sinister forces" to account for the erasure.

Men's Talk

In some cultures the lives of men and the lives of women are so separate that each has a special language to refer to the values, aspirations, and organizing principles that govern their respective interests. For the most part, men and women in America speak the same language, but this linguistic homology obscures conventional differences in their respective life-spaces. The division of labor and the separation of home and work have effectively produced two distinct versions of reality in America—a man's world and a woman's world—and each is characterized by its own organizing principles and value hierarcy.

The locus of the men's world is the community, the broader social network. The locus of the women's world is the family, the narrow domestic circle. Classic Judeo-Christian thought sanctions this division of practical affairs. In that interpretation of reality woman's sole purpose in life is to breed, to reproduce new members who could be deployed originally in the service of the tribe, and as society became more complex in the service of various social institutions such as the military, business, or government. Though the network of social institutions expanded through the centuries, the opportunities for women remained restricted. The only institutional domain in which they had an unquestioned place was the family. Yet this place is of little consequence. Even though the family is routinely invoked as a moral virtue when accounts are called for in the men's world, it is rarely influential in determining men's actions. Instead, the sentiments associated with domestic life and with the women who make that institution possible, are routinely denigrated. The family may offer periodic refuge from the competitive principles that govern men's affairs, but the compassion and humanitarian sentiments women are expected to embody have no value beyond the domestic circle. Rather, achievement, competition, authority, dominion, power, and will characterize the masculine world view, and masculine interests dominate most social institutions in America.

While exceptional women may live their lives as independent agents, most women play an auxiliary role to men. A woman's status in society is defined by being her husband's wife, and her duty is fulfilled by being the mother of his children and the caretaker of his domicile. Outside the family setting women may be encouraged to cultivate humanitarian interests, such as providing aid and comfort to the sick, the aged, the orphaned, and the distressed. But even here women are at best nurses for the casualties of the masculine world, where the dominant imagery is warfare and combat. In this world of men there is no place for compassion or pity except after the fact. To get by you have to be tough; to get ahead you have to be ruthless.

Since the everyday affairs of business and government, military and the media are governed by masculine interests, women who participate in these enterprises are expected to pay deference to male virtue and suppress any soft sentiments they may naturally harbor. Thus men who excell in the competitive arena are ultimately respected by both sexes. In the argot of the prison, they are *real men.*

Portrait of a Real Man

G. Gordon Liddy exemplifies the model of the *real man.* Of the seven men originally indicted in the Watergate break-in, only Liddy refused to cooperate with the prosecution. In his refusal he demonstrated that principled devotion to masculine duty that is the male ideal. At that time he was 42 years old, and although his career had not been spectacular, he had been steadily rising in authority and power in the federal bureaucracy. His prison sentence seriously interrupted his life.

The son of a professional father, Liddy had been to prep school, college, and law school, with time out for war in Korea. After his gradua-tion from law school he joined the FBI, where he worked as a special agent for five years. In fundamental ways his early manhood is dominated by the same social institutions that played a part in Richard Nixon's development: law school, warfare, the FBI, and eventually politics.

Accounts vary as to why he left the FBI. Some say he was too zealous as an agent, and he was terminated lest he embarrass the organization (Roemer, 1973). Others—such as his wife—say he left for financial reasons, that the pay of an FBI agent was not adequate to support his family in a fashionable manner (Liddy, 1973). For whatever reason, in 1962 Liddy moved his family to New York, where he joined his father in private law practice in the city, and his wife looked after his children and took care of his suburban home.

Public visibility of the counterculture was at its peak in 1966. Poets and sages like Bob Dylan and Timothy Leary were articulating an ideo-logical alternative to the gothic world view. Auto bumpers blossomed with maxims such as "Make Love Not War." This was also the year Gordon Liddy decided to begin a career in politics. He was a man in his mid-thirties with a secure professional position and a wife and five children to support. Nevertheless, he chose to take a position as Assistant District Attorney in Dutchess County, New York, at a considerable cut in pay. His wife had worked her way through college before her marriage, and now she was forced to return to work to help support her family. She suffered deprivations, but in her role of wife, her first duty was to be loyal to her husband's interests, and at this time his interests lay in politics and drugs.

As a prosecuting attorney, Liddy was responsible for numerous police raids on Timothy Leary's Dutchess County estate, as well as for arrests, indictments, and general harassment of the counterculture guru and his associates. Liddy himself became an outspoken foe of the "international drug conspiracy," and on this platform he ran for public office. He did not win a congressional seat, but he did win a reputation as a tough fighter in the battle against the drug menace. Soon after he ran for public office, he was offered a position as a special assistant to the Secretary of the Treasury, in charge of the federal drug enforcement program. So he moved his family again, this time to an affluent suburb of Washington. In his position with the Treasury Department, he organized and directed Operation Intercept, an abortive attempt to curb the drug traffic by inspecting every vehicle that crossed the Mexican border. As many anticipated when the program was first proposed, it was a fiasco. It congested traffic, brought business to a standstill, and upset the Mexican tourist economy. It did little to stop the drug traffic, although it drove up the price of drugs on the street. The only manifest success of Operation Intercept was in public relations. It made headlines daily and thereby provided demonstrable evidence that the federal government and the incumbent administration were actively doing something against the threat of illegal drug use.

Useful to the Treasury Department as a drug fighter, Liddy had a personal pride in, and outspoken position on, guns that eventually brought him into conflict with his superiors, who advocated control and restraint. Dismissed from the Treasury Department, within weeks he secured a position as the "drug expert" on John Ehrlichman's domestic staff.

At meetings of the Bureau of Narcotics and Dangerous Drugs, Liddy claimed to represent "the White House," although his official position was assistant to Egil Krogh, himself but the President's assistant's assistant. Yet slender ties are sufficient ties for a man of ambition. In his niche in the White House he gradually made a name for himself.

Under Krogh's direction he was involved in programs of domestic espionage and, later, when assigned to the CRP, he was mastermind of the break-in of the DNC. For his part in that operation and for his refusal to cooperate with the authorities, he was sentenced to a 6-to-20-year term in prison and served the longest sentence of any of the men convicted in the Watergate scandal.

Liddy's personal career exemplifies the ascent to power of an ambitious, aggressive man who saw an issue in the drug scare and found a way to capitalize on it. But Liddy was more than just opportunistic. He was also principled. Although his arrest on criminal charges critically jeopardized his career opportunities, he refused to cooperate with the prosecution to mitigate his own circumstances. He showed himself the loyal soldier who gives only his name, rank, and serial number. His wife described him as a hero. The administration he served expressed respect:

> NIXON: How the hell does Liddy stand up so well?
>
> DEAN: He's a strange man, Mr. President.
>
> NIXON: Strange or strong?
>
> DEAN: Strange and strong. His loyalty is—I think it is just beyond the pale . . .
>
> NIXON: He hates the other side, too, doesn't he?
>
> DEAN: Oh, absolutely! He is strong. He really is. (*Transcripts*, p. 150)

Professional criminals also held Liddy in high esteem. Interviewed in prison, they praised his qualities by comparing him with another ambitious, aggressive man—Charles Colson.

> Liddy is a man among men . . . Look at Colson. A successful young man on the go. Without scruples, as long as he's wielding the hammer . . . but when it goes against him, he runs like a scared tabby cat. Where to? To Jesus. (Terkel, 1974, p. 34)

For two years Liddy's principled silence stood as the mark of his dedicated loyalty. Then, in a letter ostensibly written to his wife though paid for and published by *Harper's* magazine, Liddy gave his own interpretation of the masculine virtues he embodied.

In that letter he describes life as a battlefield, a contest, a struggle. In support of his vision of the universe, he quotes poetry: how in accordance with the law of the Yukon, the weak perish and the fit flourish. He writes that in a hostile, indifferent world the individual finds himself absolutely alone with only his strength and his will to pit against the forces that oppose and oppress him. So the contest not only weeds the fit from the unfit, it tests each individual's character in the process. Eventually, through this embattled process of natural selection, only the elite survive, and the world is a better place because of it. Liddy concludes that the application of compassion or pity only slows the inevitable law of nature; it can never arrest it.

What motivates a man to endure hardships is the simple desire to win. Here Liddy's vision is shared by many others, even those less principled than himself. For Richard Nixon and the White House and CRP staffs, all that mattered was winning. Nixon's successor shared the same ambition. Ford is quoted as saying:

> I sincerely doubt if I ever suited up (for college football) without the the total commitment of going out there to win. Not to get exercise, gold or glory, but simply to win. (*San Francisco Examiner*, 12/11/74)

When success consists only in overcoming the opposition, it is rational to be ruthless, tough, aggressive, and strong; and these are the virtues Liddy extols in his letter to his wife. She, in return, respects his version of the universe:

> Gordon writes me really beautiful love letters, one every day. He also writes the children and on the outside of their envelopes he always prints the same message: "Win!" (Liddy, 1973, p. 138)

Acceding to his definition of reality his wife will teach his children how to interpret his incarceration as akin to his being a prisoner of war. And they, in turn, will defend their father whenever the opportunity arises.

Men's Talk in the Oval Office

Liddy was useful to the White House because he represented the ideal of a *real man*. His reputation gave him entre to positions where closer scrutiny of his credentials might have barred him. Despite the questionable termination of his positions at the FBI and the Treasury Department, he was attractive to the Nixon team insofar as he embodied the virtues the administration admired: strength, perseverence, ruthlessness. Like the prisoners in the penitentiary mess, the speakers in the Oval Office referred to him with admiration, and their own talk exemplified the norms he represented.

In the talk in the Oval Office the speakers routinely invoke the masculine imagery of conflict and competition. Metaphors are drawn from warfare and sports, zero-sum games in which the only outcome is winning and losing. The speakers do not represent themselves as responsible agents in any *collective* enterprise, such as "government." Instead, they see themselves engaged in mortal combat with the Justice Department, the Congress, and the Courts. The President says:

> This is war. We take a few shots and it will be over. We will give them a few shots and it will be over. (*Transcripts*, p. 64)

They worry about "missions," "overkill," "troops," and "bombshells." They say, "That's the end of the ball game" and talk about "the big play," "having the ball in your court," and "staying one step ahead of the curve." What gestures of conciliation there are, are employed to gain strategic advantage, such as favorable PR or motivated compliance. In short, the world these speakers inhabit is tough, and there is little room for soft sentiments. In evaluating the advice of his long-time friend William Rogers, the President says:

> I know Rogers like the back of my hand and Rogers does not like real, mean, tough problems. (p. 45)

So Rogers' advice will not do.

References to toughness permeate the transcribed talk. They are used synonymously with *hard, difficult, unfortunate, advantageous, strong, smart,* and *good:*

> NIXON: Kalmbach is a decent fellow . . . He is smart.
>
> DEAN: He has been tough thus far. He can take it . . . (p. 105)
>
> NIXON: Rush is smart and he is tough. He's a good man . . . (p. 446)
>
> NIXON: Play it tough. That's the way they play it and that's the way we are gong to play it. (*Washington Post* Staff, 1974, p. 210)

One way to play it tough is to "stonewall," to studiously ignore the imputations and inferences in the situation, to refuse to cooperate beyond giving minimal information. Other ways to play it tough include "pushing," "pressuring," "kicking butts," and "breaking asses."

Those who play it tough expect the other side to play the same way. Thus they must be prepared to "bite the bullet," "take the heat," and "take gas" in the face of an enemy offensive. Dean says in reference to the Ervin Committee:

It will be *hot*. I think they are going to be *tough*. I think they are going to be *gory*. (*Transcripts*, p. 93, emphasis added)

Antonyms of *tough* are *weak, dumb, stupid,* and *soft*. The compulsion to surrender to the principles of justice and the desire to cleanse the soul are both the antitheses of toughness. Patrick Gray, after having cooperated freely with the investigators at his confirmation hearing, is routinely referred to as "damned, dumb Gray." Nixon uses the same expression to describe his brother, Donald, and anyone else on his side who was not ruthless and unyielding, tight-lipped and callous.

A pattern of masculine imagery is clearly embedded in this talk of the Oval Office. It organizes the world into competing forces locked in mortal combat, each out to get the other for the sheer goal of winning. In such a world the participants must be ruthless, callous, strong, and unyielding. They must be moved by no other passion than the all-consuming desire to overcome the obstacles posed by their enemies. Regardless of what such speakers may *say* about the importance of the family to the structure and organization of society, there is no room in their world for soft domestic sentiments.

Writing about the lower-class milieu's contribution to crime and delinquency, Walter Miller (1958) identifies a cluster of values he argues are both characteristic of lower-class life and conducive to deviant behavior. Like the amoral familism discussed earlier, the pattern Miller identifies among lower-class American males is discernible in the Oval Office as well.

The constellation of lower-class values is as follows:*

TROUBLE: The consequence of breaking the law. Concern with the law itself rather than the social agreements it stands for.

TOUGHNESS: Being callous. The ability to take it. The "tough guy" is the one who can exert himself in the face of oppressive odds.

*Miller also includes "autonomy" as a focal concern, but on close analysis, it is not possible to separate indices of "autonomy" from indices of the other dimensions, and so I have ommitted it from the discussion as a separate dimension.

SMARTNESS:	The ability to con, dupe, or outsmart the other guy and, at the same time, avoid being conned, duped, or outsmarted yourself.
EXCITEMENT:	The exhilaration produced from thrills, kicks, danger, or risk. The thrill as an end in itself.
LUCK:	Alienation, powerlessness; a lack of control over one's ultimate fate and the ascription of success to luck.

With the exception of the last element, clear parallels exist between the talk of the President's men and the talk of lower-class men.

Over 1300 pages of transcripts the speakers in the Oval Office are consumed by trouble. Members of their organization, and in some cases the speakers themselves, have engaged in perjury, blackmail, destruction of evidence, and other forms of criminal malfeasance. Almost all of their talk focuses on the consequences of breaking the law and how to evade those consequences by continuing to break the law. Much like the lower-class delinquents in Miller's study, the President and his men are more concerned with the literal wording of the legal codes than with the symbolic significance of the law.

Concern with toughness and smartness is routinely evidenced in conjunction with their problems. The President says:

> You know what I mean . . . I believe in playing politics hard, but I am also smart. (*Transcripts*, p. 331)

> I know Murray (Chotiner) like the back of my hand. He's smart. (p. 914)

> That's a good tough way. What can he do? (p. 1021)

Excitement is less patently obvious in the transcripts, although elements of danger and risk are clear. Early in the spring, when the Nixon team still had a clear advantage, the following exchange took place:

> NIXON: I want the most comprehensive notes on all those who tried to do us in . . . We have not used the power in this first four years as you know . . . but things are going to change now . . .
>
> DEAN: What an exciting prospect.
>
> NIXON: Thanks. It has to be done. (pp. 65-66)

As things go from bad to worse, there is no more talk of thrills and excitement, but danger and risk are routinely considered. "Biting the bullet," "taking the heat," "taking gas" all allude to the dangers of prospective lines of action. The transcripts do not bear evidence of the speakers' relishing these dangers as ends in themselves. Rather, they are seen as the unfortunate consequences of necessary maneuvers. However, if the transcripts do not demonstrate adrenaline-inspired exhilaration as a desirable end in itself, Nixon's first autobiography routinely attests to the thrill he gets from crises and challenge. Furthermore, in the talk in the Oval Office, Nixon makes frequent reference to *Six Crises* as an inspirational book. For example, he tells Haldeman to be sure to reread it for guidance in the current crisis. In *Six Crises* Nixon repeatedly tells of how he thrives on sleeplessness, exhaustion, and hunger; how the moment of truth in a crisis is a peak experience, a theme he reiterates in *Memoirs*. So again, the similarities between Richard Nixon and common crooks are more evident than the differences social class alone suggests.

The speakers in the Oval Office do not invoke luck in any recognizable form. Instead, they make reference to authority, influence, and manipulation. In this dimension alone they are different from lower-class men. They are powerful rather than powerless; they see their fate as a function of their own conduct rather than as a function of forces outside their control. Their survival is testimony not to their good fortune but to their superior fitness.

Biographers note an occasional reference on Nixon's part to a belief in fate and destiny, and examples can be found in his *Memoirs*. But more often we note his belief in his own capacity to capitalize on opportunity when it occurs. So, what most clearly separates the lower-class world view from the Nixon administration is the latter's belief in their own prowess. For lower-class men the activating principle in the world is luck; for the Nixon administration the activating principle of life is power. Beyond this point of disagreement, patently a function of the opportunities provided by social class resources, there is nothing but fundamental agreement. What Miller may have tapped in his analysis of the focal concerns of lower-class culture are the focal concerns of the male sex as they are manifest in a lower-class setting.

If, in fact, these features are uniquely characteristic of the masculine world view, we should expect them to dominate wherever male interests dominate—government, the military, business, and so on. As I will suggest in the final section of this chapter, they are fundamental elements in the world view of the criminal subculture, and the Nixon men make extensive use of this metaphor in their backstage talk.

Gangster Talk

The tough guy in American folklore is found on both sides of the law: there is the tough cop and the tough killer. What distinguishes the two is not their attitude toward life but their attitude toward law. The representative of civil society is expected to have attitudes favorable to upholding the law; the denizen of the underworld is expected to have attitudes disposed to breaking the law. As the Chief Executive of the nation, Nixon should be expected to reflect a commitment to upholding the law. But in fact there is little evidence in his speech to demonstrate attitudes favorable to the law as a system of principled justice, and considerable evidence to demonstrate attitudes that support contravening the law as though it were no more than a technical impediment.

Throughout the transcripts the speakers are dominated by their involvement in activity indictable under the federal criminal code. The "problems" they constantly refer to—their "trouble"—is that they and their agents have broken the law and will continue to break the law in an attempt to cover up the first indictable offenses.

The specific crimes Nixon is interested in are obstruction of justice, perjury, blackmail, bugging, and bribery. Occasionally breaking and entering and being an accessory after the fact capture his attention. Beset by such monumental problems, he does not reflect on the inherent powers of his office as a means of overruling the law and so in this sense he does not sound like a dictatorial tyrant. Rather, he and his associates accept working within the law in order to evade its precepts. He is more like a gangster than a tyrant.

Members of the criminal underworld recognize the inherent powers of the state in the laws it attempts to enforce. But they do not see themselves duty-bound to recognize those laws as honorable and just. They desire to understand the law, but only in order to elude it. In a similar sense, the President laments he is not a criminal lawyer and cannot comprehend the subtle nuances of the criminal codes. He recognizes that he needs a technical consultant, and Dean suggests Henry Peterson:

> Yes, Peterson. It is awkward for Peterson. He is the head of the criminal division (at the Justice Department). To discuss some of these things with him, we may want to remove him from the head

> of the criminal division and say, "Related to this case, you will have
> no relation." Give him some special assignment over here where
> he could sit down and say, "Yes, this is an obstruction
> (of justice) but it couldn't be proved." So on and so forth.
> (pp. 246-247)

The Attorney General is called upon to explain the law to the President:

> KLEINDIENST: If I committed a crime and you know about it
> and you say, "Kleindienst, you go in the court and plead guilty
> to the commission of that crime. Here is ten thousand dollars . . .
> to tide you over and so forth."
>
> NIXON: That isn't a crime?
>
> KLEINDIENST: No. On the other hand, if you know I committed
> a crime . . . and you say, "Go in there and plead guilty.
> Here is twenty-five thousand dollars on the condition you say
> nothing. You just . . . take the Fifth Amendment." The judge
> cites you for contempt; you've got to continue to testify. You
> don't . . . Now, you are in a position of obstructing justice.
>
> NIXON: Excuse me. If you'd explain that again. (p. 705)

To elude the law the criminal must know the moves the law is
likely to make. Thus the objective of the copious legal advice the
President demands from the Justice Depatment is not to provide him
with guidance to formulate his own conduct and meet his responsibility
to obey the law. It is to provide him with advance intelligence, so he
can plan a strategy to beat the rap. Nixon considers bluffing and
sacrifice plays. He deliberates the difficulties the government will have
making a case, and the possible penalties that may be involved if the
Justice Department is successful.

In all cases, he wants to know what his odds are for various moves,
and this is the purpose of his "legal advice." In no case is this legal
counsel any more than a resource in a game of all-out competition.
Nowhere does the Chief Executive reflect on the official commitment
he has as the President of the nation, sworn to support the Constitution, elected on a platform of law and order. At best, his commentary
on justice is sardonic. When subordinates at the CRP are forced to
perjure themselves repeatedly, the President says, "I suppose we can't
call that justice, can we?" (p. 146)

Richard Nixon not only thinks like a gangster, he and his henchmen
talk as though they were habitues of the underworld. Speech in the
Oval Office is infused with terms such as:

bag job	cover-up
bag man	deep six
black bag operation	freewheeling
blackmail	gang
bloodthirsty	jail
bloody	kidnapping
blowing the whistle	killers
broker	Mafia
bugging	pistol
bug out	ringleaders
caper	shook him
cap on the bottle	sold out
common crook	thievery
coming clean	trigger man
cop-out	

More often than they employ the imagery of warfare, sports, or westerns, the speakers employ the argot of the criminal underworld. Exchanges like the following are typical:

> DEAN: Well, first of all, there is the problem of the continued *blackmail* which will not only go on now, but will go on while these people are in prison and it will compound the obstruction of justice. It will cost money. It is dangerous. People around here are not pros at this sort of thing. This is the sort of thing *Mafia* people can do: washing money, getting clean money, and things like that. We just don't know about these things because we are not *criminals* and not used to dealing in that business.
>
> NIXON: That's right.
>
> DEAN: It is a tough thing to know what to do.
>
> NIXON: Maybe it takes a *gang* to do that.
>
> DEAN: That's right . . . Plus there is a real problem in raising money . . .
>
> NIXON: How much money do you need?
>
> DEAN: I would say these people are going to cost a million dollars over the next two years.
>
> NIXON: We could get that. On the money, if you need the money you could get that. You could get a million dollars. You could get it in cash. I know where it could be gotten. It is not easy, but it could be done. But the question is who the hell would handle it? Any idea on that? (p. 193-194; emphasis added)

Argot plays a special role in the criminal underworld. It is used to classify and order experience in ways that are relevant to the speakers' illicit business. Those who adopt such patterns of speech come to see the world in terms that are structured by their language. When they use that language in talking with one another, they make manifest their subscription to the world view embodied in their cant. Thus people who speak the same language know what to expect from one another.

In using the language of the criminal underworld, the speakers in the Oval Office communicated to one another just where they stood with respect to the law at the same time that they interpreted their experience in ways that were unfavorable to upholding the law.

Theorists of criminology, such as Edwin Sutherland (1960) argue that criminal behavior is learned, just as any other behavior is learned. Originally writing before the massive expansion of media, Sutherland argued that in order to become a professional thief a person must learn both the language and the behavior of the underworld in the tutelage of others who practice the profession. But by mid-century the argot and attitudes of the criminal underworld had been broadcast across the nation in the nightly crime shows that dominated the airwaves, the movies, headlines, novels, and the comic strip. So in certain respects no one in America is ignorant of attitudes unfavorable to the law or unaware of the criminal world view that sustains such notions. At the same time, not everyone in America talks like a hoodlum. Depite the prevalence of such imagery, the language patterns are more restricted. So individuals *must* have more intimate links with the criminal underworld if they are to adopt that argot as their own. Or at least this is what Sutherland's theory would lead us to predict.

An indisputable case for Nixon's ties to the underworld has not been made. But circumstantial evidence exists. To begin with, his stint with the carnival in adolescence provided an opportunity to be introduced to attitudes unfavorable to the law, even if such experiences did not convert him at the time. Secondly, writing on the relationship between Nixon and organized crime, critics make note of the following facts and inferences:

> While assistant district attorney for the city of Whittier, Nixon went to Havana on business. At that time (c. 1940) Meyer Lansky, the reputed head of organized crime in America, was deeply involved with gambling interests in Cuba. Lansky and Nixon *may* have met.

> Before he enlisted in the Navy, Nixon worked as a lawyer with the OPA, in charge of tire rationing. He *may* have first met Bebe Rebozo in this connection, and then met him again through George Smathers.

> Through Bebe Rebozo and a number of Florida land speculators, there are *links* between Nixon and organized crime.

> During the time Murray Chotiner was managing Nixon's political career, Chotiner and his brother were managing the defense of numerous persons involved in organized crime. Chotiner *may* have served as a broker between political and criminal interests.

> There are *links* to organized crime through Walter Annenberg, Nixon's appointee to U.S. Ambassador to Great Britain, whose father was Moses Annenberg, an important figure in organized crime.

> Through Howard Hughes and Frank Sinatra as well as lesser known personalities, a *circumstantial* case can be made for Nixon's involvement with a network of organized crime. (See Gerth, 1972; Kunkin, 1974; Kohn, 1976)

In sum, it has been suggested that the connections between Nixon and organized crime are numerous and varied. If such *were* the case, there would have been ample opportunity for Richard Nixon to learn how to talk like a gangster.

But, of course, it was not just Richard Nixon who talked like a gangster in the Oval Office. His aides and associates employed the same metaphors. So however he came by his private speech patterns, he was influential in teaching his young companions the same world view. His aides have attested that he set the tone and style of the White House, and often subordinates pick up speech habits in paying deference to their superior. In so doing, they could become socialized to the world view their President presented. The following exchange exemplifies the socialization process:

> DEAN: You have to wash the money. If you get $100,000 out of a bank, it all comes in serialized bills.
>
> NIXON: I understand.
>
> DEAN: That means you have to go to Vegas with it or a bookmaker in New York City. I have learned all these things after the fact. I will be in great shape for the next time around. (*Transcripts*, p. 238)

Richard Nixon sold himself to the American public as a dedicated President and a pious family man. He claimed to stand for all that was noble and good, honorable and true, decent, righteous, and just. Yet in the privacy of his office he routinely adopted the language and mentality of a common crook. What history will make of this disparity is yet to be written. Certainly those who tend toward a psychological explanation will see the hiatus between his public image and his private self as symptomatic of some mental aberration. But those who choose to interpret Nixon's conduct as evidence of mental instability must acknowledge that his illness was manifest in the company of high-level government functionaries, and not in the social isolation of a mental hospital ward. Richard Nixon is not the classic model of a paranoid schizophrenic.

Furthermore, his symptomology was chronic, not acute. Some have argued that it spanned his entire career in politics; few would deny that if there were symptoms of sickness to be recognized, they could be seen from the summer of 1972 on. Yet during this period Nixon was overwhelmingly reelected to office, where he continued to make consequential decisions in both domestic and foreign affairs. He was repeatedly exposed to public scrutiny through the media, occasionally to direct questioning by the press corps. Now.and again he spent time in intimate conversations with correspondents like Theodore White. Yet so subtle were the symptoms of this illness that while he invokes it to account for Nixon's high crimes and misdemeanors, White could not recognize it except in retrospect. Not until the (more or less) complete tale of Watergate came out and the President resigned in disgrace was it known that the Chief Executive had been sick in the first place (cf. White, 1961, 1970, 1973, 1975). Thus those who explain the disparity between Nixon's public image and his private self by invoking mental illness or any other idiosyncratic aberration are missing the point. *If the backstage talk in the Oval Office reveals an administration with a Mafia mentality, it is not because the President is crazy. It is because the culture in which that position of leadership is embedded is organized in such a way that what was once considered criminal is now common practice.*

In New England in the 17th century hucksterism and other sharp business practices were defined as crimes, and persons who practiced them could be fined or sentenced to the stocks or pillory. By the 19th century, as material interests began to supplant spiritual concerns, sharp business practices were conventionalized; and by the time of Nixon's birth, the mentality of the marketplace held sway as the dominant ideology.

During Nixon's boyhood organized crime emerged alongside the growth of the conventional marketplace as a system of providing illicit goods and services on a large scale. Within half a century the thugs and hoodlums that once beset the local community rose to national stature and, in an ironic way, gave testimony to America as a land of open opportunity.

Throughout the period of Nixon's personal growth and development, organzied crime and the conventional marketplace flourished. Bookmakers and bankers both made profitable use of the telephone, while the automobile was a boon to bank robber and branch salesman alike. By the time Nixon reached maturity, the interests of the underworld and the interests of the conventional world had merged in a variety of common enterprises such as land speculation, gambling casinos, banks, and hotels. When Nixon came into power, it was difficult to separate the interests of organized crime, the interests of the conventional marketplace, and the interests of the United States government. Nixon's political supporters used principles of extortion to extract campaign contributions from legitimate business corporations (Breslin, 1975), and known figures of the underworld made cash contributions to his cause (Gerth, 1972).

In the nation as a whole sharp business practices routinely tested the law. Conventional business interests affected how the law was written and illegal business interests affected how the law was enforced. Where the technology of the 20th century had broken down the old barriers of time and space, the social practices organized to deal with that technology broke down old notions of truth and morality. Truth became what sells, morality what you can get away with.

If he took advantage of these changes, Nixon was not crazy, just crafty. He and many others like him saw where they could capitalize on the opportunities of the new order. For some the profit was found in wealth, for others in influence or fame. But for large numbers of people in the 20th century the possibilities of material profit expanded at an unprecedented rate, while at the same time their ties to the local community receded. Thus freed of the informal social controls traditionally exerted by friends and neighbors, the individual truly came into his own. The old ethical standards that once restricted the individual's options lost their locus and then their force, and in their place vague notions of societal expectations were embodied in media messages.

The old attitudes did not disappear entirely. Rather, they were transformed into sentimental symbols, manipulated to give the appearance of traditional respectability and so provide an acceptable cloak for contemporary opportunism. But the old values were no longer effective guides to action; they were invoked only after the fact, as public accounts. In intimate conversation, the values were those of less lofty aspirations.

·reflections·

Chapter 11
Nixonian Logic

Every way of talking about the world presupposes some logic that directs the use of the language and leads to reasoned conclusions. If language is likened to a map of reality, logic is the key that explains the connections between various named places.

Consider the following example of logic in action. The President and the Chief Prosecuter from the Justice Department are discussing what happened to evidence taken from the White House office of one of the Watergate defendants.

> PETERSON: Pat Gray (acting head of the FBI) took (the envelopes) back, and I said Pat where are they, and he said I burned them. And I said —
>
> NIXON: He burned them?
>
> PETERSON: I said that's terrible . . . I said Pat why did you do it.
>
> NIXON: Pat's naive.
>
> PETERSON: He said—well, I suppose because I took them at their word. (Nixon, 1974, pp. 1098-1099, hereafter referred to as *Transcripts*)

What emissaries from the White House told Pat Gray when they gave him the incriminating evidence was "This is political." In so naming the contents of the envelopes, they divested them of the legal protection they would have had were their evidentiary status known. As acting head of the FBI, Gray could agree to destroy the documents only if he were assured they had no relevance to the investigation before the law. However, he did not have to be told to destroy the envelopes; he only needed to be told they were "potentially embarrassing." People who speak the same language can expect others to understand what is required without having to say it in so many words, for the function of logic is to lead to just those conclusions.

It is possible to describe the logic behind the language of the 37th President as a set of structural principles and thereby critique its assumptions and see its limits. Simplified, Nixonian logic can be expressed as taken-for-granted ideas leading to conclusions that are neither inevitable nor safe.

Nixon's *Memoirs* provide a rich source for the structural study of language. Like *Six Crises,* the *Memoirs* were written in the years immediately after his retreat from the public arena. Proclaimed an important historical document by the publisher, the book purports to give the most intimate account of Nixon's career, administration, and downfall. Yet even a casual reading suggests these are not so much the intimate reflections of a public figure as they are the author's attempt to rationalize his life to himself and justify it to others.

For example, although *Memoirs* is an autobiography, it is not a personal account insofar as it relies for the most part on the public record for the facts it brings forth. We expect the subject/author of autobiography to present much more about his own life than what finds its way into public sources. Yet few intimate revelations appear in this weighty tome. Most of the text is drawn from the same sources I had access to, or from transcriptions of tapes not yet made public.

A few bits of personal insight appear between the descriptions of well-publicized encounters (for instance, Nixon's dream of Rockefeller upstaging him, on p. 686). The pages are sprinkled with quotes from diary notes, giving the impression of an inside perspective. But these quotes are as apt to be taken from his daughter Tricia's dairy as they are from Nixon's own. Furthermore, the fact that Nixon's diary entries are not dated makes them less useful to the historian than they would be if the dates of these reflections were appended, as they are on the bedside notes he occasionally duplicates in their original handwriting. Here the handwriting—its loops and constraints, its starts and its spacing—tells the observant reader more about Nixon's psyche than does the content of the text.

Despite their length, these memoirs are highly selective. Some things every biographical source documents are omitted from Nixon's personal account of his life, such as the role of the Teapot Dome scandals in his youthful decision to become a lawyer. Other events of great historical significance—Henry Kissinger's replacement of William Rogers as Secretary of State, or the institution of wage and price controls—are passed over with one or two sentences and no insight or background on what the author of that decision had in mind. The pattern that governs the selection of events and the detail of description suggests that these are not the intimate memories of a mature man but a PR job for history.

The chronological organization of the text permits Nixon to review the first six crises of his career, as well as set the record straight about his boyhood and youth, topics not covered in his earlier attempt at autobiography. However, this historical review is misleading, for if we measure the space dedicated to the various phases of his career, it is the events of Watergate that dominate his *Memoirs* and not the cumulative experiences of a lifetime.

Like the published transcripts of his taped conversations, his autobiography is a sanitized version of the events it represents. It was produced to document the claim that the 37th President was unfairly hounded from office by his political enemies, even though he did nothing others have not done, including his more respected predecessors in the Oval Office. Instead of being titled *Memoirs* the volume would have been more appropriately titled *Apologia*.

Understanding the objective that lay behind claims made in a document provides the key to interpreting what it says. Nixon's autobiography cannot be read at face value, as the personal reflections of a historic figure, for at this level it portrays an idealized version of a political career enacted by a weak, bumbling man, more pitiful than powerful. Nixon's *Memoirs* must be read between the lines and beneath the surface for a full appreciation of his role in the 20th century. *Memoirs* must be treated as a work of rhetoric if it is to make history.

★   ★   ★

The principles of Nixonian logic I have drawn from this text are not stated in the form I present them. Nowhere, for example, does Nixon write THE SELF IS USEFUL FOR PURPOSES OF EXAMPLE. IT IS NOT A SUSTAINED EXPERIENCE OF CONSCIOUSNESS, BUT AN ON/OFF SWITCH. Rather, I have inferred this principle from statements such as the following:

> All that was left to me was to try to get myself into a position to be able to claim that I had cracked the case, trying to garner some credit for leadership that I had failed to exert. (Nixon, 1978, p. 819, hereafter referred to as *Memoirs*)

> If I had given the true answer I would have had to say that without fully realizing the implications of my actions I had become deeply entangled in the complicated mesh of decisions, inactions, misunderstandings, and conflicting motivations that comprised the Watergate cover up; I would have to admit that I still did not know the whole story and therefore did not know the full extent of my involvement in it . . . (pp. 849–850)

Again, from statements like the following I have inferred the principle EVERY HAIR CAN BE SPLIT FINER THAN THE ONE BEFORE:

> Another choice was to *abide* by the Court's ruling without actually *complying* with it. (p. 1043; emphasis in the original)

> As certain as I was that we had done everything we could to *contain* the scandal, I was equally as confident that we had not tried to *cover it up*. (p. 773; emphasis added)

> As John Dean would say to me a few months later, "The intent when Segretti was hired was nothing evil, nothing vicious, nothing bad, nothing. Not espionage, not sabotage. It was pranksterism that got out of hand." (p. 775)

If we are to understand Richard Nixon's repeated claims that he was acting in a principled fashion when he made his decisions, then it is this logic, or some similar set of principles, that must describe the assumptions he made about the world; the way he ordered, arranged, and interpreted evidence; and the conclusions he was inescapably drawn to.

NIXONIAN LOGIC

ALL THINGS ARE POSSIBLE.

MOST THINGS ARE BAD.

BEING BAD IN DEFENSE OF GOOD IS NOT SO BAD; BEING GOOD IN DEFENSE OF BAD IS OK.

ERROR DOES NOT NEGATE GOOD. A GOOD ACT CAN HAVE ANY NUMBER OF ERRONEOUS SCENES WITHOUT DISPROVING THE ACTOR'S MOTIVE.

THE SELF IS USEFUL FOR PURPOSES OF EXAMPLE. IT IS NOT A SUSTAINED EXPERIENCE OF CONSCIOUSNESS, BUT AN ON/OFF SWITCH.

EVERYBODY HAS A RIGHT TO A PERSONAL BELIEF. YOU CAN'T FAULT A FELLOW FOR ACTING ON WHAT HE BELIEVES.

PROJECTION IS RATIONAL; THE OTHER SIDE IS EXACTLY LIKE YOU, ONLY MEANER.

TO EACH HIS OWN. UNDER PRESSURE IT IS RATIONAL TO ABANDON ANYTHING TO SAVE YOURSELF.

SPEED COUNTS. FAST AND FIRST ARE ALL THAT MATTER; #1 IS EVERYTHING.

THE OBJECTIVE OF ALL LIFE IS WINNING.

TIME, CASH, AND ENERGY GIVE A STRATEGIC ADVANTAGE IN THE GAME OF LIFE.

TIME IS ELASTIC. IT CAN BE SPED UP, SLOWED DOWN, EDITED, AND CREDITED.

ONLY TIME WILL TELL. THE MEANING OF THE PRESENT IS DETERMINED BY THE EVENTS OF THE FUTURE; NOT UNDERSTANDING WHAT IS HAPPENING IS NORMAL.

BLACK HOLES EXIST. REALITY CAN APPEAR AND DISAPPEAR.

MEMORY IS COMPOSED OF BLACK HOLES SURROUNDED BY LUCID DETAIL.

EVERY HAIR CAN BE SPLIT FINER THAN THE ONE BEFORE. THE FASTER YOU ARE, THE FINER THE DISTINCTIONS YOU CAN MAKE. IF YOU ARE VERY FAST, YOU CAN SPLIT THIN AIR.

LIES ARE LINES. IF SOME FISH FALLS FOR THEM, WHOSE FAULT IS IT—THE FISHERMAN WHO WAS JUST DOING HIS JOB, OR THE SUCKER WHO WAS LOOKING OUT FOR #1?

ALL BLAME IS RELATIVE.

Understanding the "method in his madness" puts passages like the following in perspective:

> If I had indeed been the knowing Watergate conspirator that I was charged as being, I would have recognized in 1973 that the tapes contained conversations that would be fatally damaging. I would have seen that if I were to survive, they would have to be destroyed . . . on Saturday, July 21, I made a note outlining this rationale: "If I had discussed illegal action, I would not have taped. If I had discussed illegal action and had taped I would have destroyed the tapes once the investigation began." (p. 902)

"Therefore, I must have been innocent" is the obvious conclusion of this syllogism. Innocence is known to Nixon only as the bottom line of a memorandum written to the self.

Nixonian logic is familiar, but it is not the same as the logic taught at school. It has more in common with the deception of the carnival shell game than it has with the intellectual puzzles that have fascinated Western thinkers from Aristotle on.

The ways Nixonian logic differs from schoolroom logic are instructive. First of all, Nixonian logic is not a contemplative logic. It is not constructed to lead independent thinkers to the same conclusions, but to confuse different people in the same way. The objective of Nixonian logic is to string together words into propositions that resemble schoolroom logic if they go by fast enough. Speed is as important as authority. What is said is not as important as who said it and what it sounded like.

Whether Aristotelian or quantum, schoolroom logic rests on truth value: the ability to assign YES or NO to propositions. For Richard Nixon truth is not absolute, but variable. He writes:

> I believe that a totally honest answer would have been neither a simple yes or no. (p. 849)

In Nixonian logic the meaning of language rests not on publicly acknowledged relationships between words and facts, but on special relationships between words and the speaker's interests. The classic example of this style of thought is found in *Alice in Wonderland*, when Humpty Dumpty says, "When I use a word, it means just what I choose it to mean . . ."

The foundation of Nixonian logic is not truth or falsehood, but advantage and risk. Propositions that advance the speaker's interests are true, and those that expose the speaker to risk are false. Consider the following excerpts:

> I wanted (a written report from Dean) as proof of the truth of my public statements that there was no one in the White House involved in Watergate. I wanted a document that would show I had said it because I had been told it and believed it. (p. 801)

> Everything was growing more and more fluid on Watergate. I still sought some actions that would put the White House out in front of the controversy—some symbols to demonstrate that *we* . . . were on the side of right. (p. 808; emphasis in the original)

Nixonian logic does not so much duplicate schoolroom logic as it emulates that classic form of thought. It sounds reasoned because it is intended to mimic traditional patterns of thought while it disregards the customary content. You can get from one point to another using Nixonian logic, but in the last analysis all the points are self-serving. There is no way to transcend the speaker's interest in, among other things, divesting himself of moral responsibility for his acts. Free of blame in any customary sense, he is free to reassert the virtues of his character in the future.

Nixonian logic is not totally disconnected from the classic traditions of Western philosophy. Incorporating the idea of relativity, it is in the vanguard of 20th century thought. Relying on the principle of self-interest, it is aligned with the core of Western tradition.

In Nixonian logic relativity resolves the apparent contradiction in the use of base means to achieve lofty objectives. It does so by arguing that relative to any apparent conflict between ends and means there is some perspective in which things look different. The traditional categories of good, bad, right, wrong, true, false are no longer absolutes. Rather, they are nominal labels affixed for self-serving purposes. Thus in Nixonian logic if someone calls you a crook, you do not deny his allegations. Rather, you respond by showing the interests your enemy has in discrediting you, while you quickly preface your remarks with an affirmation of your own pure motives.

What made the 20th century different from every century that preceded it was the introduction, dissemination, and incorporation of relativistic thinking. Just as the introduction of perspective had radically altered thinking about what was possible and profitable in the Renaissance, so did the introduction of relativity transform modern thought in contemporary times.

Introduced at the same juncture in history as Freud was describing the unconscious, Einstein's algebraic vision of the universe liberated tremendous forces that heretofore had been locked in the microcosmic world of the atom.

In the universities philosophers deliberated the existential wonder of being and nothingness, while theologians developed the concept of "situational ethics" to adjust Christian morality to modern thinking. But the university was not where the action was. The consequential decisions for modern life were being made by political, military, and industrial specialists, who were adapting the new way of thinking to different objectives. In business the sophisticated reasoning of relativity became another way to say *caveat emptor*. In politics it permitted speakers to justify their selfless dedication to office by claiming they acted in good faith, but were misunderstood by others, and that is normal. In the combined military and industrial interests relativity was reflected in the design, creation, testing, and stockpiling of nuclear weapons, tools of destruction built out of a new way of looking at what is fixed and what is variable.

★　　★　　★

By the time the theory of relativity was being introduced to Western thought, the idea of enlightened self-interest had become so routinized as to be thought basic human nature. However, not every society makes a firm distinction between self and other, a distinction that is at the root of self-interest. The unique self taken for granted as the right and obligation of every Westerner is not so much an attribute of human nature as it is a special idea that took root when new opportunities were on the horizon and old traditions were being transformed.

The idea of a self as an independent agent choosing between different values emerged in the same historic context as the gothic imagination. (Morris, 1972) Those whose economic or political power gave them choices saw their selves as distinct, unique, special. They became conscious in a new way.

Traditional people experienced or "found" themselves by affiliation, by identifying with others with whom they shared the same circumstances, be it family, work, church, or social position. In the new social order emerging in the West, people "found" themselves by differentiation, by pursuing a personal agenda of private interests.

In the new vision that was emerging to justify the new order similarities were disregarded in favor of accentuating the differences between people. Self and other were no longer mirror images; instead they were set in opposition.

The idea of a self composed of unique features was as liberating a force as were the technological advances that permitted such a notion in the first place. In the perpetual differentiation of self and other, innovation became institutionalized. To maintain the illusion of uniqueness, each person had to keep a wary eye out for the special opportunities that would permit him—and with the democratization of Western culture, her—to stand apart from the crowd. The new and the different became valued; modernity was on the way.

The Protestant Reformation furthered the process of individualization that began around the end of the Middle Ages and by the 18th century the idea of a rational self, capable of knowing the world by personal experience, became advanced thinking. In the writings of those men who, taken collectively, represent the Enlightenment, the concept of self-interest was legitimized.

At first it was only the aristocracy whose economic and political advantages gave them resources to claim distinction. Tied to the church's interest in the old order, clerics preached the deadly sins of human vanity to no avail. Practical advantage was quickly seized by individuals acting in ways they saw to be in their personal interests. Then, with the rise of the middle class, the aristocracy lost its monopoly on assertiveness, and ultimately self-interest became a bourgeois notion.

Around the same time, the radical new ideas of the Enlightenment were introduced into the New World. Just as America saw itself as a Christian nation from its inception, so too did it see itself as an enlightened nation, providing contractual rights to independent selves in pursuit of their special interests, government regulating the traffic.

The ideas of the Enlightenment were not simply radical, they were revolutionary. They gave those who believed them the confidence to take on their betters and grasp political power for themselves. In both the Old World and the New, the idea of an enlightened self became a forceful vision that dethroned the hereditary aristocracy and redistributed its special powers and privileges.

In the democratic revolutions of the 18th century, the notion of self-interest met itself coming around the other way. The aristocratic order had distinguished itself by assuming it was special and then acting in defense of its special interests. In so doing, it spawned an intellectual movement that subsequently contributed to its demise.

Such is the irony of history.

By the 20th century self-consciousness had been heightened to obsession. Academic disciplines studied the development and dis-stresses of the self, while medical specialties and pharmaceutical companies expanded to treat these dis-eases and abnormalities of the self as "pathology." Advertisers pitched their sales to selves longing to stand out from the crowd, if only they could find the right formula, potion, product, or ploy.

By the 20th century the self had become the measure of all things, growing in direct proportion to the atrophy of community.

The opposition between self and other is not so much a fact of human nature as it is a figment of Western imagination. Traditionally, human beings have identified themselves in terms of class membership: family, tribe, occupation, class, community, station. These traditional concepts began to break down in the West about the time gothic imagery first appeared at the end of the Middle Ages. From the 18th century on authoritative thought has presupposed that my interests and yours are in diabolical opposition, and Nixonian logic reflects this basic assumption.

★   ★   ★

Technology is often treated as the *sine qua non* of human intelligence. It represents the transformation of earthly possibilities to fit human desire. Every innovation alters the natural elements that preexist human intervention and reforms those elements into tools to accomplish and extend human intention.

Archaeologists looking at cultures long lost often have only the tools a people fashioned to reconstruct their way of life, and so entire histories are written on the basis of the technological accomplishments of a particular people. In a similar fashion, museums are built to display the material achievements of past and present cultures, though we rarely see the beliefs and practices that accompany the artifacts housed in glass cases. The tool is separated from its maker, from its use, and from the ideas that conceived it, to stand as a symbol of culture: to represent a way of life.

However, technologies are always entwined with ideologies. A tool is symbolic of culture only insofar as it also elucidates the beliefs of the people who fashioned it or exemplifies the ideas that came to mind after the prototype was developed. Just as the technological innovations of an era transform the culture they emerge from, so do the beliefs of that era direct the pursuit of innovation.

In the present study I have been concerned with the relationship between technology, opportunity, and routinization. I have suggested that new tools open new vistas, create options not envisioned by the traditional way of doing things. The clever, the quick, the shrewd, the ambitious, those who are excluded by the old system as well as those who have used up all their options, adventurers and visionaries—all are quick to grasp the implications of the new opportunities that follow in the wake of technological innovation. They become the proponents of social change, the human potential that transforms the impersonal culture.

As much as change is an integral part of the historical process, powerful interests are always committed to the status quo, to the continuity of the old system that gives them their relative advantage. So the most difficult historical change is the change that gives the ruling elite an advantage in the new order without jeopardizing their position in the old. It is change that is radical *without* being revolutionary.

Richard Nixon's biography and the course of American history coincided in the early decades of the 20th century when the products of domestic technology were beginning to flood the marketplace, when the tools of communication and transportation were reducing space and speeding time, when electronics and image projection were creating possibilities never before conceivable. Richard Nixon's biography and the course of American history coincided just about the time human consciousness was being transformed, when the small community was dissolving under the onslaught of consumer culture and mass society was emerging to fill the void.

This was a period when individual thought, local dialect, and regional character all gave way to national interest, and the image of the vigorous, youthful couple advertisers used to portray the good things in life became everyone's ideal. Celebrities replaced heroes; getting ahead replaced being good; substance was sacrificed to style.

As fundamental as these changes were, descendents of the bourgeois industrialists and financiers who had secured their economic and political advantages in the 19th century had a vested interest in maintaining a sense of continuity with the old order, lest the opportunities they saw to capitalize on the future be denied them by revolutionary coup—by some fundamental change in who was making the decisions, the language they spoke, and the logic they invoked. In Richard Nixon, a provincial West Coast lawyer, they found the perfect pitchman. The economic elite backed and supported his career while he sold their interests to the public. When he began to discredit himself in office, his backers withdrew their collective support, and Nixon's power quickly aborted.

While Nixon was in office, his greatest achievement was to manage the transition between the old and the new. He did so by first selling the American people a vision of enemy forces bent on destroying the traditional freedoms that made America great in the past. Once people were sold on the idea that their personal investment in the American dream was threatened by some named enemy—commie, pinko, hippie, bum—Nixon sold the public on his personal candidacy as salvation from those demonic forces he conjured. He was adroit. Whether he was acting the Cold War warrior of his youth or the dignified statesman of maturity, every campaign was a moral crusade, with challenges and obstacles to overcome, a ruthless enemy who played by no known rules, and the multitude, always waiting to praise him and cheer him, to urge him on, offer him God's blessing, or accept God's blessing from him.

For more than a quarter-century Nixon played the role of the gothic huckster, the evangelical salesman whose only product was himself.

★　　★　　★

The evangelical salesman is an American archetype. Traveling from one outlying community to another, taking advantage of slow-witted yokels, making a profit from a glib tongue and a quick wit, the Yankee peddler and the fundamentalist preacher both contribute to the image. What distinguishes the gothic huckster of the 20th century from his predecessors is the technological arsenal that enhances his prowess and mesmerizes his audience. Television is perhaps the most powerful tool of 20th century salesmanship in a warehouse of sales technology that spans the gamut from four-color rotary printing presses to plastic credit cards.

Beyond technology, what the 20th century contributed to the pitchman's performance is a new way of thinking to justify an old way of acting. The radical new theory of relativity, introduced by scientists at the beginning of the century, was quickly assimilated to everyday talk and then became a feature of ordinary thought. The absolutes that once dominated the human mind were being replaced by an infinitely branching network of alternatives that all came back to the same place: the self.

Chapter 12
Gothic Heroes

Watergate was a severe test of the American system. For more than two years crime in the executive suites dominated the media and excited the imagination. Discrediting revelation after discrediting revelation cast doubt on the presidency and the entire structure of the federal government. It was shown that the man in the Oval Office was an unscrupulous fraud and that the executive agencies assigned to the task of investigating the original break-in and subsequent cover-up were easily diverted from the path of justice. Yet the response of the nation was not one of heightened self-criticism. Instead, citizens of all persuasions were reassured by reputable speakers that America was a good nation and eventually virtue would win. At each stage of the investigation evidence was found to validate the belief that the idealized version of the system was real.

When Richard Nixon finally uttered his words of resignation, the nation experienced a sense of relief. With reassuring calm, his successor declared the Watergate nightmare over and the Constitution victorious.

Like Teapot Dome and Wounded Knee, Watergate quickly passed into the common language. After Watergate there was Koreagate, and after Koreagate there was Lancegate. When the Carter peanut factory finances came under congressional examination, cynics began to refer to Goobergate.

The jazzed-up rhythm introduced at the beginning of the century as an attribute of time and space had become an attribute of consciousness. By the last quarter of the century events of monumental consequence with ramifications that could and would alter the very system they were a part of, were noted, labeled, and filed for oblivion in that all-purpose category, The Past. Crises had become commonplace, unremarkable, routine.

Certainly Richard Nixon was counting on the rapid tempo of 20th century time to give him a strategic advantage in the future. A healthy man in his early 60s, he could count on another decade or two of active life. Rather than surrender to the Constitutional principles he had twice sworn to uphold, he stonewalled the nation. In a final telecast he proclaimed he was not quitting the presidency, but rather putting the best interests of the nation before his personal interests by stepping down from office so the nation could have a full-time president.

In his last public performance as President, Nixon spoke at great length of the contributions he made to peace during his years in office. As in previous television performances, his demeanor was cool and controlled. For a man who had broken into tears on past public occasions, there were few signs of visible weakness. He was tough.

He was considerably more emotional when he said his personal good-byes to the White House staff. In a rambling, disconnected style he thanked them profusely for their dedicated service in the interests of good government. He acknowledged the role of his family in his own career. He mentioned his ordinary father and his saintly mother, but never once did he mention his long-suffering wife. He compared losing an election with losing a loved one, and then he cautioned his audience about the perils of hate:

> Never get discouraged. Never be petty. Always remember: others may hate you. Those who hate you don't win unless you hate them. And then you destroy yourself. (*Washington Post* Staff, 1974, p. xxi)

He ended his performance by bestowing God's blessings on the attendant audience and the Nixon presidency was over. He was humble but not defeated.

After the emotionally charged speech in the East Room, he boarded a helicopter waiting on the White House lawn,* still the most influential man in the nation. By the time his plane set down in Southern California, he was technically just another citizen, though not an ordinary one. Crowds of well-wishers attended his arrival. He assured them of his high hopes, his good spirits, and his prayers for their well-being. The man who had just resigned from the office of the United States Presidency showed no evidence of embarrassment, shame, guilt, or despair. Instead, he appeared vital and healthy, ready to begin all over again when the time was right.

Had Richard Nixon permitted the Constitutional system to work its way through the massive revelations of malfeasance in his office and on his part, he would have forfeited his government pension. Though he repeatedly vowed he was not a quitter, it made sense to quit rather than to be impeached. It was a strategic setback, not a surrender. Similarly, while Nixon had been uniquely healthy through a quarter-century of politics, it made sense to get sick in the fall of '74 when the judicial trials of his closest aides and associates began. When the existence of the tapes became known the previous summer, Nixon suddenly came down with pneumonia, requiring immediate hospitalization and eliciting the sympathy due those in the sick role. Nixon is a man of enormous will, singular determination, and consummate skill at displaying the proper response at the proper time. His postresignation phlebitis was convincing to professional diagnosticians, and their professional judgment was convincing to the court. Pardoned of all crimes of commission and omission by his successor, he was further excused from any public testimony under oath by the court. He could leave office with a pension and without having to acknowledge his complicity in the subversion of justice.

*Up to this point I have refrained from embellishing the text with commentary and asides. However, the ascending helicopter as the symbol of the end of Watergate is so ubiquitous that it deserves comment. Nixon ends his *Memoirs* with a description of his last moments before boarding the helicopter, and the final photograph in his book is a full page shot of a helicopter ascending in front of the Washington monument on a smoggy day. Whether they are written from the perspective of participant or that of observer, virtually all accounts of Watergate end with the helicopter lifting off from the White House lawn. What makes this imagery remarkable is the way it parallels the imagery Fellini used to introduce 20th century life in *La Dolce Vita*: the helicopter flying over the eternal city of Rome, transporting an enormous statue of Christ, arms outstretched.

The trials of Haldeman, Ehrlichman, Mitchell, and others continued through the fall of '74. The new year began with the announcement of their convictions, accompanied by their protestations of innocence. Soon afterward, Nixon began to recuperate. Though he was reported to be near death in the fall, old friends like Elmer Bobst and Bebe Rebozo began to visit him and report on his improving health. He made his first public appearance at a party at Walter Annenberg's desert estate, attended by Hollywood notables, the former California governor, and others of corporate and political influence. A man always dressed for a formal occasion, he took barefoot walks along the beach at San Clemente, shaking hands with well-wishers and posing for photographs with the tourists who frequent the base of the cliffs. He played golf with Teamster boss Frank Fitzsimmons at the La Costa Country Club, a place long associated with underworld figures and organized crime. Eventually he visited the old haunts of his days of public power—China, Europe, New York, Washington. And everywhere he went there was always a crowd to affirm what people believed he represented.

Rumors began to circulate about a second resurrection, yet another New Nixon waiting in the wings, ready to take an encore, a replay of '68.

The man who retired in disgrace to exile and seclusion the summer before was a man making a reentry into society, and the doors were not closed. Republican leaders like Charles Wiggins from California and Barry Goldwater from Arizona made harsh judgments about his conduct in office, but soon they began to have charitable things to say about the former President.

Citizens followed their leaders' example. Of people polled after his resignation a slender majority believed he had suffered enough, while most Republicans believed he was still being persecuted by his enemies: the liberal establishment, the popular press, agents of the Communist Party.

Through his years of exile his name was remembered, but the details of his reputation grew vague.

Over the years, millions of loyal supporters have continued to make their devotion to Richard Nixon known. Every day, Republican volunteers from the nearby retirement community travel to San Clemente to sort the messages sent by the public. On special occasions, such as Christmas and Easter, the former President's birthday or his wife's birthday, up to 50 volunteers may be recruited to review and catalogue the public response. Volunteers estimate the mail to be 98 percent in Nixon's favor. Crank letters are few, and the occasional threat is passed on to the Secret Service.

For the most part, people send Nixon medical cures and mass cards, invitations to public functions and requests for public appearances, as well as requests for his favorite recipes, his autograph, his blessing. They write letters expressing their appreciation of all he has done for the country, bestowing their best wishes on him and his family. They send unsolicited gifts of money to help defray the costs of his legal and medical bills. They send a multitude of presents: flowers, candy, and fruit; canes and lap robes; silver and crystal. The receipt of such gifts is acknowledged, and autographed pictures are sent out. The names of well-wishers are then catalogued and filed for future reference. Volunteers at San Clemente estimate they have millions of names on file, and that many of these people have indicated they would vote for the man again.

Despite the revelations surrounding his resignation, untold millions remain loyal to Richard Nixon. They believe he won consummate glory in foreign affairs, but unfortunately was undone by malevolent forces on his domestic staff. They explain what they know in the following way: involved as he was in the tremendous effort to bring peace to a global community and estabish America's moral leadership in the world, he necessarily delegated authority for domestic affairs. The men he trusted and loyally tried to protect betrayed their President's lofty objectives for sinister ambitions of their own. Greedy for personal power, coveting influence, unscrupulous underlings undermined a great man. If Nixon erred, he erred in his judgment of his subordinates. But his poor judgment of associates does not reflect on his judgement in foreign policy. Those who remain loyal to him personally claim that his vision was far-sighted. He had a small blind spot, but that's only human. Thus they continue to affirm his basic integrity and overall moral worth, making sense of the facts by splitting the logical foundation they rest on.

Long after the man fell from power in disgrace, Nixon's popularity lingers. By 1977 he began to make the most admired man list once more, while his wife continued her uninterrupted popularity among women.

★   ★   ★

Nixon's political career began in the small Southern California town of Whittier. After a quarter of a century in politics, he returned to Southern California again, to reside in exile only an hour's drive from his birthplace.

In the 19th century Whittier was an intentional Quaker community. From the hill above the original site, one could see the mountains to the east and the ocean to the west. Now the community is ringed by pornographic bookstores and topless bars. The genteel propriety that once characterized the town has given way to forces of history and circumstance. In Nixon's youth Whittier was a prosperous business community, but now the economy is stagnant, and there are few opportunities for local people, much less for newcomers. The tree-lined streets of the residential districts are still broad and clean, but the air is often foul with industrial pollutants, and one can hardly see the mountains, much less the sea. From its origins as a spiritual community, Whittier has become just another small town in the mass society of the 1970s.

Public signs acknowledging the relationship of Nixon to Whittier are few, vandalism of Nixon artifacts routine. After his resignation, the only public testimonies to their native son were presidential portraits hanging in city hall and the chamber of commerce, and a small plaque on the East Whittier Friends Church proclaiming "Church Home of President Nixon." In the special collections room of the Whittier College library, Nixon documents and artifacts share space with those of poet John Greenleaf Whittier for whom the community was named and author Jessamyn West, the town's other notable. There are public thoroughfares named for Whittier and West but local detractors blocked the movement to name a street after Nixon. At the city library there is a special Nixon room, but the Nixon memorabilia it once housed were removed during renovations, and the local Library Commission voted not to return them for fear of vandalism.

The malicious mischief of Nixon detractors is significant, for Whittier is a respectable community heavily dominated by conservative Republican interests. For a quarter-century those interests supported Nixon's career, and they continued to support his image long after he resigned in disgrace. There were always detractors in the community, people who did not care for Nixon's campaign tactics or who did not believe his claims of dedication to community interests. But they have been a minority compared to his outspoken supporters, and many, from the mayor to the Nixon family's local minister, remain staunch loyalists. Others have become disillusioned over time, but their disillusionment is mitigated by conflicting interests and masked by various devices.

For as long as most people can remember, Nixon's fortune has been Whittier's entertainment. The community that was influential in molding him took pride in his success and was anxious about his misfortune. He provided a regular topic of talk as well as their hope for cosmopolitan recognition.

Nixon also provided the possibility of an economic windfall, the possibility of a renaissance of the prosperity Whittier knew in the 1920s and again in the 1950s, for during the 20th century the practice of building presidential libraries as monuments of public testimony had begun and Whittier saw the economic opportunity implicit in such a monument to their native son.

Such edifices house the documents, tapes, and innumerable memorabilia acquired through a man's tenure in office. They serve as resources for historical researchers as well as public museums where ordinary people can visit and be informed of that period in history represented by a particular President's tenure. When Richard Nixon took office, the precedent of the presidential library was already established, and he and his supporters assumed one would be constructed to his memory. Therefore, early in his administration negotiations began to select the site where the monument would be erected. The Nixon Foundation was created to manage the negotiations and the city of Whittier was one of the bidders.

The Nixon Library would be an economic windfall for a dying community. Disneyland, a colossal Southern California tourist attraction, is only 20 minutes away from Whittier; tourists could easily include it on their itinerary. Thus the Nixon Library could be expected to draw millions of people no matter what it housed. So even after Nixon resigned from office in disgrace, the community that nurtured him continued to have an economic interest in his image.

People manage the disparity between what they know about the man and what they desired from his image in various ways. No one has become openly vindictive. No one publicly condemns Nixon as a betrayer. Most (although not all) refuse to speak about Watergate and Nixon's downfall, either in public or among their intimates. They prefer silent denial to any open discussion of the complexities of the man's rise to power and their own loyal support of his career. Few speak from their hearts about their experiences or feelings. Time has been edited; black holes appear.

The disillusionment of Nixon's supporters was a gradual process. At first loyalists said that what he did was nothing new, that the Democrats did it too. As more and more discrediting facts were revealed, they acknowledged that Nixon's conduct was extreme; but they claimed he must have had good reasons to do what he did. Many remained behind him—if hesitantly—until the revelation of his income taxes and the publication of the taped conversations. A professor at the local college gives the following account of the disillusionment of one of his colleagues:

> Professor X is an administrator at the college. A classmate of Nixon's in youth, he was a long-time supporter and counts himself a personal friend.
>
> Professor X has always believed in the Protestant ethic, especially as it is translated into economic profit. He and his wife lived frugally all their lives, saved their money, and invested in land that eventually became the industrial parks of the outlying area. Over the years Professor X made millions of dollars in land speculation.
>
> However, Professor X is also a man of principle and integrity, and so year after year he paid his federal, state and local taxes without looking for loopholes. When Nixon's tax data were revealed, Professor X was horrified at how mean and petty Nixon had been in respect to his social obligations. After the tapes were revealed, he was scandalized by Nixon's corrupt practices and vulgar language. (Personal interview, 1975)

Professor X moved from loyalist, to dubious, to ambivalent, to disillusioned. Others in the community followed the same course.

However, *what* they were disillusioned with was never clear. Professor X's response to the Watergate revelations was not a critical analysis of himself, the man he once believed in, or the system that gave meaning and legitimacy to both. Rather, he was beset by an undifferentiated illness that gave focus to his anxiety and reason to avoid critical assessment of the past. Others less habituated to logic and reason retreated into mute silence. If Nixon's name could not be spoken sympathetically, it would not be spoken at all.

This response was buttressed by the traditional principle of Christian charity. Asked how he guides his parishioners' thinking about Watergate, the minister of the East Whittier Church replied:

> I counsel them to have compassion and not be vindictive. I explain that vindictiveness would be more damaging to the country . . . there has been irresponsibility shown by the media in the publicity given the case, distorted reporting. This divisiveness has hurt the country. (Personal interview, 1975)

He acknowledges Nixon has been an issue for the church, but the issue was reconciled by reaffirming that the church cares for its deviants;

it will not cast them out. This does not mean they condone the acts, only that they do not condemn the actor. Instead, they pray for Nixon and try to understand him.

There has been a move on the part of East Coast Quakers to disown Nixon (Mayer, 1973), but the ritual of denunciation had to be instigated by Nixon's own church. In Whittier the membership decided not to enact the degradation ceremony. They argued that Christian charity extends even to those who would most severely test the canons of righteousness. Thus the ritual acts that would have served to discredit Nixon's reputation for once and for all were systematically avoided. Resignation precluded impeachment, illness precluded testimony. The vested economic interests of his home town precluded religious ostracism. Richard Nixon was home free.

The community of Whittier does not deny that Watergate represents the malicious perversion of the democratic principles the country stands for. Indeed, they find the locus of evil embodied in H.R. Haldeman, who, they agree, along with his aides and underlings subverted the system for insidious selfish ambitions. His minister says Nixon is a sensitive, compassionate man. The PR and advertising men who surrounded him built up an image of him in their own interests, rather than letting him "be himself," that is, be a basically good person. That he selected poor advisers is a failing on Nixon's part, but certainly not a sin of commission. The mayor insists that Watergate is a product of the self-serving calculations of H.R. Haldeman; influential women in the Republican Party reiterate the same theme, or they speak of sinister agents of the Communist Party ceaselessly seeking revenge for Alger Hiss. They do not see Richard Nixon as a bad man, only as a victim of circumstances. They can envision a day when Nixon will be remembered for his greatness in foreign affairs, and the significance of Watergate will have been forgotten, like Teapot Dome or Wounded Knee.

Despite the crystallization of attitudes about their native son, the people of Whittier disclaim any particular interest in Nixon. Since Watergate they say "He is no more concern to us than he is to anyone else in the country." Among the youth, in particular, there is studied indifference to the man and lack of interest in the lessons Watergate might have revealed. Some, like their parents, express respect for Nixon's image and refuse to cast aspersions on his character. Others

acknowledge the hypocrisy and cynicism he represents, but they insist
this is the only game in town, and they eagerly await the opportunity
to make their own claims to money, fame, and power. Those who speak
disrespectfully of the former President or the system at large do not
speak passionately. Instead they talk about "apathy with honor,"
and they resign themselves to a life of misery and frustration. There
are few visionaries among the youth of Whittier. Few disgusted by
the past or dismayed by the present can conceive of alternatives for
the future, or, if they can, can convince others to share their vision.

The response of Whittier mirrors the response of the nation as a whole.
Critics' belief in Nixon's basic evil is reaffirmed, while loyalists' belief
in his virtue is sustained. The ambiguity surrounding his fall from
power permits such polar opinions to exist side by side, without means
for their resolution. In exile Richard Nixon has not been cast as
a sinister figure in American history. Rather, he is portrayed as a poor
unfortunate caught in the web of circumstances. Whatever his sins of
commission and omission, his fall from power is considered punishment
enough. Those who ask more are chastised for being vindictive. Americans
can hate when necessary, but they do not hold a grudge.

Few soul-searching statements have come forth to propose a critical
analysis of the events of Watergate. Instead, Nixon's resignation from
office has been taken as proof that the system works, that righteousness
is routinely victorious, that only the good guys win. The disillusioned
do not speak of disillusionment with the traditional principles of the
nation and loyalists provide a benign interpretation of the man they still
support. In short, the post-resignation mood of the nation has been one
of collective denial.

Under the Nixon administration, massive perversions of the Constitutional principles of law and order took place at home while the President
waged and then expanded an illegal war abroad. But the end of the war
did not signal a critical reappraisal of national objectives. Rather,
Vietnam was treated as an unfortunate interlude in the past of a basically
peaceful nation whose citizens essentially agree on what constitutes
the collective good. In the same sense, Nixon's resignation from
office did not signal a critical reappraisal of the democratic process by
which the collective goals of the nation are achieved. Rather, Watergate
was treated as an aberration on the part of one or a few unscrupulous

men, dedicated to their own egoistic gratification. The Mayor of Whittier counsels: "The problem with American society today is that it is attuned to negativism, to criticism. We must learn to look at the positive side of life." (Personal interview, 1975) In so doing, the Mayor sustains the mood of collective denial.

Collective denial permits conflict to be resolved by ignoring contradictions. It permits a group to disregard any embarrassing, discrediting, or disgusting aspect of its past in order to maintain the present illusion of its virtue. Collective denial is like tact in that people may know or suspect the worst, but it is never openly acknowledged. It is like repression in that a line is maintained with a moral fervor, despite the facts of history or biography.

In George Orwell's vision of the 20th century—written while the consequences of Hitler's rise to power smoldered through the Old World—collective denial is organized in a systematic manner. The past is officially denied, and the language of the present obscures any way of recapturing that knowledge. "Newspeak" is the language of a society that cannot deal with alternatives but is singularly dedicated to maintaining illusion. In striking ways, Newspeak is similar to what has been identified as the "D.C. Dialect," a variant of ordinary English spoken by the Nixon administration; most congressmen, senators, and federal officials; and, to a lesser extent, corporation executives, computer technicians, the military, promotion and sports people (Morgan and Scott, 1975). The D.C. Dialect is a language of obscurity and evasion. It gives the impression of candor as it misrepresents facts and intentions. (See figure 5.)

The language of 1984 and the language of 1974 differ in one significant respect. The goal of Newspeak is to establish one clearly understood concept in association with one staccato term. The goal of the D.C. Dialect is a multiplicity of meanings associated with multisyllabic terms. Where the objective of Newspeak is to direct thought, the objective of D.C. Dialect is to obscure thought. Despite this difference, both languages provide the speakers with an effective way to collectively deny the facts of their past or the circumstances of their present.

Collective denial is not the simple psychological mechanisms of suppression or repression distributed on a wide scale. Large numbers of people who want to suppress the past or avoid the present are a necessary precondition. But that denial only becomes collective when responsible leaders provide public examples of how the discrediting past can be repudiated, invalidated, interpreted, edited, or otherwise made congruent with present intentions. And those intentions must be phrased

Figure 5. **Totalitarian Prose**

LINGUISTIC DEVICE	NEWSPEAK* c. 1984	D.C. DIALECT** c. 1974
Any word can be used as a verb, noun, adjective, or adverb.	**Speedwise (n.)** (Quickly) [adv.]	**Funding (v.)** (Money) [n.]
The meaning of words can be transformed by adding the proper prefix or suffix.	**Unlight** (Dark)	**Misspoke** (Lied)
Words are deliberately constructed for practical purposes.	**Joycamp** (Forced labor camp)	**Intelligence community** (Spies)
There are a great many euphemisms.	**Goodsex** (Chastity)	**Game plan** (Criminal conspiracy)
Words often mean the opposite of what they suggest.	**Ministry of peace** (Ministry of war)	**Peace with honor** (Extended warfare)

*Orwell, 1948
**Morgan and Scott, 1975

in terms of the collective good. Critical appraisal of self and others gives way to forces of denial, and denial is legitimized by respectable community leaders in the name of national interest.

A traumatic event in the history of the nation is at the heart of collective denial. Repression takes place where individuals cannot accept the role they played in the disgrace of the nation. Suppression takes place where citizens recognize their role in historical destiny, but cannot resolve their actions with their expressed intentions or their idealized images. Influential speakers organize national ambivalence in ways that are meaningful to the confused citizenry; that is, in traditional terms. They reaffirm the status quo and thereby avoid cause for purposive change. As long as traditional values are in the interest of influential speakers, their reaffirmation both pacifies the populace and furthers the speakers' ambitions. Collective denial is thus eminently conservative.

Examples of collective denial abound in American history. From the massacre of the Indians to the pollution of the environment, the sensibilities of the citizenry have been assaulted by death, doom, destruction, and nihilism. Yet the principled version of what America stands for is peace, freedom, justice, and good will. Thus every American child must undergo a process of disillusionment when he or she reaches maturity and becomes wise to the ways of the world. Each must recognize betrayal as a routine fact of life and learn to cope with its predictability. Some become cynical, others bitter. Some become resigned, others vindictive. But one way or another, each must adjust to betrayal. Collective denial facilitates the process of adjustment.

Collective denial is not unique to American society. For a quarter of a century, as Nixon's star rose in the west, Germany practiced its own version of the same routine.

In the years immediately after World War II, Germany was a conquered nation, demoralized and discredited before the rest of the world. These were chaotic years for the German people, during which salvation was found in renewed dedication to work and the marketplace. Economic recovery eased the transition from the 1940s to the 1950s. Once defeated and disgraced, Germany soon renewed its place in European affairs. However, Germany's speedy return to economic prosperity was not accompanied by any critical reassessment of the past. Influential speakers ritually repudiated all ties between the past and the present, and with the official line of denazification came the public belief that, at worst, fascism and Hitler were an aberration in German history and not a natural manifestation of any latent tendencies in Western culture. There was no critical analysis of the roles played by petit bourgeois fears, scapegoating, elitism, or unquestioned obedience to authority. Hence there was no principled repudiation of the tendencies that contributed to the growth of the Nazi Party and the rise of Adolph Hitler. Ambiguity surrounded the meaning of the period between 1933 and 1945, and collective denial was possible.

If the reasons Germany followed Hitler should have been the most burning issue for postwar recovery, they were quickly forgotten in the wake of economic affluence. Until 1960 no attempt was made to incorporate the catastrophe of the past into the German stock of knowledge and experience. Public school texts made cursory references to the war and no mention of the atrocities surrounding it. University libraries were as barren. Although memoirs of Hitler's generals proliferated in the popular press, the German intelligentsia produced few critical accounts of the Fuehrer, the Nazi Party, or German society. From kindergarten through college, German youth were socialized to collective denial. Either they knew nothing about Hitler, or they believed that his major contribution to German history was curing unemployment and building the *Autobahnen*.

Lest embarrassing questions be asked at home, parents put pressure on teachers to avoid the issues at school. As a result young people did not begin to learn the truth until the German war crimes trials began in the 1960s. The elders strongly objected to the airing of the Nazi atrocities so long after the war, while the youth were deeply shocked by what they learned about their nation's past. Ironically, authoritarian Germany was characterized by a growing split between the young and the old about the same time more permissive industrial nations were also experiencing a fracture in the relations between generations.

With the exception of dissident youth, the postwar history of Germany has been characterized by collective denial of the immediate past. Guided by responsible leaders in school, church, politics, and business, Germans believe that Hitler did more good than harm for Germany, or that the Jews got no worse than they deserved, or that the German people were only following orders, or that what Germany did was no worse than what other nations do. Most Germans remain silent on the question of their involvement in the events of World War II, content to reap the benefits of the postwar prosperity. Many are apathetic, believing they are powerless to affect their own fate in the modern world. Some have become bitter and cynical, rejecting all ideals as illusion. Others have become pessimistic, fearing that their unconquered past is destined to repeat itself. But there is no evidence of any new enlightenment flowing from a critical assessment of the past. There is just the traditional order of renewed dedication to the ethic of hard work and the symbols of material success.

The similarities between the collective denial practiced in postwar Germany and the collective denial practiced in post-Watergate America bring into focus the similarities of Hitler and Nixon as 20th century figures. The malicious destruction Hitler waged through Europe from 1933 to 1945 far overshadows Nixon's subversion of the democratic process in America, and at first it makes comparison of the two seem disproportionate. However, without suggesting there is any equivalence in their historical place, there are clear similarities in the biographical development and style of these two world leaders.

To begin with, both came from provincial, petit bourgeois families, although each subsequently described his childhood as though it were one of poverty and privation. Each saw himself as the underdog, disadvantaged and oppressed.

As a youth, Adolph Hitler is described as energetic, ambitious, and irresponsible; while Richard Nixon is described as energetic, ambitious and organized. This difference in self-discipline is reflected in their respective educational careers: Hitler's formal education ended with high school; Nixon went on to complete college and law school. Despite these differences, in the same period in their life cycle, each experienced the conflict of global warfare waged with the most sophisticated technology of the time. Combat, contest, struggle, dominion, and will were the essential experiences of their early manhood, and this metaphor became the lietmotiv of their subsequent careers. In the context of global warfare, each came to embrace the basic tenet of gothic imagery: the sinister enemy bent on destroying traditional virtue. In his own way each subsequently elaborated that ancient world view.

While Nixon's wartime experiences were associated with national victory, Hitler's were associated with defeat, and therein may be the key to the differences in the lengths each would go in asserting his manhood in maturity.

Despite the fact that young Hitler had evinced an interest in architecture and young Nixon an interest in law, each was drawn to politics as a vocation after the war. In the demoralized ferment of Germany after World War I, Hitler was instrumental in forging a new political party, while in the heady victory of America after World War II, Nixon rose in the established party system. Hitler's star rose faster. By the age of 44 he was Chancellor, while Nixon did not achieve the presidency until 55, although he came close when he was younger. Ultimately, each took control of his respective nation and in so doing made unilateral decisions that altered the course of world history.

The social forces that cull one man out from the crowd suggest that all those who make it to the pages of history have something in common. If we look closely, we can find similarities, but these similarities do not reveal any fundamental truths about personality or any necessary conclusions about history.

In suggesting that there were important similarities between Germany in the 1920s and America in the 1950s, I do not wish to obscure the myriad of differences that are obvious. I do wish to suggest that the two cultures represent Old World and New World versions of the same cultural strain.

The political growth of fascism in 20th century Europe has been treated as an historic aberration in Western life. In labeling that force as "deviant," historians have neutralized its significance. Instead of focusing on the changing conditions of Western life and how these changing conditions are related to the rise of tyranny, contemporary critics and academic historians have assumed that such an aberration of Christian democratic principles cannot happen again—or it cannot happen here. However, both Germany and America share an ancient historical tradition and that tradition is the generic strain of many powerful modern nations.

The techniques of bureaucratic organization that had lain dormant for a millenium after the fall of Rome reemerged with the birth of bourgeois society in medieval times. By the 20th century these organizational skills had been transformed from an art to a science. Loudspeakers and radio, rapid print and rapid transportation all contributed to increased efficiency in the manipulation of people. Ears, eyes, and entire bodies could be captured on a massive scale, and the *manipulation of all social life became possible.* In the 1920s Hitler was quick to grasp the significance of the moment and exploit it to annihilation. Nixon was equally adept if more restrained.

Just as fundamentalist religious revivals proliferated in America in the 1920s, mass political rallies proliferated in Germany. In such settings, Hitler cultivated his personal style, and ultimately he cultivated the world view of his nation. He began by adopting an evangelical demeanor. In his public harangues he played upon the emotions of the crowd, first invoking sacred traditional values, then directing the heightened emotions those sentiments evoked toward a named enemy: the Jews, the Communists, the Slavs, the decadent West. The emotional contagion generated in his presence before the crowd was attributed to his person, and his reputation grew.

This same evangelical style of politics was repeated by Richard Nixon in midcentury America. Each man was believed by the masses because of the personal courage, resolve, vitality, heroism, and will he made claim to. Neither demonstrated leadership on the basis of any plans for the future. Rather, each claimed the right to leadership on the intrinsic worth of his being. That worth was validated by the genuine feelings it elicited from the mass audience. However, their personal charisma was a function of their ability to control people's deepest emotions by using the sophisticated technology of the 20th century to manipulate traditional sentiments of a fundamentalistic order.

What Adolph Hitler discovered in the 1920s and Richard Nixon discovered in the 1950s were the possibilities of impression management in the context of the 20th century. Each discovered how the basic techniques of the carnival pitchman could be transformed by modern technology and then used to move the masses through the ritual of the democratic process. Through this new technology old skills of interpersonal manipulation were magnified millionfold, and the globe was tipped to the speaker's advantage.

In both the 1920s and the 1950s techniques of advertising had developed in the interests of business, and these techniques were subsequently applied to the interests of party politics (Lasswell, 1930). Propaganda became a weapon by which the free citizens of a nation could be captured in the interests of a ruling elite. Directed by Herman Goebbels in Germany, an enormous propaganda machine was developed on principles such as the following explicated by Leonard Doob (1954):

It is more important for a propagandist to plan an event than to rationalize one that has occurred.

Credibility alone must determine whether propaganda output should be true or false.

News policy is a weapon of war. Its purpose is to wage war and not to give out information.

Propaganda is facilitated by leaders with prestige. It must label events and people with distinctive phrases and slogans. It must create an optimum anxiety level, facilitate the displacement of aggression, and evoke desired responses that the audience already possesses.

Under H.R. Haldeman, these same principles were employed in America, except the machine was labeled "PR" and newer technology made dissemination of the message more effective.

Like propaganda, PR is a sophisticated form of control. It does not rely on bondage or discipline, threat or force. Rather, it uses the natural intelligence of the subjects to control their own behavior. Through the manipulation of language and thought, image and metaphor, the logical conclusions people are drawn to are determined in advance. While each individual achieves the illusion of free will, what can be willed is narrowly circumscribed and artfully designed by others.

Similarities in the life, times, and political styles of Adolph Hitler and Richard Nixon suggest that both can be seen as gothic heroes of the 20th century.

In Germany and in America the seeds of gothic imagery were cultivated, and each country produced a leader who in turn elaborated and repropagated that sinister version of reality.

In his own way each man played on the anxieties, insecurities, stresses, and distresses of a society inundated by monumental change.

Each objectified evil as the threat to tranquility and order, evoking a named enemy to account for the fears and misfortunes of the masses.

Each used the sophisticated technology of the times to secure and maintain his own power.

Each unified his respective nation without offering a positive direction to guide the collective emotions so aroused.

Finally, each tested the limits people would tolerate as expressions of their collective will.

While clear differences separate the historical influence of these two 20th century figures, a family resemblance remains.

Like the Frankenstein monster, the gothic hero is both awesome and tragic. He is awesome in that he embodies the forces of change, new technological accomplishments that can transform old economic, political, and social structures. But he is tragic in that he uses those forces for destructive ends. Ultimately he destroys himself, but not before he has destroyed others.

★

Methodology

In *Life History and the Historical Moment,* Erik Erikson notes that the motives and influences of the analyst of biography are as relevant as the motives and influences of the subject of study. I intend this appendix as an "objective," that is, neutral, account of the methodological procedures I employed in writing *20th Century Gothic,* but Erikson's remarks suggest I begin that statement with an account of my own biography.

I was born in 1938 in the suburbs of New York City, the only child of a petit bourgeois Jewish family. Gloria Bennet and Lester Goldberg were first-generation Americans whose roots lay in eastern and western Europe and whose most immediate experiences were forged by the Great Depression. Drawn to the West Coast by promises of economic opportunity, my parents migrated from Long Island to Long Beach, California just before the end of World War II. I grew up in the postwar prosperity of Southern California; my childhood experiences and first knowledge of the world were thus cultivated in the milieu of a provincial port town.

I started college in Los Angeles in the mid-1950s. Between my junior year and my Ph.D. a decade later, I married, divorced, had a son, and moved to the more cosmopolitan port of San Francisco. I attended U.C.L.A. at the end of the McCarthy era and U.C. Berkeley at the beginning of the Free Speech movement. Like the subject of my study, I was influenced by the prevailing forces of my own historical moment.

The most significant influence was my encounter with sociology. I started college as an international relations major with a minor in Russian, preparing to go out in the 1950s world as a Cold War warrior: an international spy. I was very much a child of the times. By my sophomore year I discovered that the simple syllogisms I learned in youth were not the only accounting of reality, and I turned to sociology for insight into the world around me. Since then sociology has become my passion, my pastime, and my profession, while my interest in politics has been episodic.

In high school I participated in student politics, but marriage and child care dominated my everyday affairs throughout college and graduate school. I took a lively interest in local, state, and national political contests and engaged in the ritual of voting until 1964, when I withdrew from the political process in dismay having voted for the "peace candidate" and seen the war expanded. Later, I reregistered and became a precinct worker in San Francisco for a few years. Watergate revived the political fervor of my adolescence.

After completing my doctoral thesis in 1965, I took a position at San Francisco State University, where I have been ever since. I rose through the ranks to full professor, teaching courses in deviant behavior, qualitative methods, sociolinguistics, American society, social psychology, the sociology of television, and similar topics at the undergraduate and graduate level. I became active in various professional associations, serving on committees and holding office. I pursued research interests in the counterculture, intoxicants, television, and grooming behavior. Some of this research was subsidized by government grants; most of it was not. The present research was financed out of my household budget and the time not otherwise claimed by my teaching duties.

In June 1972 I had completed another semester teaching deviant behavior at San Francisco State. Three years earlier that campus had been wracked by conflict and dissention. I had witnessed armed police in the hallways and watched students being beaten in front of the library steps. My sense of what was normal—that childhood vision cultivated in the years after the Second World War—would never be the same again, even though the campus eventually returned to its more traditional form and my tenured position permitted me to continue to speak my mind.

When the newspapers began carrying accounts of the break-in at the Democratic National Committee headquarters, I found the story curious. I began to follow its progression and contemplate the implications of the growing corpus of facts, both alleged and denied. I found Watergate a provocative test of various theories of deviance that I was teaching, and, as more and more evidence began to amass through the following fall, I bought examples into the classroom to share with my students. A few years earlier students considered accounts of injustice and corruption relevant to the academic discussion of deviance. Yet through 1972 and far into 1973, my students were manifestly uninterested in the Watergate revelations. They told me, "That's the kind of man Richard Nixon is," and "Every politician does that," and insisted that we discuss instead what they, and hundreds of millions like them, believed were more pressing examples of crime and malfeasance: juvenile delinquency, drug addiction, prostitution.

Colleagues and friends were more willing to discuss the stories that dominated the popular press and television news. Their interest sustained my own.

In the spring of 1973 the papers reported that John Dean, the counsel to the President, was meeting with officials from the Justice Department. By then it seemed obvious that the facts of Watergate were yet to be revealed, and I began to take a systematic interest in the Nixon administration. I continued to collect clippings from the popular press and follow the television coverage. Through the summer months I watched the West Coast broadcasts of the Ervin Committee hearings in the morning, and some days I watched the rebroadcasts at night, taking notes and thinking about the implications of these revelations. By the time of the Cox firing I began to order my observations into a set of questions that eventually developed into the themes of the present book.

Once such questions were formulated, I began a systematic search of relevant documentary sources for answers. Bay Area public and university libraries (and their librarians) as well as the public and college library in Whittier (and their librarians) provided copious material on the career of Richard Nixon, on the social influences that pervaded his lifetime, and on the historical forces that molded these social influences. For two years I was immersed in politics and history.

The resultant portrait of Richard Nixon is thus filtered through the biographical influences of the analyst. My personal knowledge of Nixon dates back to the 1950s; his career was part of the political panorama of my youth. My sociological interest in his affairs is of more recent vintage, but not unaffected by my past. As a matter of methodological discipline, I have tried to suppress my personal feelings and consider the facts, sifted and sorted from various sources, on their own terms. My success is a matter of judgment for the reader.

In the fall of 1974 I began to outline the text, and writing began the following February, after my first visit to Whittier and San Clemente. Writing forced me to order and objectify my impressions, ideas, insights, and intuitive responses. I began to create an historical perspective in which Richard Nixon, American society, and the Watergate scandals were inevitable scenes in a progression of events whose beginnings are only dimly recognizable and whose future was either invariant or problematic. In the process of such objectification I began to experience a change in perspective. My personal animosity for the man and his way of life began to fade as my sense of tragic irony expanded. I did not feel more comfortable than I did when I could simply blame a particular individual and ignore the forces that created the individual in the first place. But I did feel that I had grasped, in some fundamental way, the larger picture in which both Richard Nixon and I were inextricably bound.

With this caveat, the following pages outline the methods and procedures this particular analyst employed in assessing the life and times of Richard Nixon.

Most of the facts of history and biography have been sifted from public documents of one sort or another: accounts from the popular press, as well as the writings of biographers, sociologists, historians, political scientists, anthropologists, psychologists, and economists.

Not all facts considered significant to a pattern could be found in more than one source. In such cases, I treated accounts from intimates—his mother, his wife, his speechwriter, for instance—as valid, independent of any other documentation. Facts *observed* by biographers as eyewitness accounts were also treated this way, although facts *inferred* by biographers were held problematic. The facts about Nixon's involvement with organized crime are of this order, and they are noted as circumstantial in the text.

Another body of evidence consisted of live television coverage of presidential speeches, press conferences, and congressional committee hearings: transcripts of the presidential tapes made by the Judiciary Committee and transcripts of congressional committee hearings. These were treated as primary sources, eyewitness accounts not heretofore sifted by the perspective of previous analysts. Notes were taken of various televised events, and standard procedures of content analysis were used to organize transcript materials.

Of particular interest were three sources of information: the White House *Transcripts* of presidential conversations, and Nixon's two autobiographical books, *Six Crises* and *Memoirs*. These documents were treated as the closest an outsider could get to the intimate thought and style of the man in question. In no case were these eyewitness accounts unordered by human motive. The White House *Transcripts* were edited, most likely by Nixon himself, to show the Judiciary Committee and the public at large that Nixon had committed no impeachable offense. With the exception of the last chapter, *Six Crises* was ghostwritten, and his *Memoirs* involved the assistance of a staff of researchers and a full-time historian. Both autobiographical accounts were written by a man out of office to justify and rationalize the actions he took while in office. In the first Nixon uses the metaphor of "crisis" to organize the significant events of his life; in the second he uses more traditional chronology as the organizing principle. Though all are self-serving statements, each was treated as an authoritative source.

Observations and interviews in the community that nurtured Richard Nixon and the community to which he retreated in exile constitute another body of evidence. In both communities standard anthropological field-work techniques were used to generate a description of the day-to-day life of Whittier during Nixon's boyhood and youth and the response of this community to his resignation. In San Clemente I wanted to know how people made sense of the historic events they had just witnessed and how they explained the turn Richard Nixon's career had taken. In January and June of 1975 I made trips to Southern California. In Whittier I interviewed shopkeepers and students, matrons and officials, people on the street and people in public office. The community that nurtured Richard Nixon still contains many who knew him in youth and in his first years of law practice; some of these were among the people I interviewed. Contacts in Whittier introduced me to people who had served in Nixon's campaign and in his first administration, and their cooperation contributed to the lore of eyewitness accounts. In San Clemente I interviewed residents and tourists as well as the volunteers who handle Nixon's mail.

Finally, interviews with William Rogers' daughter and Murray Chotiner's son provided additional resource material covering a long period of Nixon's career.

In addition to the documentary material in the archives at Whittier College Library and Whittier City Library, I scanned microfilm copies of *The Whittier News* for the period of Nixon's youth until he left for law school. Knowing that he was a reader in childhood, I sought to see what he might have read. I also reviewed accounts of *The Whittier News* at key points in his political career to assess community sentiments and opinion.

The search for archival material was itself noted as an item of information. Nixon materials routinely "get lost" in the community of Whittier. An oral history, done by a professor at the local college through funds from the Nixon Foundation and deeded to Whittier College, was, according to one informant, "confiscated as government property."

Another informant says Whittier is supposed to get a copy of the oral history, but she does not know where it is. There are no special funds provided for Whittier College to maintain the special collections library, and so memorabilia are scant, and much of what is available is sarcastic and scurrilous. Inquiries about special Nixon collections at the newspaper morgue and the City Library produced the same response. "Nixon material gets lost" in the archives of Whittier. When the city librarian finally found the public library's special Nixon collection, it consisted almost entirely of newspaper clippings chronicling Nixon's involvement with the Methodist Church in Washington and his friendship with Billy Graham. This discovery, along with the facts of his evangelical experiences in childhood, was fundamental in my questioning his commitment to the Quaker faith.

With respect to Nixon's formative years, the documentary record is scant. The more removed Nixon becomes from the masses, the richer the evidentiary resources, until he reaches the Oval Office, where we find almost verbatim accounts of his intimate conversations. The character of the accessible data partially dictated the model of analysis. I assumed that for the formative years of his life, he was indistinguishable from any other boy born in his generation; that the forces he was subject to were forces that any male child might experience at the same time, in the same situation. As he moved from one in millions to one in four hundred, then one in a hundred, one in two, and finally into the number one position, particular influences were identified as residing (1) in his own style an ambition, and (2) in the associates he dealt with on a routine basis.

With the addition of the concept of significant others, Erikson's model provided the framework for analyzing the interrelation of history and biography. A model of Richard Milhous Nixon as a person was constructed in the following way. Biographical facts were reviewed. Pictures of the prevailing culture and its characteristic changes were drawn from various historical accounts. The influence of the prevailing culture on Nixon's personal biography was then assessed by the hypo-thetico-deductive model: *How would this factor* (e.g., the veneration of business in the 1920s) *affect this person* (a boy between the the the formative ages of 7 and 17, bright, ambitious) *in these particular circumstances* (from a petit bourgeois family, with links to the inner circle of the community, etc.)? Conclusions about the influence of prevailing cultural forces were then reincorporated into the model of the man at varying stages of his life cycle, and the influence of the next historical era was assessed on this expanded model. In this methodical, systematic way, I tried to ignore what I knew about the subject's future as I reconstructed the phases of his development. I tried to be guided by the facts of the evidentiary record and not by my personal knowledge or ad hoc conclusions.

Not all facts have the same significance to the biographer. In order to assess the importance of some facts, discount the validity of others, and assign many to the region of irrelevance, I employed general principles drawn from the theories of symbolic interaction and class conflict. Sociological theories were implicit in all that I did, but since the text was written for a more general audience, I shall not detail the theoretical concerns that lay behind my practical decisions other than to note that the significance of facts was assessed by theoretical models of individual and societal process.

Since the text was intended for a general audience, I have avoided copious footnotes and citations. With the exception of direct quotations, I have cited sources to emphasize rather than to document the facts. Furthermore, I have taken the liberty of editing quotations from the transcripts of the President's tapes to facilitate reading. Throughout the transcripts Nixon continues to hem and haw, starting a sentence, changing it mid-clause, repeating, and rewording. Other speakers often talk in a circuitous fashion, making a paragraph do for a sentence. In such cases I have edited the statements into clearer, more concise English, trying to preserve the particular flavor of the sequence whenever possible. The following example of the original and the edited version of an exchange between Kleindienst and Nixon demonstrates the procedure, although not all changes were as extensive as this example.

ORIGINAL
(Transcripts, pp. 705-706)

KLEINDIENST: And likewise in this case. If I had committed a crime and you know about it and you say, "Kleindienst, you go in the Court and plead guilty to the commission of that crime and here is ten thousand dollars, you know, to tide you over and so forth."

NIXON: That isn't a crime?

KLEINDIENST: No. On the other hand, if you know that I committed a crime.

NIXON: Right.

KLEINDIENST: And you say, "You go in there and plead guilty, and here is twenty-five thousand dollars on the condition that thereafter you'll say nothing. You just make the plea, take the Fifth Amendment, the judge cites you for contempt, you've got to continue to testify, you don't. You do not take it." Then you are now in a position of obstructing justice.

NIXON: Excuse me. If you'd explain that again. If you tell 'em —if you tell 'em—if you raise the money for the purpose of telling them *not* to talk.

KLEINDIENST: After he's pleaded guilty. Let's take the—

NIXON: Well . . . (etc.)

EDITED VERSION
(Text, p. 247)

KLEINDIENST: If I committed a crime and you know about it and you say, "Kleindienst, you go in the Court and plead guilty to the commission of that crime. Here is ten thousand dollars . . . to tide you over and so forth."

NIXON: That isn't a crime?

KLEINDIENST: No. On the other hand, if you know I committed a crime . . . and you say, "Go in there and plead guilty. Here is twenty-five thousand dollars on the condition that you say nothing. You just . . . take the Fifth Amendment. The judge cites you for contempt; you've got to continue to testify. You don't . . . Now you are in a position of obstructing justice.

NIXON: Excuse me. If you'd explain that again.

Bibliography

Able, Theodore
  1938   *Why Hitler Came into Power,* Englewood Cliffs, New Jersey, Prentice-Hall, Inc.

Editors
  1973   "Adding Up Watergate," *Time Magazine,* 102: Aug. 20, 8-22.

Abrahamsen, David
  1976   *Nixon vs. Nixon: An Emotional Tragedy,* New York, New American Library.

Adler, Bill
  1969   *The Wit and Humor of Richard Nixon,* New York, Popular Library.

Ahern, M.B.
  1971   *The Problem of Evil,* New York, Schocken Books.

Allan, Frederick Lewis
  1959   *Only Yesterday,* New York, Bantam Books.
  1969   *The Big Change: America Transforms Itself 1900-1950,* New York, Perennial Library.

Allen, Gary
  1971   *Richard Nixon: The Man Behind the Mask,* Belmont, Massachusets, Western Islands.

Alsop, Stewart
  1958   "Nixon on Nixon," *Saturday Evening Post,* July 12, 13.

American Heritage Magazine (ed)
  1969   *The Inaugural Story 1789-1969,* New York, American Heritage Publishing Co.

Amlong, William
  1973   "Bebe and Dick on a Houseboat," *The Nation,* Nov. 12, 217: 489-493.

Arendt, Hannah
  1950   "The Aftermath of Nazi Rule," *Commentary,* Oct., 10: 342-353.
  1958   *The Origins of Totalitarianism,* New York, Meridian Books.
  1975   "Home to Roost: A Bicentennial Address," *New York Review of Books,* June 26, 2-6.

Arora, Satish K. and Harold D. Lasswell
1969   *Political Communication: The Public Language of Political Elites in India and the United States,* New York, Holt, Rinehart and Winston.

Arterton, F. Christopher
1974   "The Impact of Watergate on Children's Attitudes Toward Political Authority," *Political Science Quarterly,* 66(2): 269-287.

Arguelles, Jose A.
1975   *The Transformative Vision,* Berkeley, California, Shambala.

Ashman, Charles and Sheldon Englemayer
1973   *Martha: The Mouth That Roared,* Berkeley, California, Medallion Books.

Atkins, Ollie
1977   *The White House Years,* Chicago, Playboy Press.

Banfield, Edward C.
1958   *The Moral Basis of a Backward Society,* New York, Free Press.

Barber, James David
1972   *The Presidential Character: Predicting Performance in the White House,* Englewood Cliffs, New Jersey, Prentice-Hall, Inc.

Bark, William
1958   *Origins of the Medieval World,* Stanford, California, Stanford University Press.

Barton, Bruce
1924   *The Man Nobody Knows,* Indianapolis, Indiana, Bobbs-Merrill Co.

Becker, Howard S. (ed.)
1964   *The Other Side: Perspectives on Deviance,* New York, Free Press.

Bendiner, Robert
1956   "The Chotiner Academy of Scientific Vote-Catching," *The Reporter,* Sept. 20, 15: 28-29.

Bernstein, Carl, and Bob Woodward
1975   *All the President's Men,* New York, Warner Paperback
        Library.

Bethell, Tom
1977   "The Myth of an Adversary Press," *Harper's,* Jan.
        254: 33-40.

Boorstin, Daniel J.
1973   *The Americans: The Democratic Experience,* New York,
        Random House.

Booth, Wayne
1973   "Loathing and Ignorance on the Campaign Trail: 1972,"
        Columbia Journalism Review, Nov./Dec., 12: 7-12.

Boroson, Warren
1958   "What Makes Nixon Run?" *Avant-Garde,* Jan., 1: 1-9.

Bottomore, T.B.
1966   *Elites and Society,* Middlesex, England, Penguin Books.

Bradlee, Benjamin C.
1975   *Conversations with Kennedy,* New York, Norton.

Branch, Taylor
1974   "Crimes of Weakness," *Harper's,* Oct., 248: 40-43

Brandenburgh, Donald
1960   *A Comparative Study of Social Rank and the Nixon Papers,*
        unpublished M.A. thesis, Department of Sociology, Whittier
        College, California.

Brashear, Ernest
1952   "Who Is Richard Nixon?" *New Republic,* Sept. 1,
        127: 9-12 and Sept. 8, pp. 9-11.

Breslin, Jimmy
1975   *How the Good Guys Finally Won: Notes from an Impeachment
        Summer,* New York, Viking Press.

Brown, J.A.C.
1967   *Techniques of Persuasion: From Propaganda to Brainwashing,*
        Middlesex, England, Penguin Books.

Bryant, Traphes, and Frances Leighton
1976   *Dog Days at the White House,* New York, Pocket Books.

Bullock, Allan
1971   *Hitler: A Study in Tyranny*, New York, Perennial Library.

Burlingham, Bo
1974   "Paranoia in Power," *Harper's*, Oct., 248: 26-37.

Calic, Edouard (ed.)
1971   *Secret Conversations with Hitler*, New York, The John Day Co.

Campbell, Anne
1969   *The Picture Life of Richard Milhous Nixon*, New York, Franklin Watts, Inc.

Carter, Jimmy
1976   "To Establish Justice in a Sinful World: Excerpts from Jimmy Carter's Law Day Speech, May 4th, 1974," *Rolling Stone*, Dec. 16, p. 72.
1977   *A Government as Good as Its People*, New York, Pocket Books.

Cater, Douglass
1958   "Who Is Nixon, What Is He?" *The Reporter*, Nov. 27, 19: 9-13.

Chambers, Whittaker
1952   *Witness*, New York, Random House.

Chesen, Eli S.
1973   *President Nixon's Psychiatric Profile*, New York, Peter H. Wyden.

Cheyney, Edward
1961   *European Background of American History 1300-1600*, New York, Collier Books.

Chotiner, Murray
1960   "Managing the Campaign," in J.M. Cannon (ed.), *Politics U.S.A.*, Garden City, New York, Doubleday & Co.

Cohen, Richard M., and Jules Witcover
1974   *A Heartbeat Away: The Investigation and Resignation of Vice President Spiro T. Agnew*, New York, Viking Press.

Cohen, Yehudi A.
1961   *Social Structure and Personality*, New York, Holt, Rinehart and Winston.

Cohn, Norman
1975   *Europe's Inner Demons,* New York, New American Library.

Colson, Charles
1976   *Born Again,* Old Tappan, New Jersey, Chosen Books.

Cordtz, Dan
1973   "The Imperial Life Style of the U.S. President," *Fortune Magazine,* Oct., 88: 143-147 ff.

Costello, William
1960   *The Facts About Nixon,* New York, Viking Press.

Cox, Tricia Nixon
1974   "My Father and Watergate," *Ladies Home Journal,* April, 136, 164.

Crouse, Timothy
1974a   *The Boys on the Bus,* New York, Ballantine Books.
1974b   "The Long Ear of the Law: The White House Tapes," *Rolling Stone,* Dec. 5, pp. 36-38.

Dash, Samuel
1976   *Chief Counsel: Inside the Ervin Committee—The Untold Story,* New York, Random House.

Davis, Fred
1975   "A Watergate Afterthought: Muted by the Media or the Anesthetisation of Chaos." Unpublished paper.

Dean, John
1976   "Rituals of the Herd," *Rolling Stone,* Oct. 7, 38-58.

DeToledano, Ralph
1956   *Nixon,* New York, Holt, Rinehart and Winston
1969   *One Man Alone,* New York, Funk and Wagnalls.

Diamond, Edwin
1974   "Psychojournalism," *Columbia Journalism Review,* March/April, 13: 7-11.

Dibble, Vernon K.
1963   "Four Types of Inference from Documents to Events," *History and Theory,* 3: 203-226.

Donovan, Richard
1952   "Birth of a Salesman," *The Reporter,* Oct. 14, 7: 29-33.

Doob, Leonard W.
1954   "Goebbels' Principles of Propaganda," pp. 508-521 in
D. Katz, et al. (eds.), *Public Opinion and Propaganda*,
New York, The Dryden Press.

Dornberg, John
1961   *Schizophrenic Germany*, New York, Macmillan.

Drew, Elizabeth B.
1970   "The White House Hard Hats," *The Atlantic*, Oct., 226:
51-57.

Dulles, Foster Rhea
1965   *A History of Recreation: America Learns to Play*, New York,
Appleton-Century-Crofts.

Dunham, Roger and Armand Mauss
1976   "Waves from Watergate: Evidence Concerning the Impact
of the Watergate Scandal upon Political Legitimacy and
Social Control," *Pacific Sociological Review*, 19: 469-490.

Dworkin, Ronald
1972   "The Jurisprudence of Richard Nixon," *New York Review
of Books*, May 4, 27-35.

Eck, Marcel
1970   *Lies and Truth*, London, MacMillan.

Edmondson, Madeline, and Alden Cohen
1976   *The Women of Watergate*, New York, Pocket Books.

Ehrlichman, John
1976   *The Company*, New York, Simon & Schuster.

Eisenhower, David
1975   "The Last Days in the Nixon White House," *Good Housekeeping*, Sept., 89: 179-184.

Eisenhower, Julie (ed.)
1972   *Eye on Nixon: A Photographic Study of the President
and the Man*, New York, Hawthorne Books.

Eisenstadt, Abraham, Ari Hoogenboom and Hans Trefousse
1979   *Before Watergate: Problems of Corruption in American
Society*, New York, Brooklyn College Press.

Eisenstadt, S.N.
1956   *From Generation to Generation: Age Groups and Social Structure,* New York, Free Press.

Erikson, Erik
1950   *Childhood and Society,* New York, Norton.
1975   *Life History and the Historical Moment,* New York, Norton.

Erikson, Kai T.
1969   *Wayward Puritan: A Study in the Sociology of Deviance,* New York, Wiley.

Ermann, M. David, and Richard Lundman
1978   *Corporate and Governmental Deviance: Problems of Organizational Behavior in Contemporary Society,* New York, Oxford University Press.

Evans, Les, and Allen Myers
1974   *Watergate and the Myth of American Democracy,* New York, Pathfinder Press.

Evans, Rowland Jr., and Robert D. Novak
1971   *Nixon and the White House: The Frustration of Power,* New York, Vintage Books.

Fairlie, Henry
1974   "Lessons of Watergate: An Essay on the Possibility of Morality in Politics," *Encounter,* Oct, 8-29.

Feldman, Trude B.
1974   "The Quiet Courage of Pat Nixon," *McCalls Magazine,* May, 94-95 ff.

Fest, Joachim C.
1975   *Hitler,* (tr. Richard and Clara Winston), New York, Vintage Books.

Finch, Gerald
1974   "Impeachment and the Dynamics of Public Opinion: A Comment on 'Guilty, Yes; Impeachment, No,' " *Political Science Quarterly,* 89(2): 301-304.

Flew, Anthoney (ed.)
1965   *Logic and Language,* Garden City, New York, Doubleday Anchor Books.

Foley, Charles
1975   "Richard Nixon's Comeback Plan," *The Observer*, Oct, 16-18

Fox, Frank, and Stephen Parker
1974a   "Why Nixon Did Himself In: A Behavioral Examination of His Need to Fail," *New York Magazine*, Sept. 9, 26-32.
1974b   "Is the Pardon Explained by the Ford-Nixon Tapes?" *New York Magazine*, Oct. 14, 41-45.

Frady, Marshall
1979   "The Use and Abuse of Billy Graham," *Esquire*, April 10, 25-44.

Friedman, Leon (ed.)
1974   *United States V. Nixon*, New York, Chelsea House Publishers.

Frost, David
1978   *I Gave Them a Sword: Behind the Scenes of the Nixon Interviews*, New York, Ballantine Books.

Galbraith, John Kenneth
1960   *The Affluent Society*, Boston, Houghton Mifflin.

Gardner, Lloyd C.
1973   *The Great Nixon Turnaround*, New York, New Viewpoints.

Gardner, Richard
1952   *Fighting Quaker*, unpublished manuscript, Whittier College Library, Whittier, California.

Gerth, Hans, and C. Wright Mills (eds.)
1958   *From Max Weber: Essays in Sociology*, New York, Oxford University Press.

Gerth, Jeff
1972   "Nixon and the Mafia," *Sundance*, Nov./Dec., 30-42 ff.

Gleckner, Robert F., and Gerald E. Enscoe (eds.)
1962   *Romanticism: Points of View*, Englewood Cliffs, New Jersey, Prentice-Hall.

Goffman, Erving
1959   *The Presentation of Self in Everyday Life*, Garden City, New York, Doubleday Anchor Books.
1969   *Strategic Interaction*, Philadelphia, University of Pennsylvania Press.

Goodman, Mary Ellen
1967   *The Individual and Culture,* Homewood, Illinois, Dorsey Press.

Gorey, Hays
1974   "Dean's Dilemma," *Harper's,* Oct., 248: 63-65.

Gregor, A. James
1969   *The Ideology of Fascism,* New York, Free Press.

Greider, William
1974   "The Trouble with Rocky," *Rolling Stone,* Dec. 5, 32-44.

Haldeman, H.R., with Joseph DiMona
1978   *The Ends of Power,* New York, New York Times Book Co.

Harris, Mark
1964   *Mark the Glove Boy,* New York, Macmillan.

Harris, Neil
1973   *Humbug: The Art of P.T. Barnum,* Boston, Little, Brown.

Editors
1974   "Has the Press Done a Job on Nixon?" *Columbia Journalism Review,* Jan.-Feb., 50-58.

Hearings Before the Committee on Judiicary, House of Representatives
1974a   *Comparison of White House and Judiciary Committee Transcripts of Eight Recorded Presidential Conversations,* Washington, D.C., U.S. Government Printing Office.

1974b   *Presidential Statements on the Watergate Break-In and Its Investigation,* Washington, D.C., U.S. Government Printing Office.

1974c   *Testimony of Witnesses, Book II,* Washington, D.C., U.S. Government Printing Office.

1974d   *Transcripts of Eight Recorded Presidential Conversations,* Washington, D.C., U.S. Government Printing Office.

Henderson, Charles P.
1972   *The Nixon Theology,* New York, Harper & Row.

Hess, Stephen
1974   *The Presidential Campaign,* Washington, D.C., Brookings Institution.

Higgins, George V.
1974   "The Friends of Richard Nixon," *Atlantic*, Nov., 234: 41-52.

Hoffman, Paul
1970   *The New Nixon*, New York, Tower Publications.

Hofstadter, Richard
1952   *The Paranoid Style in American Politics and Other Essays*, New York, Vintage Books.
1972   *The Idea of a Party System*, Berkeley, University of California Press.

Editors
1970   "How Nixon's White House Works," *Time Magazine*, June 8, 15-20.

Huizinga, Johan
1950   *Homo Ludens: A Study of the Play Element in Culture*, Boston, Beacon Press.

Editors
1956   "Investigations: The Friends from California," *Time Magazine*, May 14, 28-29.

Jaworski, Leon
1976   *The Right and the Power: The Prosecution of Watergate*, New York, Reader's Digest Press.

Jeness, Linda, and Andrew Pulley
1973   *Watergate: The View from the Left*, New York, Pathfinder Press.

Johns-Heine, Patricia and Hans H. Gerth
1957   "Values in Mass Periodical Fiction, 1921-1940," p. 226-234 in B. Rosenberg and D. Manning (eds.) *Mass Culture*, Glencoe, Ilinois, Free Press.

Joint Committee on Internal Revenue Taxation
1974   *Examination of President Nixon's Tax Returns for 1969 through 1972*, Washington, D.C., U.S. Government Printing Office.

Jones, Elizabeth Jensen
1958   *A Content Analysis of the Nixon Papers*, unpublished M.A. thesis, Department of Sociology, Whittier College, Whittier, California.

Jones, Howard Mumford
1970   *The Age of Energy: Varieties of American Experience, 1865-1915*, New York, Viking Press.

Editors
1974   "Julie: Her Father's Daughter," *Newsweek*, Oct. 14, 39-43.

Kautsky, Karl
1972   *Foundations of Christianity*, New York, Monthly Review Press.

Keogh, James
1972   *President Nixon and the Press*, New York, Funk and Wagnalls.

Kerns, Doris
1976   *Lyndon Johnson and the American Dream*, New York, Harper & Row.

Kipling, Richard
1973   "Fascism: Myths and Possibilities," *Journal of Contemporary Revolution*, Winter 1973-1974, 6: 56-66.

Kissinger, Henry
1976   "America and the World: Principle and Pragmatism," *Time Magazine*, Dec. 27, 41-43.

Klein, Alexander
1960   *The Magnificent Scoundrels*, New York, Ballantine Books.

Kohn, Howard
1976   "The Hughes-Nixon-Lansky Connection: The Secret Alliances of the CIA from World War II to Watergate," *Rolling Stone*, May 20, 40-50, 77-92.

Kohn, Howard, and Lowell Bergman
1976   "Reagan's Millions," *Rolling Stone*, Aug 26, 46-50.

Korff, Baruch
1974   *The Personal Nixon: Staying on the Summit*, Washington, D.C., Fairness Publishers.

Kornitzer, Bela
1960   *The Real Nixon*, New York, Rand McNally.

Kraus, Sidney (ed.)
1962   *The Great Debates: Background, Perspective, Effects*, Bloomington, Indiana University Press.

Krige, J.D.
1947   "The Social Function of Witchcraft," *Theoria,* 1: 8-21.

Kroeber, A.L.
1963   *Style and Civilization,* Berkeley, University of California Press.

Kunkin, Art
1974   *Organized Crime Behind Nixon!,* City of Industry, California, Therapy Productions.

Lasky, Victor
1977   *It Didn't Start with Watergate,* New York, Dell Publishing Co.

Lasswell, Harold
1930   "The Propagandist Bids for Power," *American Scholar,* 8: 350-357.

Lefebvre, Henri
1971   *Everyday Life in the Modern World,* New York, Harper & Row.

Leinster, Colin
1970   "Nixon's Friend Bebe," *Life,* July 31, 69: 21-25.

Lerner, Max
1957   *America as a Civilization,* New York, Simon & Schuster.

LeShana, David C.
1969   *Quakers in California,* Newberg, Oregon, The Carclay Press.

Levine, Herbert
1974   "The Culture of Fascism," *The Nation,* Aug. 17, 219: 103-107.

Lewis, Arthur H.
1971   *Carnival,* New York, Pocket Books.

Lewis, Finlay
1973   "Some Errors and Puzzles in Watergate Coverage," *Columbia Journalism Review,* Nov./Dec., 12: 26-32.

Lewis, Sinclair
(1922)
1961   *Babbit,* New York, Signet Books.
(1927)
1970   *Elmer Gantry,* New York, Signet Books.

Liddy, G. Gordon
1974   "A Patriot Speaks," *Harper's*, Oct., 249: 45-51.

Liddy, Mrs. G. Gordon
1973   "Watergate Wife," *Ladies Home Journal*, Sept., *90: 79, 132-138.*

Lilley, Samuel
1965   *Men, Machines and History*, New York, International Publishers.

Lorenz, J.D.
1978   *Jerry Brown: The Man on the White Horse*, Boston, Houghton Mifflin Co.

Luechtenberg, William
1958   *The Perils of Prosperity: 1914-1932*, Chicago, University of Chicago Press.

Luethy, Herbert
1952   "Behind Reawakened German Nationalism," *Commentary*, Feb., 13: 115-123.
1954   "The Wretched Little Demon That Was Hitler," *Commentary*, Feb. 17, 129-138.

Lukas, J. Anthony
1973   *Nightmare: The Underside of the Nixon Years*, New York, Viking Press.

Lundberg, Ferdinand
1975   *The Rockefeller Syndrome*, New York, Kensington Publishing Corp.

Lurie, Leonard
1971   *The King Makers*, New York, Coward, McCann and Geoghegan.
1972   *The Running of Richard Nixon*, New York, Coward, McCann and Geoghegan.
1973   *The Impeachment of Richard Nixon*, New York, Berkeley Publishing Co.

Lyman, Stanford M., and Marvin B. Scott
1970   *A Sociology of the Absurd*, New York, Appleton-Century-Crofts.

Lynd, Robert S., and Helen Merrell Lynd
  1929   *Middletown: A Study in American Culture,* New York, Harcourt Brace and Co.
  1937   *Middletown in Transition: A Study in Cultural Conflicts,* New York, Harcourt Brace and Co.

Magruder, Jeb Stuart
  1975   *An American Life: One Man's Road to Watergate,* New York, Pocket Books.

Mankiewicz, Frank
  1973   *Perfectly Clear: Nixon from Whittier to Watergate,* New York, Popular Library.
  1975   *U.S. vs. Richard M. Nixon: The Final Crisis,* New York, Ballantine Books.

Manning, Jonathan R.
  1973   *The Propaganda of Adolph Hitler,* Phoenix, Arizona, O'Sullivan Woodwide & Co.

Maurer, David W.
  1962   *The Big Con,* New York, Signet Books.

May, Rollo
  1974   "The Fall of Richard Nixon: What We Must Not Forget," *Redbook,* Nov., 144: 92, 165-168.

Mayer, Milton
  1973   "Disownment: The Quakers and Their President," *Christian Century,* Oct. 10, 1000-1003.

Mazlish, Bruce
  1973   *In Search of Nixon: A Psychohistorical Inquiry,* Baltimore, Penguin Books.

Mazo, Earl
  1959   *Richard Nixon: A Political and Personal Portrait,* New York, Avon Books.

McCarthy, Mary
  1973   *The Mask of State: Watergate Portraits,* New York, Harcourt Brace Jovanovich.

McCartney, James
  1973   "The Washington Post and Watergate: How Two Davids Slew Goliath," *Columbia Journalism Review,* July/Aug. 12: 8-22.

McGeever, Patrick
1974   "Guilty Yes; Impeachment No: Some Empirical Findings,"
        Political Science Quarterly, 69: 2, 289-301.

McGinnis, Joe
(1968)
1970   *The Selling of the President,* New York, Pocket Books.

McNall, Scott G., and Sally O. Margolin
1974   "A Preliminary Study of the Linkage Between U.S. Multi-
        national Corporations and U.S. Foreign Policy Making
        Agencies," paper presented at Pacific Sociological Asso-
        ciation, April.

Merriam, Eve
1970   *The Nixon Poems,* New York, Atheneum.

Meyer, Donald
1966   *The Positive Thinkers,* Garden City, New York, Double-
        Day Anchor Books

Miller, Marvin
1974   *The Breaking of a President, Vol. 1 - Vol. 4,* City of Industry,
        California, Therapy Productions.

Miller, Merle
1973   *Plain Speaking: An Oral Biography of Harry S. Truman,*
        New York, Berkeley Publishing Corporation.

Miller, Walter
1958   "Focal Concerns of the Lower Class," *Journal of Social
        Issues,* 14: 5-19.

Mills, C. Wright
1956   *White Collar,* New York, Oxford University Press.

Editors
1956   "Mr. Chotiner's Clients," *The New Republic,* May 21
        134: 3-4.

Mitgang, Herbert
1972   *Get These Men Out of the Hot Sun,* " New York, Arbor House.

Mitscherlich, Alexander, and Margarete Mitscherlich
1974   "The Inability to Mourn," pp. 257-70 in R.J. Lifton
        (ed.), *Explorations in Psychohistory,* New York, Simon &
        Schuster.

Morgan, Paul, and Sue Scott
1975   *The D.C. Dialect,* New York, Washington Mews Books.

Morris, Colin
1972   *The Discovery of the Individual: 1050-1200,* New York, Harper & Row Torchbooks.

Mowry, George (ed.)
1963   *The Twenties: Fords, Flappers and Fanatics,* Englewood Cliffs, New Jersey, Prentice-Hall.

Murray, Stephen O.
1975   "Styles of Sociolinguistic Power and Solidarity in the Oval Office," paper presented at 70th annual meeting of the American Sociological Association, Aug.

Myers, Robert J.
1973   *The Tragedie of King Richard the Second,* Washington, D.C., Acropolis Books, Ltd.

Myerson, Michael
1973   *Watergate: Crime in the Suites,* New York, International Publishers.

Nadeau, Remi
1963   *California: The New Society,* New York, David McKay.

National Commission on the Causes and Prevention of Violence
1969   *Rights in Concord: The Response to the Counter-Inaugural Protest Activities,* Washington, D.C., U.S. Government Printing Office, Jan. 18-20.

Neaman, Judith
1975   *Suggestion of the Devil: The Origins of Madness,* New York, Doubleday Anchor Books.

New York Times Staff (ed.)
1973   *The Watergate Hearings: Break-In and Cover-Up,* New York, Bantam Books.
1974   *The End of a Presidency,* New York, Bantam Books.

Nixon, Hannah M.
1960   "Richard Nixon: A Mother's Story," *Good Housekeeping,* June, 150: 54-57, 207-216.

Nixon, Patricia Ryan
1952   "I Say He's a Wonderful Guy," *Saturday Evening Post,* Sept. 6, 225: 17-19 ff.

Nixon, Richard M.
1961   *The Challenges We Face,* New York, Popular Library.
1962   *Six Crises,* New York, Pocket Books.
1974   *Submission of Recorded Presidential Conversations to the Committee on the Judiciary of the House of Representatives,* Washington, D.C., U.S. Government Printing Office, April 30.
1978   *RN: The Memoirs of Richard Nixon,* New York, Grosset & Dunlap.

Editors
1975   "Nixon's New Life," *Newsweek,* Oct. 20, 85: 21-24.

North-Broome, Nicholas
1972   *The Nixon-Hughes "Loan": The "Loan" No One Repaid,* New York, APAI Books.

O'Brian, Robert
1974   *The Night Nixon Spoke,* unpublished manuscript, Whittier College, Whittier, California.

O'Brien, Robert, and Elizabeth Jones
1976   *The Night Nixon Spoke: A Study of Political Effectiveness,* Los Alamitos, California, Hwong Publishing Co.

Orwell, George
(1948)
1949   *1984,* New York, Signet Books.

Ortega y Gasset, Jose
1932   *The Revolt of the Masses,* New York, W.W. Norton.

Osborne, John
1972   *The Third Year of the Nixon Watch,* New York, Liveright.
1973   *The Fourth Year of the Nixon Watch,* New York, Liveright.
1974   *The Fifth Year of the Nixon Watch,* New York, Liveright.
1975   "Was Nixon 'Sick of Mind'?" *New York Magazine,* 37-45, April 21.

Ossowska, Maria
1970   *Social Determinates of Moral Ideas,* Philadelphia, University of Pennsylvania Press.

Packard, Vance
1957   *The Hidden Persuaders,* New York, David McKay.

Peckham, Morse
1962   "Toward a Theory of Romanticism," pp. 212-227 in
        R. Gleckner and E. Enscoe (eds.), *Romanticism: Points of
        View,* Englewood Cliffs, New Jersey, Prentice-Hall.

Perry, James M.
1973   *Us & Them: How the Press Covered the 1972 Election,* New
        York, Clarkson N. Potter.

Pike, Nelson (ed.)
1964   *Good and Evil: Readings on the Theological Problem of Evil,*
        Englewood Cliffs, New Jersey, Prentice-Hall.

Playboy Interview
1975   "John Dean," *Playboy Magazine,* Jan., 22: 65-80

Porter, Herbert L.
1974   "My Little White Lie," *Harpers,* Oct., 248: 73-76.

Powdermaker, Hortense
1950   *Hollywood the Dream Factory,* New York, the Universal
        Library.

Powers, Thomas
1976   "The Rise and Fall of Richard Helms," *Rolling Stone,*
        Dec. 16, 46-55.

Rather, Dan, and Gary Paul Gates
1974   *The Palace Guard,* New York, Harper & Row.

Raven, Bertram H.
1974   "The Nixon Group," *Journal of Social Issues,* 30(4):
        297-320.

Reedy, George E.
1970   *The Twilight of the Presidency,* New York, Mentor Books.
Reeves, Richard
1976   "What Ehrlichman Really Thought of Nixon," *New York
        Magazine,* May 10, 40-56.

Reich, Wilhelm
1970   *The Mass Psychology of Fascism,* (tr. Theodore Wolfe),
        Sebastopol, California, Masters of Perception Press.

Richardson, Elliot
1976   "The Saturday Night Massacre," *The Atlantic,* March,
        237: 40-44, 69-72.

Riesman, David, et al.
1955   *The Lonely Crowd,* Garden City, New York, Doubleday Anchor Books.

Rischin, Moses
1965   *The American Gospel of Success: Individualism and Beyond,* Chicago, Quadrangle Books.

Roemer, John
1973   "Gordon Liddy: He Bungled into the White House," *Rolling Stone,* 1, July 19, 24-28.

Rosenbloom, David
1973   *The Election Men: Professional Campaign Managers and American Democracy,* New York, Quadrangle Books.

Rossiter, Clinton
1960a   *The American Presidency,* New York, Mentor Books.
1960b   *Parties and Politics in America,* Ithaca, New York, Cornell University Press.

Rowe, Robert
1967   *The Bobby Baker Story,* New York, Parallax Publishing Co.

Rowse, Arthur Edward
1957   *Slanted News: A Case Study of the Nixon and Stevenson Fund Stories,* Boston, Beacon Press.

Russell, Edward F.
1969   *Return of the Swastika?* New York, David McKay.

Saffell, David C.
1974   *Watergate: Its Effects on the American Political System,* Cambridge, Massachusetts, Winthrop Publishers.

Safire, William
1975   *Before the Fall: An Inside View of the Pre-Watergate White House,* Garden City, New York, Doubleday.

Sandeen, Ernest R.
1970   *The Roots of Fundamentalism: British and American Millenarianism 1800-1930,* Chicago, University of Chicago Press.

Sanford, Nevitt, and Craig Comstock (eds.)
1971   *Sanctions for Evil,* Boston, Beacon Press.

Scammon, Richard, and Ben J. Wattenberg
1970   *The Real Majority,* New York, Coward, McCann, and Geoghegan.

Schell, Jonathan
1975   "Reflections: The Nixon Years," parts I-VI, *New Yorker Magazine,* June 2, 9, 16, 30, and July 7.

Seid, Steven
1977   "Descent into Decadence," *Zenger's,* April 13, 12.

Shannon, David A.
1960   *The Great Depression,* Englewood Cliffs, New Jersey, Prentice-Hall.

Sheridan, Terence
1973   "Nixon's Heartbreak Kid: From Wooster to Watergate," *Rolling Stone,* June 21, 32-34.

Sherrill, Robert
1969   *Gothic Politics in the Deep South: Stars of the New Confederacy,* New York, Ballantine Books.

Sidey, Hugh
1972   "The Big Win: What Will Nixon Do with It?" *Life* Nov. 17, 73: 4-8.

Sipes, Richard
1973   "War, Sports and Aggression: An Epirical Test of Two Rival Theories," *American Anthropologist* 75: 64-86.

Spalding, Henry D.
1972   *The Nixon Nobody Knows,* Middle Village, New York, Jonathan David, Publishers.

Sprague, Richard E.
1975   "Nixon, Ford and the Political Assassinations in the United States," *Computers and People,* Jan., 1: 27-31.

Stans, Maurice
1979   *The Terrors of Justice: The Untold Side of Watergate,* New York, Everest House.

Stein, Benjamin
1976   "If You Liked Richard Nixon, You'll Love Jimmy Carter," *Penthouse,* Nov., 62-68, 98.

Stein, George H. (ed.)
1968   *Hitler,* Englewood Cliffs, New Jersey, Prentice-Hall Spectrum Books.

Stein, Howard
1973   "The Silent Complicity at Watergate," *American Scholar* Winter 1973-74, 43: 21-37.

Stern, J.P.
1975   *Hitler: The Fuhrer and the People,* Berkeley, University of California Press.

Stokes, Geoffrey
1974   "The Story of P," *Harper's,* Oct., 249: 6-12.

Stone, Gregory P.
1972   *Games, Sport and Power,* New Brunswick, New Jersey, transaction books.

Stratton, William
1964   *A Content Analysis of the Responses to the Nixon Speech,* unpublished M.A. thesis, Department of Sociology, Whittier College, Whittier, California.

Streiker, Lowell, and Gerald Strober
1972   *Religion and the New Majority: Billy Graham, Middle America and the Politics of the 70s,* New York, Association Press.

Stroud, Kandy
1974   "Pat Nixon Today," *Ladies Home Journal* March, 91: 77, 132-133.

1975   "The Sad New Life of Rose Mary Woods," *McCall's Magazine* June, 102: 46-50 ff.

Stupp, V.O.
1961   *The Debating Techniques of Richard M. Nixon: 1947-1960,* unpublished M.A. thesis, Department of Speech, Pennsylvania State University.

Sussman, Barry
1974   *The Great Cover-Up: Nixon and the Scandal of Watergate,* New York, Signet Books.

Sutherland, Edwin, and Donald Cressey
(1924)
1960   *Principles of Criminology,* 6th ed., Chicago, Lippincott.

318

Sykes, Gresham M.
1966   *The Society of Captives,* New York, Atheneum.

terHorst, Jerald F.
1974   *Gerald Ford and the Future of the Presidency,* New York, The Third Press.

Terkel, Studs
1974   "View from the Second Story: Two Pros on the Break-In," *Rolling Stone,* Nov. 7, 32-36.

Thimmesch, Nick
1975   "David Eisenhower: 'Our Hardest Year'," *McCall's Magazine,* Aug., 102: 24-31 ff.

Thompson, Fred
1975   *At That Point in Time: The Inside Story of the Watergate Committee,* New York, Quadrangle Books.

Thompson, G.R. (ed.)
1974   *The Gothic Imagination: Essays in Dark Romanticism,* Washington State University Press.

Thompson, Hunter S.
1973   *Fear and Loathing on the Campaign Trail '72,* New York, Popular Library.
1974a   "The Scum Also Rises," *Rolling Stone,* Oct. 10, 28-52.
1974b   Interview, *Playboy Magazine,* Nov., 21: 75-90 ff.

Tiger, Lionel
1970   *Men in Groups,* New York, Vintage Books.

Time Life Books (eds.)
1970   *This Fabulous Century,* Vols. 1-6, New York, Time-Life Books.

Tolchin, Martin, and Susan Tolchin
1971   *To the Victor: Political Patronage from the Clubhouse to the White House,* New York, Random House.

Trotter, Robert J.
1974   "Watergate: A Psychological Perspective," *Science News* Dec. 14, 106: 378.

Tuck, Dick
1973   "The Bugging of Mack the Knife," *Rolling Stone,* Oct. 11, 27-32.

Tuckman, Howard
1973   *The Economics of the Rich,* New York, Random House.

Tyler, Parker
1970   *The Hollywood Hallucination,* New York, Simon & Schuster.

Voorhis, Jerry
1972   *The Strange Case of Richard Milhous Nixon,* New York, Popular Library.

Walsh, Vivian Charles
1961   *Scarcity and Evil,* Englewood Cliffs, New Jersey, Prentice-Hall Spectrum Books.

Walters, Robert
1974   "What Did Ziegler Say, and When Did He Say It?" *Columbia Journalism Review,* Sept./Oct., 13: 30-35.

Warner, W. Lloyd
1962   *American Life: Dream and Reality,* Chicago, University of Chicago Press.

Warriner, Charles
1958   "The Nature and Functions of Official Morality," *American Journal of Sociology,* 64: 165-168.

Washington Post Staff
1974   *The Fall of a President,* New York, Dell Publishing Corp.

Weissman, Steve
1974   *Big Brother and the Holding Company: The World Behind Watergate,* Palo Alto, California, Ramparts Press.

White, Theodore H.
1961   *The Making of the President: 1960,* New York, New American Library.
1970   *The Making of the President: 1968,* New York, Pocket Books.
1973   *The Making of the President: 1972,* New York, Bantam Books.
1975   *Breach of Faith: The Fall of Richard Nixon,* New York, Atheneum.

Wills, Garry
1970   *Nixon Agonistes: The Crises of the Self-Made Man,* New York, Mentor Books.
1974   "The Hiss Connection Through Nixon's Life," *New York Times Magazine,* Aug. 25, 8-9 ff.

1976a   "Anti-Papa Politics," *New York Review of Books,* June 10, 12-16.

1976b   "Carter on His Own," *New York Review of Books,* Nov. 25, 30-32.

Wilson, Bryan

1963   "Millennialism in Comparative Perspective," *Comparative Studies,* Oct., 6: 93-114.

Wilson, Monica

1951   "Witch Beliefs and Social Structure," *American Journal of Sociology,* 55: 307-313.

Wise, David

1978   *The American Police State: The Government against the People,* New York, Vintage Books.

Witcover, Jules

1970a   *The Resurrection of Richard Nixon,* New York, G.P. Putnam and Sons.

1970b   "Salvaging the Presidential Press Conference," *Columbia Journalism Review,* Fall, 9: 27-34.

1972   *The White Knight: The Rise of Spiro Agnew,* New York, Random House.

Wolin, Sheldon

1976   "Consistent Kissinger," *New York Review of Books,* Dec. 9 20-40.

Wood, Charles T.

1971   *The Quest for Eternity: Medieval Manners and Morals,* Garden City, New York, Doubleday Anchor Books.

Woodstone, Arthur

1972   *Inside Nixon's Head,* New York, Popular Library.

Woodward, Bob, and Carl Bernstein

1976   *The Final Days,* New York, Simon & Schuster.

Woodward, C. Vann (ed.)

1974   *Responses of the Presidents to Charges of Misconduct,* Dell Publishing Co.

Wycoff, Gene

1968   *The Image Candidates,* New York, Macmillan.

Young, T.R.
1976   "Critical Dimensions in Dramaturgical Analysis: Part II,
        Backstage at the White House," paper presented at the 71st
        annual meeting of the Americal Sociological Association,
        San Franciso, California.

Index

324